P9-ARG-505

THE DICKENS COMPANIONS

[1]

The Companion to *Our Mutual Friend*
MICHAEL COTSELL

[2]

The Companion to *The Mystery of Edwin Drood*
WENDY S. JACOBSON

THE DICKENS COMPANIONS

General editor Susan Shatto, Associate editor Michael Cotsell

The Companion to *The Mystery of Edwin Drood*

WENDY S. JACOBSON

London
ALLEN & UNWIN
Boston Sydney

Allen & Unwin (Publishers) Ltd,
40 Museum Street, London WC1A 1LU, UK

Allen & Unwin (Publishers) Ltd,
Park Lane, Hemel Hempstead, Herts HP2 4TE, UK

Allen & Unwin, Inc.,
8 Winchester Place, Winchester, Mass. 01890, USA

Allen & Unwin (Australia) Ltd,
8 Napier Street, North Sydney, NSW 2060, Australia

First published in 1986

British Library Cataloguing in Publication Data

Jacobson, Wendy S.
The companion to the mystery of Edwin Drood.—
(Dickens companions)
1. Dickens, Charles, *1812–1870.* Mystery of Edwin Drood
I. Title II. Dickens, Charles, *1812–1870.*
Mystery of Edwin Drood III. Series
823'.8 PR4564
ISBN 0-04-800063-9

Library of Congress Cataloging in Publication Data

Jacobson, Wendy S.
The companion to The mystery of Edwin Drood.
(Dickens companions)
Bibliography: p.
Includes index.
1. Dickens, Charles, 1812–1870. Mystery of Edwin Drood.
I. Dickens, Charles, 1812–1870. Mystery of Edwin Drood. 1986.
II. Title. III. Series.
PR4564.J35 1986 823'.8 85-22855
ISBN 0-04-800063-9 (alk. paper)

Set in 10 on 11 point Erhardt by Fotographics (Bedford) Ltd
and printed in Great Britain by Anchor Brendon Ltd, Tiptree, Essex

CONTENTS

LIST OF ILLUSTRATIONS

GENERAL PREFACE BY THE EDITORS

The Dickens Companions series provides the most comprehensive annotation of the works of Dickens ever undertaken. Separate volumes are devoted to each of Dickens's fifteen novels, to *Sketches by Boz* and to *The Uncommercial Traveller*; the five Christmas books are treated together in one volume. The series will be completed by a General Index, making nineteen volumes in all.

The nature of the annotation is factual rather than critical. The series undertakes what the general editors of the Clarendon Dickens have called 'the immense task of explanatory annotation' of Dickens's works. Each Companion will elucidate obscurities and allusions which were doubtless intelligible to the nineteenth-century reader but which have changed or lost their meaning in a later age. The 'world' of Dickens passed away more than a century ago, and our perceptions and interpretations of his works can be sharpened by our having recalled for us a precise context or piece of information.

The annotation identifies allusions to current events and intellectual and religious issues, and supplies information on topography, social customs, costume, furniture, transportation, and so on. Identifications are provided for allusions to plays, poems, songs, the Bible, the Book of Common Prayer and other literary sources. Elements of Dickens's plots, characterization and style which are influenced by the works of other writers are also identified. When an aspect of the text can be shown to have been influenced by Dickens's own experience this is indicated. The work of Dickens's illustrators is also discussed. Finally, although the Companions do not attempt the work of a modern scholarly edition, material from Dickens's manuscripts and proofs is included when it is of major significance.

The main part of the information in each Companion is arranged in the form of notes presented for convenient use with any edition of Dickens's works. The information is thus placed where it is most relevant, enabling the notes to be used to elucidate a local difficulty, or to pursue the use of a certain kind of material or the development of a particular idea. To facilitate the last purpose, the notes are cross-referenced, and each Companion contains a comprehensive index. The introduction to each Companion traces the major influences and concerns revealed by the annotation and, where appropriate, demonstrates their place in the genesis and composition of the text.

Dickens's vital and imaginative response to his culture is a familiar fact, but The Dickens Companions demonstrate and explore this response more fully and in far greater detail than has ever been attempted. Hitherto, Dickens's works have been annotated only on a modest scale. Many modern editions of the novels contain some notes, but there is not space in one volume for both the text of a novel and a comprehensive annotation of the text. Because most volumes of The Dickens Companions are devoted to a single work, the series can provide the full-scale, thoroughgoing annotation which the works of Dickens require. The completed series will compose a uniquely comprehensive archive of information about Dickens's world, affording the modern reader an unparalleled record of Dickens's concerns and the sources of his artistry. For many kinds of scholar, not merely Dickensians, The Dickens Companions will provide a fundamental tool for future critical and historical scholarship on various aspects of nineteenth-century British culture.

To undertake the 'immense task' of annotation, the Editors have assembled a team of Dickens scholars who work closely together and with the Editors in order to enhance the depth and scope of each Companion. The series is not a variorum commentary on Dickens: it does not consist of a survey or a selection of comments by other annotators and scholars. Previous scholarship is, in general, cited only when it is considered to identify an important piece of information about the historical, literary and biographical influences on Dickens's works.

The annotation in The Dickens Companions is based on original research which derives for the most part from the writings of Dickens's own time, the reading available to him and the books he is known to have read. The annotation is not perfunctorily minimal: a large number of notes are substantial essays and all are written in a readable style. Nor does the annotation consist of narrow definitions of what the reader (in the opinion of another reader) 'needs to know' in order to 'understand' the text. Rather, the annotation attempts to open up the actual and imaginative worlds which provided the sources and the backgrounds of Dickens's works in the belief that what interested, engaged and amused Dickens can hardly fail to interest, engage and amuse his readers. Our largest hope for The Dickens Companions is that the volumes will be read with a pleasure akin to that with which Dickens's own writings are read, and that they will be genuine Companions to both his works and his readers.

The idea of providing each of Dickens's major works with a companion volume of annotation originated with the late Professor T. J. B. Spencer. It is to his memory that the series is gratefully and affectionately dedicated.

SUSAN SHATTO
MICHAEL COTSELL

ACKNOWLEDGEMENTS

Margaret Cardwell has edited the Clarendon and World's Classics editions of *The Mystery of Edwin Drood* with an authority that has lightened and illuminated my own work. The studies of opium by Virginia Berridge, Griffith Edwards and Alethea Hayter have been invaluable. The Pilgrim Edition of *The Letters of Charles Dickens* has earned the respect of all Dickens scholars, but for annotators of Dickens these volumes are especially helpful. My own work has also relied substantially on the scholarship of John Butt, Philip Collins, K. J. Fielding, Edgar Johnson and Kathleen Tillotson, to all of whom I am grateful.

To the editors of the series, Susan Shatto and Michael Cotsell, I owe an extraordinary debt of gratitude for the generous and extensive assistance they have given me at every stage. Susan Shatto in particular spent an immeasurable amount of time on the research and revision of the volume and further assumed the tasks of preparing it for the press and substantively amending the index. Her work on the index depended greatly on the advice of Kevin Harris, the indexer of The Dickens Companions, to whom I am also indebted.

I should like to thank the librarians at Rhodes University, Sue Arnott and Betty Clark, without whose help this volume would not have been completed. A grant from Rhodes University is gratefully acknowledged. To David Bunyan and Arthur Morgan I owe thanks for advice on parts of the manuscript, and to Nick Visser, the antithesis of 'an old Tory Jackass', I am particularly grateful for his hours of good-humoured patience in teaching me how to use a computer. Thanks are also due to Ken Masters for his proof-reading.

Acknowledgements for kind assistance are offered to Lady Elinor Birley, Jim Binns, Joan Bohl, J. T. Boulton, Colin Brewer, Geoffrey Carnall, Elsie Duncan-Jones, Lynne Meredith, Christopher Price, R. L. Ratcliffe, Paul Schlicke, I. A. Shapiro and Stanley Wells. I am also indebted to the Librarian of the Shakespeare Institute, University of Birmingham, and to the staff of the National Library of Scotland. The Dickens House Museum, the Tate Gallery, London, and the Victoria and Albert Museum have kindly given permission to reproduce illustrations and manuscript material in their collections.

This series is dedicated to the memory of T. J. B. Spencer, whose guidance and imagination continue to inspire those of us who worked with him. This book is dedicated to his memory, and to the memory of my father, Nathaniel Jacobson. It is offered in loving thanks to the University of Rhodesia – in particular, Anthony Chennells and Raymond Brown – and to members of the Shakespeare Institute. It is all the thanks I can offer to my mother, and it is given, too, to my nieces, Marice and Celean.

ABBREVIATIONS FOR DICKENS'S WORKS AND RELATED MATERIAL

1. Works: Major

AN	*American Notes*
BH	*Bleak House*
BL	*The Battle of Life*
BR	*Barnaby Rudge*
C	*The Chimes*
CC	*A Christmas Carol*
CH	*The Cricket on the Hearth*
CHE	*A Child's History of England*
DC	*David Copperfield*
DS	*Dombey and Son*
GE	*Great Expectations*
HM	*The Haunted Man*
HT	*Hard Times*
LD	*Little Dorrit*
MC	*Martin Chuzzlewit*
MED	*The Mystery of Edwin Drood*
MHC	*Master Humphrey's Clock*
NN	*Nicholas Nickleby*
OCS	*The Old Curiosity Shop*
OMF	*Our Mutual Friend*
OT	*Oliver Twist*
PI	*Pictures from Italy*
PP	*The Pickwick Papers*
SB	*Sketches by Boz*
TTC	*A Tale of Two Cities*
UT	*The Uncommercial Traveller*

2. Works: Miscellaneous Writings

CP	*Collected Papers*
MP	*Miscellaneous Papers*
RP	*Reprinted Pieces*
AYR	*All the Year Round*
HW	*Household Words*

3. Related Material: Basic Sources

Forster	John Forster, *The Life of Charles Dickens*, 3 vols (1872–4)
Letters	*The Letters of Charles Dickens*, ed. Madeline House and others, Pilgrim Edition (1965–)
Letters: Coutts	*Letters from Charles Dickens to Angela Burdett-Coutts, 1841–1865*, ed. Edgar Johnson (1953)
Nonesuch	*The Letters of Charles Dickens*, ed. Walter Dexter, Nonesuch Edition, 3 vols (1938)
Speeches	*The Speeches of Charles Dickens*, ed. K. J. Fielding (1960)

BIBLIOGRAPHICAL SYMBOLS AND ABBREVIATIONS

MS	Manuscript
< >	Deletion in MS or proof
∧ or ∧	Addition or substitution in MS
∧ OR △	Addition or substitution in proof
illegible word	Signifies an unreadable word in MS

Note: Dickens heavily revised the manuscripts of his later novels, including *The Mystery of Edwin Drood*. The annotation in the present volume includes only a small selection of the variant readings.

INTRODUCTION

Influences

The Mystery of Edwin Drood is as resonant with the experiences, reading and writing of Dickens's lifetime as Cloisterham Cathedral is with its past. Annotation of the novel has revealed the extent to which its richness, complexity and humour arise from three important kinds of influence.

One of the influences reflected in the wide range of allusions in the novel originates in Dickens's lively interest in contemporary and near-contemporary events, issues and personalities. For example, Charles Kingsley's philosophy of Muscular Christianity animates the portrait of the Reverend Crisparkle (chapter 2), just as John Bright and his involvement with philanthropy and the Governor Eyre controversy animate the portrait of Honeythunder (chapters 6, 17). The depiction of Bazzard as a frustrated playwright is a wickedly witty personal attack on R. H. Horne, with whom Dickens broke off relations in 1869 (chapter 20). The public inquiry which began in the 1840s into interment in churchyards and cemeteries is partly responsible for the recurrent concern of the novel with modes of burial. Allusions to this topical subject occur in the description of Cloisterham's 'earthy flavor', its cathedral crypt and monastic graves (chapter 3); in the character of the chronically drunk sexton, Durdles (chapter 4); and in Jasper's interest in the use of quicklime to decompose corpses (chapter 12). A related subject, the aesthetic debate among reformers of ecclesiastical art to improve the standards of sepulchral monuments, underlies the meditation of Durdles on tombstones (chapter 5) and the pride of Mr Sapsea in his epitaph for ETHELINDA (chapter 4).

Edwin Drood's decision to go out to Egypt as an engineer arises from such events as the introduction to Egypt of European influence and commerce which began in the 1830s, the opening of the Overland Route to India, and the completion of the Suez Canal in 1869 (chapter 2). The British fascination with Egypt is manifested in other ways in the novel. For example, the quantity of travel guides and history books published on Egypt, and the variety of exhibitions in London displaying Egyptian artefacts are, we can presume, the source of Miss Twinkleton's extensive knowledge of the country. More whimsically, Rosa Bud, although bored by Egypt, sucks on 'Lumps-of-Delight' – the sweetmeat as common in Egypt as in Turkey – in the midst of her complaint about Miss Twinkleton's lessons: ' "Tiresome old burying-grounds! Isises, and Ibises, and Cheopses, and Pharaohses; who cares about them?" ' (chapter 3).

It is well known that Dickens's personal experiences of opium-eating (the drinking of laudanum) and his visit to an opium den in the East End of London combine to inform the characterization of John Jasper. But an equally important influence on the depiction of the Princess Puffer's den and on her esoteric knowledge of opium-smoking are articles published in *London Society* and the

Ragged School Union Magazine in 1868: 'East London Opium Smokers' and 'In an Opium Den' (chapter 1). Many more examples of the ways in which aspects of the novel derive from biographical experience and contemporary occurrences and topics are identified in the annotation itself.

A second kind of influence on *The Mystery of Edwin Drood* is Dickens's earlier writing – his novels, stories and journalism. The most important sources in his own works of the concerns and ideas which can be seen to be reworked in his last novel are examined below in the context of how he might have intended the novel to end.

Two examples of such influence might be mentioned here, however: his Christmas stories, 'The Haunted Man' and 'Tom Tiddler's Ground'. 'The Haunted Man' deals with memory both as the cause of pain and as a source of compassion and generosity of spirit. Memory and the loss of memory are important issues in *The Mystery of Edwin Drood* on account of Jasper's opium addiction and the extent to which his addiction might influence his recollection of events on the night of Edwin's disappearance, a recollection which affects the time-scheme of the novel. One of the tales in 'Tom Tiddler's Ground' portrays a girl's school, a school-mistress and a pupil, all precursors of the Nuns' House, Miss Twinkleton and Rosa Bud. The use of a cathedral town is itself a return to an earlier setting. Many commentators have noticed how Dickens in a sense ends where he began in choosing as the original of Cloisterham the town of his boyhood, Rochester, the setting for much of *The Pickwick Papers*.

The third major kind of influence on the novel is the works of other writers. Of these, *The Moonstone* (1868) by Wilkie Collins is the most prominent. It could be said that in *The Mystery of Edwin Drood* Dickens is offering a kind of answer to the novel by his young friend, a novel which he admired but, perhaps, tried to better. *The Hunchback of Notre-Dame* (1831) by Victor Hugo features a haunting Cathedral setting much closer in atmosphere to Dickens's novel than are the Barsetshire novels of Trollope, sometimes considered to be comparable to *The Mystery of Edwin Drood*. Hugo's portrait of an intense and brilliant priest enduring a repressed and embittered passion for a young girl is also closer to Dickens than is Trollope. The third important work of influence is *Macbeth*. The novel contains many echoes of phrasing from the play, and both works have an ambiguous character at their centre. They also share a similarity of design. The opium woman, who is overtly presented as a witch, opens the novel just as the witches open the play. Moreover, Jasper's return to the den halfway through the novel to recapture the relief he derives from the spectres induced by opium parallels Macbeth's return to the coven in the central scene of the play in order to seek reassurance of his power.

Less prominent an influence, but nevertheless interesting, is *Confessions of an English Opium-Eater* (1821; 1822) and other of De Quincey's works. Southey's ballad, 'Jaspar' (1798; 1799), about a murderer of that name and his innocent associate called Jonathan, gave Dickens the name for his choirmaster and perhaps influenced the characterization. Likewise, Goldsmith's *The Vicar of Wakefield* (1766), with its ballad about the lovers called Edwin and Angelina, provided Dickens with the name for Jasper's nephew and may also have had a bearing on aspects of theme and plot. The legend of Eugene Aram, made famous by the poem of Thomas Hood (1829; 1831) and the novel by Bulwer-Lytton (1832), is echoed in the motif of the learned and talented murderer who suffers paroxysms of remorse. Finally, echoes of the Old and New Testaments and of the Book of Common Prayer reverberate in *The Mystery of Edwin Drood* as frequently as in any of Dickens's other novels.

The Mysteries

No study of *The Mystery of Edwin Drood* would be complete without a consideration of the fragmentary state of the novel and the possible hints of what was intended to follow: the danger of missing possible signals is at least as great as that of seeing significance where none exists. The title itself alerts the reader to the need to respond to the sometimes confusing and even baffling details of the narrative. The search for a solution to the mystery has often concentrated on what is not there, while ignoring the artistic integrity of the fragment. Authors, scholars and armchair detectives have been tempted to complete the work in a remarkable variety of styles. Even ghosts have been summoned by spiritualists claiming to be in contact with the dead novelist. Dickens was familiar with the productions of his novels put on the stage before he had completed them himself, and he delivered his judgement on the perpetrators of such counterfeit versions in 1838, in *Nicholas Nickleby*:

> You take the uncompleted books of living authors, fresh from their hands, wet from the press, cut, hack, and carve them to the powers and capacities of your actors, and the capability of your theatres, finish unfinished works, hastily and crudely vamp up ideas not yet worked out by their original projector, but which have doubtless cost him many thoughtful days and sleepless nights; by a comparison of incidents and dialogue, down to the very last word he may have written a fortnight before, do your utmost to anticipate his plot – all this without his permission, and against his will; and then, to crown the whole proceeding, publish in some mean pamphlet, an unmeaning farrago of garbled extracts from his work, to which you put your name as author, with the honourable distinction annexed, of having perpetrated a hundred other outrages of the same description. Now, show me the distinction between such pilfering as this, and picking a man's pocket in the street. (48).

Most attempts to complete *The Mystery of Edwin Drood* are characterized by a stubborn insistence that the proffered theory is unassailable: Droodians seem to be divided between those who believe Edwin to have died at the hand of his uncle, and those who believe that he escapes. The majority seem to believe that Edwin is murdered. But Dickens wrote the perfect mystery: it cannot and will not be finally solved for the reason that the novel is half-finished and he left almost no clues outside the text except for those reported by Forster, Luke Fildes and Charles Dickens Junior (the details if not the validity of which are not particularly helpful). If the integrity of the fragment is to be respected, the fairest method of inquiry is to ask the questions suggested by the text itself, and then make conjectures based on the possibilities implied in the text.

There are, of course, several unsolved mysteries in the novel. Perhaps the simplest of them is the identity of Datchery. To account for the new settler in Cloisterham, commentators have proposed candidates from the entire cast of characters in the novel, including Grewgious but at least excluding Rosa. Sometimes new characters have been invented, and W. W. Robson has ingeniously argued that Datchery is Dickens (' "The Mystery of Edwin Drood": the solution?', *The Times Literary Supplement*, 11 November 1983, 1246, 1259). It seems likely, however, that Dick Datchery is simply himself – but, if not, then he may be Bazzard, off-duty from Grewgious's office at about the time Datchery arrives in Cloisterham.

A more interesting question than 'Who is Datchery?' is 'Who is the Princess Puffer?' Why does she hate Jasper? What has she heard him say in the opium reverie that precedes the opening of the novel? How can she know Jasper ' "better far, than all the Reverend Parsons put together know him" ' (chapter 23)? What is her connection with Jasper that she should twice follow him with malicious compulsion to Cloisterham? What does she know about 'Ned' that she should warn him, and what does she know about his sweetheart?

Helena Landless also tempts curiosity. Her 'intense dark eyes' are 'softened with compassion and admiration' for Rosa, but what does their 'slumbering gleam of fire' signify for 'whomsoever it most concerned' and who should 'look well to it' (chapter 7)? What interpretation, moreover, can be put upon the strange mode of communication she shares with her brother? Who *are* the Landlesses? Neville speaks only of his mother, who died when they were children, but who was their father? What is the significance of the phrase in the work plans that refers to the 'Mixture of Oriental blood – or imperceptibly acquired nature – in them'? Will Helena marry the Minor Canon, or will Edwin's nascent admiration of her come to fruition?

Durdles and Deputy also present puzzles: Durdles's ability to find out 'with remarkable accuracy' where bodies are buried seems clearly to hint at some later revelation, possibly in connection with the unexplained ' "ghost of one terrific shriek" ' he heard at Christmas a year ago (chapter 12). The tapping and the dream interest and agitate Jasper, but why? As for Deputy, what could he have witnessed that could be held in evidence against Jasper, who so unreasonably loathes him? Durdles points out that the grave of Edwin's father is in Cloisterham, but where does Edwin's mother lie? Where is Tartar at the end of chapter 22 so that Rosa seems to be losing her spirits as she looks 'so wistfully and so much out of the gritty windows'? What role is he designated to play? One can assume that he is given agility and strength, as Crisparkle, his old friend, is given physical prowess, for a purpose. Is his being a sailor a clue? Why should the attitude of Grewgious towards Jasper change from geniality to implacable dislike? What has Grewgious learnt that causes him to view Jasper's fit so coldly, and how has he learnt what he knows?

The Endings

Two questions more important than these puzzles are those which concern Jasper's ambiguous personality and whether or not he kills Edwin Drood. The plot of the novel depends for its outcome not on devices, but, rather, on the character of John Jasper, and in particular upon his opium addiction and his double personality. The motif of the *doppelgänger* is ubiquitous in Dickens's fiction (see below), but is notably presented in *The Mystery of Edwin Drood* in the respectable public persona of the choirmaster who is undermined by his murderous instinct and his desire for Rosa. The motif is reflected in Miss Twinkleton's 'two states of existence' and, less comically, in the pair of twins and in the two locations, Cloisterham and London. The doubling seems to move towards integration when the Princess Puffer hobbles into the Cathedral, the antithesis of her opium den. A spectre like Banquo's ghost, she brings together the disparate parts of Jasper's life. Can this be a parody of a possible integration of Jasper's personality? Certainly, his two worlds conjoin at Morning Service in the last chapter when 'glorious light from moving boughs, songs of birds, scents from gardens, woods, and fields . . . penetrate into the Cathedral . . . and preach the Resurrection and the Life'.

One aspect of Jasper's personality is his addiction to opium. His habit is the most obvious of the novel's many similarities to *The Moonstone*, a novel in which opium-eating is the crux of the mystery. The diamond is stolen by Franklin Blake after he unwittingly drinks laudanum. Dr Jennings suspects this and, in order to persuade Blake to participate in his experiment, quotes the same passage from John Elliotson's *Human Physiology* that Dickens quotes in chapter 3. On the basis of Elliotson's principle, 'if I hide my watch when I am drunk, I must be drunk again before I can remember where', Jennings reconstructs the circumstances of the theft, administers the opium to Blake, and solves the mystery. Dickens would have known of the irony that Collins actually dictated the last chapters of *The Moonstone* under the influence of laudanum and was not able to recognize them when he read through them later.

If, like Blake, Jasper suffers from a delusion caused by opium and has not in fact killed Edwin, then Edwin's disappearance needs to be explained. He could be suffering from amnesia. An article in the *Spectator* (9 January 1869), 'The Man with Two Memories', reported the curious case of George Nickern of New Orleans: after a fall he was deprived of his senses, but on recovery he lost his memory. The prognosis is that some other trauma may return his memory to him, although he would then lose any recollection of the intervening period. In a novel by Bulwer-Lytton published in *All the Year Round, A Strange Story* (1862), the doctor who narrates the tale explains that ' "oblivion after bodily illness or mental shock are familiar enough to the practice of all medical men" '.

The works of Collins and Bulwer-Lytton may well have inspired Dickens to give Edwin amnesia, but a likelier possibility is that after the dinner at the Gate House he in fact has sought out Grewgious's aid and guardianship, as does Rosa later on. We suspect that Grewgious knows something about Jasper that motivates antipathy. Grewgious may wish to keep Edwin away from his friends in order to entrap Jasper. By the same token, he keeps an eye on Neville, as he says, in order to protect him from being victimized any further.

The supposition that Edwin is not dead but merely in hiding is based on four pieces of evidence: a deletion in the manuscript regarding Edwin's possible return to Cloisterham; the cover design for the wrapper of the monthly parts; the list of projected titles for the novel (p. 15); and a consideration of earlier themes in Dickens's works.

In chapter 14, Edwin wanders about Cloisterham before the dinner at the Gate House and wistfully looks at 'all the old landmarks. He will soon be far away, and may never see them again, he thinks. Poor youth! Poor youth!' Dickens revised this from: '<He> Poor youth! <He little, little knows how near a cause he has for thinking so.> Poor youth!' For Margaret Cardwell, this deletion means an 'impending successful murder'. She thinks that as Eugene Wrayburn escaped in *Our Mutual Friend*, so might Edwin, but that the 'argument in favour of Dickens's not using the same outcome twice is probably the stronger' (1969, 275). On the contrary: Dickens used the theme of a man returning from the dead more than once, and it therefore seems likely that he intended to do so again.

As a second piece of evidence, the cover design for the wrapper of the monthly parts suggests that Jasper would be compelled to revisit the vault in which he supposes Edwin's body to lie, and there, in the light of the lantern, find the living Edwin. The face and figure of the young man are recognizably those of the young man at the top left of the illustration: Edwin with Rosa on his arm. And he stands with one hand in his breast pocket, much as Edwin would have stood as his hand crept to the ring given to him by Grewgious for Rosa. Although it has been argued that the young man in the vault is Helena, Datchery, Bazzard or Neville disguised as Edwin, the use of disguise would weaken the impact of revelation and, anyway, Dickens denigrated disguise in a novel as mere device.

A third piece of evidence lies in the manuscript list of projected names and titles for the novel. Not all the titles are relevant: 'Sworn to avenge it' refers to Jasper's reaction to the loss of his nephew, as do 'One Object in Life' and 'A Kinsman's Devotion'. 'The loss of James Wakefield', however, suggests something else. (Is Dickens thinking of *The Vicar of Wakefield*, from which Edwin's name probably derives, and of the combination of the words 'wake' and 'field'?) There are five titles beginning with the word 'loss', the only variants being Edwin's name, which alters several times. 'Loss' changes to 'disappearance' in 'James's Disappearance' and 'The Disappearance of Edwin Drood'. 'The Mystery in the Drood Family' (alluding, perhaps, to the skeleton in the cupboard referred to in chapter 2) is only slightly less ambiguous than the title finally chosen, which is also listed towards the end. The remaining four titles point to Drood's having survived: 'Flight And Pursuit' and 'The flight of Edwyn Drood' are strong enough hints, but 'Dead? Or alive?' and in particular 'Edwin Drood in hiding' seem to be even stronger evidence that Edwin is not dead, is in hiding, and that he will return.

It must be acknowledged that the manuscript and cover design alone reveal few clues to the resolution of the novel. Further evidence can be found in Dickens's earlier works, evidence that can promote an understanding of the impetus and psychology of the novel. Indeed, a study of Dickens's reworkings of certain preoccupations manifest in his earlier writings may throw light upon the mystery. That he reworked the preoccupations so frequently and for so long suggests some inner compulsion never resolved which informed his art to the end.

His association and collaboration with Wilkie Collins curiously produced a remarkable number of stories about the return from the dead. His tale of 'The Two Robins' in *A Lazy Tour of Two Idle Apprentices*, an account of a holiday he shared with Collins, tells of a dead man who has come to life again. In 'A Message from the Sea' (*Christmas Stories*), which he wrote with Collins, a man believed to have drowned is found by a captain who prepares his wife for his return:

> 'I make up stories of brothers brought together by GOD, – of sons brought back to mothers, husbands brought back to wives, fathers raised from the deep, for little children like herself.'

The theme occurs in two of Collins's own stories for *Household Words*. 'Gabriel's Marriage' tells of a fisherman who believes he has murdered a traveller. The victim survives the assault and comes back to the fisherman's cottage:

> The door was opened. On a lovely moonlight night François Sarzeau had stood on that threshold years since, with a bleeding body in his arms: on a lovely moonlight night, he now stood there again, confronting the very man whose life he had attempted, and knowing him not. (1853, 7.188)

'Sister Rose' (1855, 11.293–303) tells of a man who betrays his wife and her brother to the Reign of Terror in France; they survive for the brother to confront Danville among friends who have come to witness his remarriage. Danville's hand goes cold in the clasp of the girl he intends to marry; he is transfixed at the sight of the man whose death he believes he arranged.

Finally, a story in *All the Year Round* on which Dickens and Collins collaborated is strikingly similar to *The Mystery of Edwin Drood*. In 'No Thoroughfare' (18, Christmas Number, 1–48), Obenreizer believes that he has murdered George Vendale, although in fact Vendale is only wounded. Bintrey discovers this and finds an opportunity to have Vendale stand 'before the murderer, a man risen from the dead'. Obenreizer had used opium 'to try' his victim, in much the same way that Jasper drugs Durdles. There are other similarities. A 'certain nameless film' would come over Obenreizer's eyes just as 'a strange film' comes over the eyes of Jasper. Joey Ladle, the cellarman who complains of the unnaturalness of working underground, is a character in the same tradition as Durdles. And Obenreizer's motive for murder is jealousy of Vendale's winning the heart of his niece, Marguerite. Like Rosa, Marguerite flees to the protection of a trusted family lawyer, Bintrey.

In Dickens's novels, the theme of the return from the dead is sometimes intertwined with another of his preoccupations, the *doppelgänger* motif. *Our Mutual Friend* in particular contains notable anticipations of *The Mystery of Edwin Drood*. Bradley Headstone's tormented, guilt-ridden mind, and his struggle to keep up the appearance and the routine of a well-regulated life prefigure John Jasper. Eugene Wrayburn is attacked, thrown into the river and rescued. After his recovery from a long illness, he feels himself to be a different person and a better man, and he becomes worthy of Lizzie. Edwin Drood, as feckless as Eugene, also seems to have something to learn before he can deserve the hand of either Rosa Bud or Helena Landless. Likewise, integration and redemption may also have been intended for Jasper.

Is Edwin Drood dead? Certainly, we are left with the impression that Eugene Wrayburn is:

> Eugene was light, active, and expert; but his arms were broken, or he was paralysed, and could do no more than hang on to the man, with his head swung back, so that he could see nothing but the heaving sky. After dragging at the assailant, he fell on the bank with him, and then there was another great crash, and then a splash, and all was done. (4.6)

And we are also left with the impression that John Harmon is dead. As to why he should have assumed the identity of another man after he has been attacked and presumed drowned, Harmon explains that because he is believed to be dead he feels he has lost his own identity:

> Next day while I hesitated, and next day while I hesitated, it seemed as if the whole country were determined to have me dead. The Inquest declared me dead, the Government proclaimed me dead; I could not listen at my fireside for five minutes to the outer noises, but it was borne into my ears that I was dead. (2.13)

The moment when he 'rises from the dead' in front of the two men who believe that he was drowned at their instigation creates the same kind of encounter as that illustrated in the cover design of the monthly wrapper of *The Mystery of Edwin Drood.* The instigators of John Harmon's 'murder' are as shocked by his reappearance as John Jasper seems shocked by Edwin's. They respond as if they were seeing a ghost:

> Bella's husband stepped softly to the half-door of the bar, and stood there . . . Mr Kibble had staggered up, with his lower jaw dropped, catching Potterson by the shoulder, and pointing to the half-door. He now cried out: 'Potterson! Look! Look there!' Potterson started up, started back, and exclaimed: 'Heaven defend us, what's that!' (4.12)

Several other of Dickens's novels feature, with varying degrees of prominence, the idea of the dead returned to life. In *The Cricket on the Hearth*, Edward Plummer, thought of as lost and dead (' "If my boy in the Golden South Americas was alive" ') returns in time to save his childhood sweetheart from an undesirable marriage. In *Dombey and Son*, the scene describing Walter Gay's last night at home contains hints of his reported loss at sea very similar to the hints given of Edwin Drood's disappearance in the scene of his farewell to Cloisterham:

> Walter's heart felt heavy as he looked round his old bedroom, up among the parapets and chimney-pots, and thought that one more night already darkening would close his acquaintance with it, perhaps for ever. Dismantled of his little stock

of books and pictures, it looked coldly and reproachfully on him for his desertion, and had already a foreshadowing upon it of its coming strangeness. (19)

Yet Walter does come home. So, too, does Walter's uncle, Solomon Gills, who has also been given up for dead. In the light of the fate possibly intended for John Jasper, it is significant, moreover, that *Dombey and Son* ultimately turns upon the redemption of Mr Dombey.

In *Bleak House*, Mr George sends a letter to Esther explaining that her father, his senior officer, 'was (officially) reported drowned', or he would assuredly have sought him out to save him from the lonely pauper's death he suffers (63). Mr George himself, incidentally, turns out to be the long-lost son of Mrs Rouncewell.

Surely the foremost example of Dickens's interweaving of the two themes is found in *A Tale of Two Cities*. What is most germane to the issues in *The Mystery of Edwin Drood* is Sydney Carton's memory of the Burial Service, presaging his vision of a redemptive sacrifice (3.9). The same words that form the burden of Carton's thoughts as he walks along the banks of the Seine on the night before his death are woven into the last chapter of *The Mystery of Edwin Drood*. The promise of redemption given in the last chapter is first made in the opening chapter when Jasper returns from his debauch in London and moves towards the intoning of Evensong. The phrase from Ezekiel, 'WHEN THE WICKED MAN . . .', seems to point to Jasper, but the words not quoted that follow these are an assurance of forgiveness after repentance. This promise is taken up in the last chapter when a note of pathos is struck in the suggestions of the Resurrection and the Life which reach symbolically into the Cathedral in the light of the 'brilliant morning' that 'shines on the old city', so that there seems to be a blessing on the world. This passage is by no means the only reference in the novel to the Bible. One important example is that Neville, after Edwin's disappearance, is repeatedly identified with Cain (chapters 16, 17). Although it is not possible to be certain of the manner in which Dickens intended to develop these associations, *The Mystery of Edwin Drood* may very well be patterned on that cycle of sin and redemption which the lesson of the Burial Service implies. The stress on the theme of integration and resurrection restores *The Mystery of Edwin Drood* to lovers of literature. The neglected artistry of the novel, a profoundly suggestive romance of great charm and beauty, rests its claim as a work of art upon its exploration of the mystery of life, not upon its being a source for literary detectives.

It is on Christmas Eve that the supposed murder of Edwin Drood takes place. That night Edwin, Neville and Jasper dine together, after which Neville and Edwin go down to the river to watch the storm. There the mystery remains. What was the state of mind, the degree of addiction, the dosage consumed of John Jasper on that night? We know that Dickens knew that the euphoric sense of power that opium can give is delusory. So instead of asking the question, 'Did Jasper attempt to murder his nephew', should we not ask: 'Did Jasper murder his nephew at all'? Indeed, did Jasper remember what had actually taken place, and when? What is the force of the power Jasper seems to wield? It may be that this power is ultimately impotent, is mere delusion. Alas, the promise of redemption, the gift of resurrection remain – as ever – the mystery of Edwin Drood.

A NOTE ON THE TEXT

The text of *The Mystery of Edwin Drood* quoted throughout this volume is that of the Clarendon Dickens edition of the novel, edited by Margaret Cardwell (1972). The annotation includes notes on the variant readings: for the most part the readings are quoted from Cardwell, but on the basis of the author's examination of the manuscript of the novel a number of significant variants not included in Cardwell are also discussed. The work plans and List of Projected Names and Titles have been transcribed by the author from the manuscript.

HOW TO USE THE NOTES

To help the reader locate in the novel the word or phrase quoted in an entry, the notes are presented in this way: the opening phrase of the paragraph which includes the entry is quoted as a guide and printed in italics; the entry itself appears in bold-face type. This system should also help the reader who turns from the novel in search of a note on a particular word or phrase.

Documentation within the notes is kept to a minimum by the use of an abbreviated form of referencing. Works of literature are referred to by their parts: *Vanity Fair* 12; *Past and Present* 3.2; *The Faerie Queene* 2.12.75.4–6; 'The Idiot Boy' 8–10. Frequently cited works of criticism and other secondary sources are referred to by author, part (where relevant) and page: '(Collins 171–2)', '(Mayhew 3.106–7)'. References to infrequently cited sources add the date of publication: '(Sala, 1859, 23)'. Complete details are given in the Select Bibliography.

The articles quoted from *Household Words* and *All the Year Round* always antedate or are contemporary with the composition of the novel unless the reference indicates otherwise.

The notes indicate the divisions of the novel in its first published form as a serial of six monthly numbers (twelve were intended but Dickens died when only half were completed), published from April to September 1870.

The Work Plans

The notes include transcripts of the sheets of memoranda on which Dickens sketched out his ideas for each monthly number. He folded each sheet once to make two pages, and he referred to the sheets as 'Mems'. In the present volume they are referred to as 'work plans'. To distinguish the pages from each other, the left page is described as the 'number plan' and the right page as the 'chapter plan'. In the notes which follow, the work plans are located among the notes to the first chapter of each monthly number.

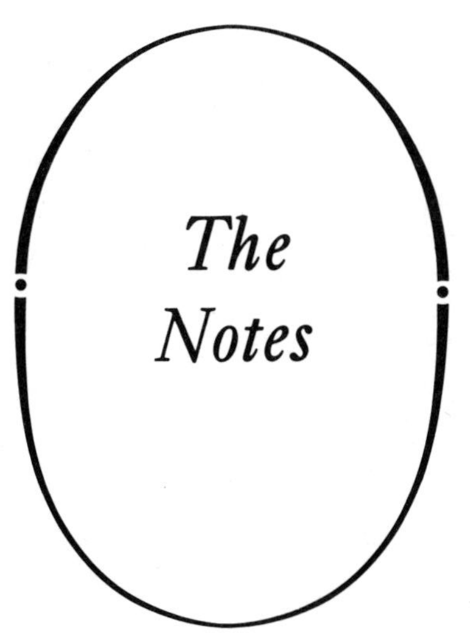

The Notes

Manuscript List of Projected Names and Titles

Friday Twentieth August, 1869.

Gilbert Alfred
Edwin
Jasper Edwyn
Michael Oswald
Arthur
Selwyn
Edgar

The loss of James Wakefield
Edwyn

Mr Honeythunder
Mr Honeyblast
The Dean
Mrs Dean
Miss Dean

James's Disappearance

Flight And Pursuit

Sworn to avenge it

One Object in Life

A Kinsman's Devotion

The Two Kinsmen

The Loss of Edwyn Brood

The loss of Edwin Brude
The Mystery in the Drood Family
The loss of Edwyn Drood
The flight of Edwyn Drood

Edwin Drood in hiding

The Loss of Edwin Drude
The Disappearance of Edwin Drood
The Mystery of Edwin Drood

Dead? Or alive?

Opium-Smoking

Touch the Key note

"When the Wicked Man" –

The Uncle and Nephew:

"Pussy's" Portrait

You won't take warning then?

Dean — Mr Jasper

Minor Canon. Mr Crisparkle

Verger

Uncle and Nephew — Peptune

Gloves for the Nuns' House — change to Tope

Churchyard

Cathedral town running throughout

Inside the Nuns' House

Miss Twinkleton, and her double existence

Mrs Tisher

Rosebud

The affianced young people. Every love scene of theirs, a quarrel more or less

Mr Sapsea Old Tory Jackass

His wife's Epitaph

Jasper and the Keys

Durdles down in the crypt and among the graves. His dinner bundle

(Mystery of Edwin Drood. – No. I.)

Chapter I

<Prologue> The Dawn

change title to The Dawn

Opium smoking and Jasper
Lead up to Cathedral

Chapter II

A Dean, and a Chapter also

Cathedral and Cathedral town   Mr Crisparkle
and the Dean

Uncle and Nephew
Murder very far off

Edwin's story and Pussy

Chapter III

The Nuns' House

Still picturesque suggestions of Cathedral Town
The Nuns' House and the young couples first love scene

Chapter IV

Mr Sapsea

Connect Jasper with him (He will want a solemn donkey
bye and bye

Epitaph brings them together, and
brings Durdles with them.

The Keys.   Stoney Durdles

1 **Rochester Cathedral from the west.** From Winkles's *Architectural and Picturesque Illustrations of the Cathedral Churches of England and Wales, 1838–42*

Chapter 1

First monthly number
April 1870

THE DAWN.

In MS the chapter was entitled 'The Prologue'.

An ancient English

An ancient English Cathedral Town? How can the ancient English Cathedral town be here!] This is the MS reading restored by Margaret Cardwell in her 1972 edition. Up until then, all published texts from 1870 onwards erroneously read 'Tower' for 'Town' and 'tower' for 'town'.

massive grey square tower] The Cathedral in Rochester, the model for Cloisterham, is built on the site of a Saxon church, on the ruins of which a Norman church and a Benedictine monastery were established (Plate 1). The Cathedral is modest in size, with double transepts, a raised choir, a presbytery containing the tombs of twelfth-century and thirteenth-century bishops, and a crypt beneath the presbytery. The crypt, Early English in style, is one of the largest and most beautiful in England (Plate 2). The central tower and spire of the Cathedral were completed in the fourteenth century. Fildes's vignette title-page for the first edition of the novel illustrates the tower as recased (by Cottingham) in 1823. (The present tower and spire are twentieth-century, although completed on the lines of the originals.) The Cathedral is described in more detail in the notes to chapter 3.

set up by the Sultan's orders for the impaling of a horde of Turkish robbers . . . the Sultan goes by . . . in long procession. Ten thousand scimitars flash . . . and thrice ten thousand dancing-girls strew flowers. Then, follow white elephants caparisoned in countless gorgeous colors, and infinite in number and attendants.] *The Arabian Nights Entertainments* is linked with opium-smoking in the article in *London Society* on which this scene is partly based (see note below, pp. 22–5). This evocation of one of Dickens's favourite books as a child does not derive from a particular *Arabian Nights* tale but conflates characteristic elements in all the tales: autocratic sultans; magnificent processions; vast numbers of attendants; hyperbolic descriptions of beautiful women and splendid jewels and fabrics. Dickens uses some licence in his imitation: many of the tales feature robbers, for example, but none of the robbers is specified as Turkish; and the most common form of execution is not to be impaled on a spike but to be decapitated with a scimitar (see the edition read by Dickens: *The Arabian Nights Entertainments*, trans. Jonathan Scott, 6 vols, 1811).

Is the spike so low a thing as the rusty spike on the top of a post of an old bedstead] Such a bedstead features in *LD* in Arthur Clennam's garret

2 The crypt in Rochester Cathedral, by H. K. Browne. From Winkles's *Architectural and Picturesque*

bedroom: the old bedstead has 'four bare atomies of posts, each terminating in a spike, as if for the dismal accommodation of lodgers who might prefer to impale themselves' (1.3).

Shaking from head to foot

the man whose scattered consciousness has thus fantastically pieced itself together] The account of the genesis of the novel which Dickens gave to Forster (3.18.425–6) mentions the double life of Jasper:

> 'I laid aside the fancy I told you of, and have a very curious and new idea for my new story. Not a communicable idea (or the interest of the book would be gone), but a very strong one, though difficult to work.' The story, I learnt immediately afterward, was to be that of the murder of a nephew by his uncle; the originality of which was to consist in the review of the murderer's career by himself at the close, when its temptations were to be dwelt upon as if, not he the culprit, but some other man, were the tempted.

The words Forster quotes partly contradict his claim that he soon after learnt just those details of the plot that Dickens said he could not, or would not, reveal. The subject of Jasper's 'scattered consciousness', his dual personality, is a critical crux of the novel.

supports his trembling frame upon his arms] In the nineteenth century large amounts of opium, imported mostly from Turkey, were sold on the London drug market as freely as any other commodity. Brokers dealt openly with importations, which varied from about 12,000 pounds in 1834 to as much as 196,000 in later decades. Persia competed with Turkey as the century wore on. The opium produced in India was exported to China, and the extent of British involvement in this trade caused growing concern in Britain.

Opium was mostly used to alleviate the symptoms of major diseases for which specific remedies were unknown, and to treat all sorts of minor ailments and anxieties. It was widely used during the cholera epidemics which began in the 1830s. Although opium was required by law in 1868 to be clearly marked as poison, it continued to be sold over the counter, not merely by chemists but by grocers and public houses. It could be bought in a variety of forms: as pills and lozenges, as laudanum (the alcoholic tincture of opium) and as chlorodyne (the active ingredient in many patent medicines). Children in particular were given opium-based syrups with names like 'Godfrey's Cordial', 'Dalby's Carminative', 'McMunn's Elixir', 'Batley's Sedative Solution' and 'Mother Bailey's Quieting Syrup'.

By the 1860s awareness of the dangers of abuse had been aroused through articles in the press and medical journals. In May 1867 a bill put before Parliament proposed that sales of opium be recorded, but this clause was excluded from the 1868 Pharmacy Act. The terms of the Act were modified partly because of anxiety that the demand for the drug, if so controlled, would cause it to fall into the hands of illegal marketeers, and partly because it was thought that having to record all sales would place unreasonable strains upon chemists. So there was no immediate check on continuing abuse, and only in the 1880s was the trade finally limited.

Dickens based his depiction of Jasper's opium addiction on popular knowledge, and on his own experience, observations and reading. The Romantic writers, notably De Quincey and Coleridge, and also Sir Walter Scott, were known to have used laudanum for medicinal and recreational purposes. The publication of De Quincey's *Confessions of an English Opium-Eater* in the *London Magazine* in 1821 created widespread interest: opium-eating came to be associated in the public mind with artistic genius and poetic imagination. The portrayal of the Cathedral choirmaster as a haunted and damaged artistic temperament dependent on opium is informed by the association. In several of Dickens's earlier novels, descriptions of heightened states of mind are similarly influenced by details from De Quincey: the illness of Esther Summerson in *BH* (35), and of Eugene Wrayburn in *OMF* (4.10); and the faces in the pavement seen by Mr Boffin in *OMF* (1.8).

Dickens's awareness of the wretchedness, rather than the romance, of opium derived in part from his personal experience of the drug. His friend Wilkie Collins used laudanum regularly, and he himself used it in his later years to counter pain and insomnia. In his last letter to his sister-in-law, Georgina Hogarth, he admits to having 'got a good night's rest under the influence of Laudanum but it hangs about me very heavily to-day' (*Nonesuch* 3.776). Opium-smoking in dens was limited to the small communities of Chinese seamen established around the London docks. (For Dickens's visit to one of these in 1869, see note below.)

Opium addiction was not identified in the nineteenth century, and was not considered a disease, but, rather, a moral issue. The physical effects experienced by addicts can vary. Jasper manifests a number of them. Small doses can stimulate the subject to a sense of vigour, while larger ones create a dream-like state of lethargy in which time and place are confused amidst images and ideas. The sleep that follows can sometimes result in coma, leading to respiratory failure and death. More usually, the subject awakens from sleep flushed and sweating, with a slow pulse and feelings of nausea, depression and headache. The symptom of contracted pupils may account for the film over the eyes mentioned several times in the novel. Opium is a delusory drug: as the initial euphoria and cessation of anxiety decline, the subject's impulse is to increase the intake, and in so doing create dependence (Hayter, 1968, 49; Lomax, 1973, 174; Berridge, 1978, 442; Berridge and Edwards, 1981, 60–1, 78; Wellcome, 1984, 16–20).

He is in the meanest and closest of small rooms.] This scene conflates the details of two actual East End opium dens, one of which was visited by Dickens in 1869. Accounts of the other one were published in *London Society* and the *Ragged School Union Magazine* the previous year. Although opium dens clearly offered similar facilities, the correspondence between the den depicted in the novel and the den described in the periodicals suggests that Dickens drew on these accounts as much as on his personal experience. In a letter of 15 May 1869, Dickens looked forward to taking a visiting American friend, James T.

Fields, on a tour of a shabby court in Shadwell, arranged 'with some of the Police, to have a glimpse of the darker side of London life' (*Nonesuch* 3.725). Fields recalled the expedition, which took place that summer:

> It was in one of the horrid opium-dens that he gathered the incidents which he has related in the opening pages of "Edwin Drood." In a miserable court we found the haggard old woman blowing at a kind of pipe made of an old penny ink-bottle. The identical words which Dickens puts into the mouth of this wretched creature in "Edwin Drood" we heard her croon as we leaned over the tattered bed on which she was lying. There was something hideous in the way this woman kept repeating, "Ye'll pay up according, deary, won't ye?" and the Chinamen and Lascars made never-to-be-forgotten pictures in the scene. (1900; reprinted 1970, 202–3)

Two other accounts of this same opium den survive. A few years before Dickens's visit, his friend, Inspector Charles Field (the original of Mr Bucket in *BH*), accompanied a group of young Guardsmen on a tour of the East End slums. One of them wrote an account of the expedition:

> We were then conducted to an opium den . . . It belonged to a woman known as "Sally the Opium Smoker". Her hair was perfectly white and she appeared to be very aged . . . When we reached the street Field asked us how old we imagined Sally to be, and we all guessed various ages, eighty being the lowest. We were then told that Sally was but twenty-six years old. (Wellesley, 1947, 75–6)

(See Collins, 1964, 88–90.) (An interesting coincidence is that Jasper, too, is twenty-six years old.)

After the publication of *MED* this den was visited by an American who sent his description of it to Forster:

> I went lately with the same inspector who accompanied Dickens to see the room of the opium-smokers, old Eliza and her Lascar or Bengalee friend. There a fancy seized me to buy the bedstead which figures so accurately in *Edwin Drood*, in narrative and picture. I gave the old woman a pound for it, and have it now packed and ready for shipment to New York. Another American bought a pipe. (3.18.427)

The fashion for gentlemen to tour the Chinese settlements in the East End was stimulated by the visit of the Prince of Wales to a den, also in Shadwell, which was reported in 'East London Opium Smokers' in *London Society* (14, 1868, 68–72; see Plates 3 and 4). The den visited by Dickens was kept by a woman. The den visited by the *London Society* reporter was kept by a Chinese and his sickly English wife. By way of introducing them to the reader, the reporter opens his article with a reference to the *Arabian Nights*:

> Of all carnal delights that over which opium rules as the presiding genius is most shrouded in mystery. It is invested with a weird and fantastic interest (for which its Oriental origin is doubtless in some degree accountable), and

3 **'The Opium-Smokers.'** From the *Illustrated London News*, 65 (1 August 1874), 99

> there hovers about it a vague fascination, such as is felt towards ghostly legend and the lore of fairy land . . . It is the vulgar supposition . . . that the thousand and one seductive stories contained in the 'Arabian Nights' were composed by writers whose senses were steeped in it. (68)

As the reporter enters the squalid house of the opium-master, Chi Ki, he notices in the parlour 'a large bedstead, with a bed made the wrong way on it'. Then he walks upstairs to the public smoking-room:

> It was an extremely mean and miserable little room . . . The chief and most conspicuous article of furniture the room contained was a large four-post bed-stead, and a bed like the one downstairs. The bed was not arranged according to the English fashion. It was rolled up bolster-wise all along the length of the bedstead, leaving the mattress bare except for a large mat of Chinese grass. The bed-hangings were of some light Chinese gauze, but very dirty, and hitched up slatternly on the hanging-rails. (69, 70)

The English wife of Chi Ki resembles in many respects Jasper's hostess, identified by Deputy in chapter 23 as the Princess Puffer. She is a 'youngish woman, very thin and pale-looking, and scarcely as tidy as she might have been':

> Poor English Mrs Chi Ki looks as though she is being gradually smoke-dried, and by and by will present the appearance of an Egyptian mummy . . . 'It is hot work I assure you when we are busy . . . It don't often make me ill; it makes me silly. I am ill sometimes, though.' (69, 72)

Another account of this woman and the den she inhabits was published the same year: 'In an Opium Den', in the *Ragged School Union Magazine* (20, 198–200). The article deplores the dens because they were frequented not only by Chinese, but also by 'British sailors, and men and women who desire to find in opium that oblivion from care which alcoholic liquors cannot give' (199). Here, Mr Chi Ki is called 'Jack', the name which must have suggested to Dickens that of the rival of the Princess Puffer, 'Jack Chinaman t'other side the court':

> By the flickering light of the fire burning in the grate I perceive the individual addressed as Jack. It is a Chinese who keeps this wretched hole, where one can get intoxicated for a few coppers. The room we enter is so low that we are unable to stand upright. Lying pell-mell on a mattress placed on the ground are Chinamen, Lascars, and a few English blackguards who have imbibed a taste for opium . . .
>
> Seated on a mattress in a room lighted by a dim lamp is an old woman with dishevelled white hair, thin face, and dull-looking eyes, blowing a cloud of smoke and coughing every now and then like a person in the last stage of consumption. She casts a stupefied gaze upon us, then throws herself back, and continues to puff away at her pipe of opium . . .
>
> . . . beyond the mattress on which the old sorceress is reclining there is not a single piece of furniture. The atmosphere is so tainted with opium that, being

4 An opium-den in the East End of London, by Gustave Doré. From *London, A Pilgrimage*, by Gustave Doré and B. Jerrold, 1872

> on the point of suffocation, I break the only window pane, through which, by the way, a kitten would find some difficulty in passing. The fresh air inundates the room, rousing up the sorceress, who gives vent to a volley of complaints in an unintelligible jargon. A shilling flung on the unclean couch mollifies the old woman, who opens her eyes to their full extent by a superhuman effort. She seizes the coin with her long, bony fingers and contemplates it with delight. A new attack of coughing, more formidable than the former, seems to tear her lungs as we retreat. (199–200)

Dickens himself describes in *BH* the wretchedness associated with opium-smoking when Tulkinghorn discovers the body of Nemo (10).

Lascar] The term applied to East Indian sailors from the Bombay region. The usage dates from the seventeenth century. Because they were cheap to hire, foreign sailors were commonly employed in the merchant marine:

> the ships are manned with motley crews of Bombay lascars, Maories, Negroes, Arabs, Chinamen, Kroomen, and Malays. There are no British or American seamen now. (Dilke, 1869, 192)

a kind of pipe] Such as the one described in *London Society*:

> Next he produced . . . an instrument like a flute, with a wooden cup with a lid to it screwed on at a distance of about three inches from the end. It was not a flute, however, but a pipe, – *the* pipe . . . It was simply an eighteen-inch length of yellow bamboo with the cup of dark-coloured baked clay before mentioned fitted into a sort of spiggot hole near the end . . .
>
> 'It's worth ten pounds,' said his wife; 'it has had nothing but the best opium smoked in it these fourteen years.'
>
> And she then went on further to enumerate the many excellences of the pipe; from which I gathered that its value was not after all so fanciful as at first appeared: since half a given quantity of opium would yield more satisfaction when smoked in a ripe, well-saturated old pipe than the whole quantity in a comparatively new one. (70)

A less detailed description appears in a *HW* article of 1851 which gives an account of opium-smoking in China (3.331). The opium woman must make do with penny ink-bottles, but Jasper, who keeps a pipe at home (chapter 5), would have a pipe made of bamboo with an ornamented stem carved in silver, gold or ivory. A smoker's outfit also required a box for storing the opium, a small lamp, scissors for trimming the wick, a knife for cleaning the bowl, and a saucer and tray (Kane, 1882, 33–5) (see Plate 4).

"Ye've smoked

"Ye've smoked as many as five] Two figures are crossed out in MS, one of which could be 'four' (not in Cardwell). Perhaps Dickens had some difficulty in deciding how many pipes would be a reasonable number. The reporter from *London Society* comments:

> What chiefly surprised me was the short time it took to consume the charging of a pipe. From the time of the young Chinaman's taking the stem in his mouth till the opium was exhausted, not more than a minute and a half was occupied. (71)

The novice smoker in the *HW* account of opium-smoking in a Chinese tea-garden comments:

> Three whiffs and it is out, and we are more than half deprived of active consciousness. Let us repeat the operation. Practised smokers will go on for hours; a few whiffs are enough for us. (3.331).

Though Jasper has taken opium for some years (chapter 23), the degree of his addiction is not clear. He has probably taken more opium in the den than he would normally smoke at home. Some smokers could take up to fifty and a hundred pipes a day, but Jasper, though a regular smoker, is not as excessively dependent.

business is slack . . . and no ships coming in] The *London Society* reporter comments: 'Sometimes, I was informed, trade was so slack that not more than two or three customers would apply all day long.' On the other hand, Mrs Chi Ki told him: ' "Sometimes two or three ships come in at once, and then we have a houseful" ' (71, 72). By the 1860s shipping in the London docks had declined on account of competition from the railways. Nathaniel Hawthorne observed in 1857: 'The aspect of London along the Thames . . . is by no means so impressive':

> The shore is lined with the shabbiest, blackest, and ugliest buildings that can be imagined, decayed warehouses, with blind windows, and wharves that look ruinous; insomuch that, had I known nothing more of the world's metropolis, I might have fancied that it had already experienced the downfall which I have heard commercial and financial prophets predict for it, within the century.
>
> ('Up the Thames', *Our Old Home*)

The same scene is noticed in *OMF* from the vantage-point of a boat on the Thames in dockland:

> Very little life was to be seen on either bank, windows and doors were shut, and the staring black and white letters upon wharves and warehouses 'looked,' said Eugene to Mortimer, 'like inscriptions over the graves of dead businesses.' (1.14)

More than three shillings and sixpence for a thimbleful!] *London Society* comments:

> Evidently opium-smoking is a more expensive enjoyment than dram drinking. Chi Ki showed me his 'measures'. They were three little ivory cups, the smallest the size of a lady's thimble. For this, full of the treacle-like opium, fourpence was charged; the next-sized cup was sixpence, and the largest a shilling. (71)

By comparison, the Princess Puffer's price seems 'dreffle high', but there were different qualities of opium and prices varied accordingly. Egyptian opium was considered less good than Turkish or Persian. Opium was often adulterated along the journey from peasant farmer to London market. Under pressure to supply, farmers would supplement the raw material with such things as dried leaves, meal, and even cow dung (Berridge and Edwards, 10, 87–91, 202–3).

the true secret of mixing it]

> It is this secret that constitutes the rarity of the luxury. To be enjoyed, the opium must be prepared by a competent hand. There are few such in London . . .
>
> The opium has to be put through a peculiar process before it is reduced to the semi-liquid state. It has to be cooked . . . the opium of the druggist is shredded into little slices, which are laid on a piece of stout coarse canvas, which is suspended in a small iron pot partly filled with water. In the process of boiling, the essence of the opium drains through the canvas and forms a sediment at the bottom of the pot, leaving on the canvas the refuse, looking not unlike tea-leaves. (*London Society* 68, 72)

A passage in the novel on Thuggee by Colonel Meadows Taylor (*Confessions of a Thug*, 1839) shows the hero enjoying the flavour of a hookah which is declared to have been prepared ' "from a choice receipt, and it is only persons of rank and taste like yourself to whom I ever give it! It would be lost on the multitude" ' (10).

She blows at the pipe

She blows at the pipe as she speaks, and, occasionally bubbling at it, inhales much of its contents.]

> He took the bamboo fairly into his mouth, and there was at once emitted from the pipe a gurgling sound . . . As the smoker heard the delicious sound, the lids of his elongated eyes quivered in ecstasy, and he sucked harder, swallowing all the black smoke except so little as he was bound to waste in the process of breathing. He was as economical as could be, however, and expelled but the merest thread of the previous smoke through his nostrils and none by means of his mouth. (*London Society* 71)

"Oh me, Oh me, my lungs

I makes my pipes of old penny ink-bottles] A cheap substitute for bowls. On 5 May 1870, Dickens assured Sir John Bowring, whom he consulted on the effects of opium-smoking, that during his visit to Shadwell he saw the opium-smoking 'exactly as I have described it, penny ink-bottle and all' (*Nonesuch* 3.775). About the illustration of this scene, 'In the Court', Fildes recorded that he had drawn the opium room from Dickens's description; the author 'recognized it as the very portrait of the place' and considered the figures were like 'photographs of the characters' (Alice Meynell, 1884, 525).

I fits in a mouthpiece, this way, and I takes my mixter out of this thimble with this little horn spoon; and so I fills] The filling of the pipe by Chi Ki is described in *London Society*:

> The stuff in the gallipot looked exactly like thin treacle, and smelt like burnt sugar and laudanum. Decidedly it seemed queer stuff to load a pipe with. But it had yet to be cooked – or grilled. Taking an iron bodkin from his little tool-chest, Chi Ki dipped the tip of it into the semi-liquid stuff, and withdrawing a little drop of it, held it in the flame of the lamp until it hardened somewhat. Keeping this still on the point of the bodkin, he dipped it again into the gallipot and again held it in the lamp flame, and repeated the process until a piece of the size of a large pea was accumulated and properly toasted. This was placed in a pipe bowl, and the hungry customer sprang up on to the bed to enjoy it.
>
> It was lit at the little lamp, and then the young Chinaman reclining at his ease . . . took the pipestem into his mouth. (70, 71)

A less detailed description is given in the *HW* article quoted previously. There a 'long stiletto' is used in place of the iron bodkin. Horn spoons were also alternatives. The MS reads 'needle'.

I got Heavens-hard drunk for sixteen year] Opium was thought to be an antidote to alcohol; indeed, it was generally administered as a remedy for delirium tremens even though fatal overdosing could occur. Another belief was that opium-eaters lived to a good age (Berridge and Edwards, 33, 40). The Princess Puffer maintains her sharpness and is nowhere actually described as 'old', although 'Mother Puffer' was the name originally given to her (chapter 23). Doctors working among the poor who took opium learnt that the drug was used in an attempt to alleviate the ills associated with poor housing, bad diet, and constant harassment (Berridge and Edwards, 26).

He rises unsteadily

the woman has opium-smoked herself into a strange likeness of the Chinaman.] Perhaps a reference to an expression, rather than a similarity, of feature. Edwin's recognition of the woman as someone who takes opium (chapter 14) suggests that there is something familiar to him in the stupor of opium trance which he had witnessed in his uncle.

"What visions can she *have?"*

"What visions can *she* have?"] Perhaps alluding to the idea behind De Quincey's claim that 'opium cannot give you dreams unless you already have the power to dream interestingly' (noted by Hayter, 1971, 21).

As he watches

unclean spirit of imitation.] That is, to be possessed by the devil, as in Mark 1.25–6: 'And Jesus rebuked him, saying, Hold thy peace, and come out of him. And when the unclean spirit had torn him, and cried with a loud voice, he came out of him.'

Slowly loosening his grasp

and draws a phantom knife.] Perhaps a hint of *Macbeth* 2.1.33–4: 'Is this a dagger which I see before me,/The handle toward my hand? Come, let me clutch thee.'

That same afternoon

That same afternoon] We do not know what becomes of Jasper between dawn and dusk; it would take only a matter of two hours to get from London Bridge Station to Cloisterham.

daily vesper service, and he must needs attend it] In *OMF* Bradley Headstone also reverts to his accustomed respectability after a sleepless night of wandering:

> Up came the sun to find him washed and brushed, methodically dressed in decent black coat and waistcoat, decent formal black tie, and pepper-and-salt pantaloons, with his decent silver watch in its pocket, and its decent hair-guard round his neck. (3.11)

The choir are getting on their sullied white robes] The boys may have had a funny or an important role to play in the resolution.

"WHEN THE WICKED MAN –"] The first verse of Evening Prayer (and Morning Prayer): 'When the wicked man turneth away from his wickedness that he hath committed, and doeth that which is lawful and right, he shall save his soul alive' (Ezekiel 18.27). The words that follow are 'I acknowledge my transgressions: and my sin is ever before me' (Psalms 51.3).

Chapter 2

A DEAN, AND A CHAPTER ALSO.

The title was altered from 'A Dean as Well as a Chapter' – perhaps because, as Trollope suggests, 'there is something charming to the English ear in the name of the Dean and Chapter' ('The Normal Dean of the Present Day', *Clergymen of the Church of England*, 1866, 35).

The Dean controls the services and, with the chapter, supervises the fabric and property of the cathedral. He is appointed by the Crown and ranks next to the bishop, although he is independent of him. Trollope provides a fine description of a dean:

> If there be any man, who is not or has not been a Dean himself, who can distinctly define the duties of a Dean of the Church of England, he must be one who has studied ecclesiastical subjects very deeply ... The dean's modest

> thousand a year sounds small in comparison with the bishop's more generous stipend: – but look at a dean, and you will always see that he is sleeker than a bishop. The dean to whom fortune has given a quaint old house with pleasant garden in a quaint old close, with resident prebendaries and minor canons around him who just acknowledge, and no more than acknowledge, his superiority, – who takes the lead, as Mr Dean, in the society of his clerical city . . . seems indeed to have had his lines given him in very pleasant places . . .
>
> The normal dean of this age is a gentleman who would probably not have taken orders unless the circumstances of his life had placed orders very clearly in his path. He is not a man who has been urged strongly in early youth by a vocation for clerical duties, or who has subsequently devoted himself to what may be called clerical administrations proper. He has taken kindly to literature, having been biassed in his choice of the branch which he has assumed by the fact of the word 'Reverend' which has attached itself to his name. He has done well at the university, and has been a fellow, and perhaps a tutor, of his college. He has written a book or two, and has not impossibly shown himself to be too liberal for the bench. (31–7)

The chapter comprises the members of the corporate body responsible for the spiritual and temporal concerns of a cathedral. In the words of Trollope, the 'highest duty' of the chapter is 'permission to choose its own bishop' (40). 'The Queen is the head of the Church, and therefore sends down word to a chapter . . . that it has permission to choose its bishop, the bishop having been already appointed by the Prime Minister', and 'the chapter makes its choice accordingly' (41).

Whosoever has observed

Whosoever has observed] Echoing the Athanasian Creed, recited at Morning Prayer:

> Whosoever will be saved: before all things it is necessary that he hold the Catholic Faith. Which Faith except every one do keep the whole and undefiled: without doubt he shall perish everlastingly. And the Catholic Faith is this: That we worship one God in Trinity, and Trinity in Unity.

that sedate and clerical bird, the rook] The MS revision from 'crow' to 'rook' is apt: the crow is not a colonial bird, for it nests in pairs. The rook's appearance is more clerical, with its bare white beak and shaggy feathered legs. The rook is a traditional image for the clergy; compare, for example, William Cowper (1731–1800), 'The Jackdaw':

> There is a bird who, by his coat,
> And by the hoarseness of his note,
> Might be suppos'd a crow;
> A great frequenter of the church,
> Where, bishop-like, he finds a perch,
> And dormitory too.

The clerical rook has found its way into the nursery rhyme 'Who Killed Cock Robin':

> Who'll be the parson?
> I, said the Rook,
> With my little book,
> I'll be the parson.

wings his way homeward] Reminiscent of *Macbeth* 3.2.50–1: 'Light thickens, and the crow/Makes wing to th' rooky wood'.

mere men] A poetic cliché, as in *Paradise Regain'd* 4.535–6: 'To th' utmost of meer man both wise and good'.

Similarly, service being

walk together in the echoing Close.] The west door beside the 'low arched Cathedral door' opens on to a small grass verge and immediately on to a roadway. With their backs to the west door, they could watch Jasper 'flit away' to the right towards the Gate House. But if they are 'in the echoing Close' they would be on the north–south axis of the Cathedral, looking towards the Priory Gate House (see Map; for the Gate House, see note on p. 36).

Not only is

the monastery ruin] A Benedictine monastery was founded in Rochester in 1082, and the now ruined buildings to the south of the nave of the Cathedral were built soon after. In *GE* Pip walks among these ruins and later stays at an inn which had once been part of an ecclesiastical house (49, 52).

Their fallen leaves lie strewn thickly about.] An echo of the passage in *Aeneid* 6, adapted by Milton:

> he stood and called
> His legions, angel forms, who lay entranced
> Thick as autumnal leaves that strow the brooks
> In Vallombrosa. (*Paradise Lost* 1.300)

seek sanctuary] A play on the tradition of the church providing sanctuary for criminals, a touch that foreshadows Neville's being denied sanctuary in chapter 16.

low arched Cathedral door] The small door adjoining the great west door, and to the north of it.

and cast them forth] The phrase is biblical; for example: 'He casteth forth his ice like morsels: who can stand before his cold?' (Psalms 147.17); 'And it grieveth me sore: therefore I cast forth all the household stuff of Tobiah out of the chamber' (Nehemiah 13.8).

a goodly key] St Peter was told by Christ: 'And I will give unto thee the keys of the kingdom of heaven' (Matthew 16.19).

a folio music-book] Music printed or written on sheets that have been folded once.

"Mr. Jasper

"Mr. Jasper] The name was suggested by Southey's ballad, 'Jaspar' (1798; 1799), a macabre tale about a murderer which inspired a poem by Thomas Hood which was also known to Dickens, *The Dream of Eugene Aram, the Murderer* (1829; 1831). Both Jasper's names derive from Southey: 'Jasper' from the murderer and 'John' from the impoverished labourer, called 'Jonathan', who is almost persuaded by Jaspar to murder his landlord. Jonathan's role is to serve as Jaspar's *alter ego.*

There are further similarities between the ballad and the novel. The body of Jaspar's victim is thrown into a river and never found, nor is the crime detected:

Jaspar raised up the murder'd man,
And plunged him in the flood,
And in the running water then
He cleansed his hands from blood.

The waters closed around the corpse,
And cleansed his hands from gore,
The willow waved, the stream flow'd on,
And murmur'd as before.

There was no human eye had seen
The blood the murderer spilt,
And Jaspar's conscience never felt
The avenging goad of guilt. (45–56)

In the closing scene of the ballad, set by the river-bank, 'a sudden light' from heaven pierces the darkness of the night. The murderer's crime is revealed to the eye of God, and Jaspar goes mad:

His cheek is pale, his eye is wild,
His look bespeaks despair;
For Jaspar since that hour has made
His home unshelter'd there.

And fearful are his dreams at night,
And dread to him the day;
He thinks upon his untold crime,
And never dares to pray.

Chapter 2, *A Dean, and a Chapter Also*

The summer suns, the winter storms,
  O'er him unheeded roll,
For heavy is the weight of blood
  Upon the maniac's soul. (169–80)

(See Shatto, 1985, 359–60.)

Sir Jasper in Fielding's *The Mock Doctor* (1733) has been suggested as a possible influence on Dickens's choice of name (Beer, 1984, 146, 185). But Sir Jasper is not an evil character. Aylmer observed that the choice of 'Jasper' 'may be due to its having become a stock name for wicked baronets in melodrama' (1964, 42), though he does not identify the melodramas. An article by Dickens in *HW* (11.434) has a pompous Member of Parliament named Sir Jasper Janus.

It is worth noting that references to the jasper stone in the Bible make an interesting pattern in *MED*. Jasper compares himself to Crisparkle, who is always training himself 'to be, mind and body, as clear as crystal' (echoing Neville's comment on the Minor Canon's 'sound mind in his own sound body' in chapter 14). The phrase is from Revelation where the city of God is described as 'Having the glory of God; and her light was like unto a stone most precious, even like a jasper stone, clear as crystal' (12.11). Also in Revelation, the throned figure is likened to a jasper, and the wall of the city is described as being built 'of jasper: and the city was pure gold' (4.3, 21.18). The coincidence that jasper is mentioned in Ezekiel is also interesting: the prophet comments on the King of Tyre that he is 'full of wisdom and perfect in beauty' and, having 'been in Eden, the garden of God', has had every precious stone adorn his covering, including jasper (Beer, 1984, 163). It seems unlikely that Dickens would have chosen to quote from Ezekiel so significantly in chapter 1, would have chosen Grewgious's name (the King of Tyre, like Grewgious, is named Hiram), and would have Jasper quote from Revelation, without an awareness that the echoes would relate to each other.

The jasper stone is accorded certain qualities in a work on gemmology which Wilkie Collins consulted during the writing of *The Moonstone* (Hennelly, 1984, 25–47). The two writers were estranged at the time so it is not likely that Collins would have shared his enthusiasm for gemmology with Dickens, nevertheless some of the qualities recorded strike a harmonious note with *MED*. The stone is green, giving a hint of Jasper's jealousy; it is 'like crystal', recalling Revelation; it is 'always opaque', which is appropriate to Jasper's impenetrable personality; and its being 'not invariably of one colour' also accords with the double personality. That the stone is familiar in the East and is used by Egyptians as amulets, particularly against spectres, is an interesting fact with regard to the Eastern elements in *MED*; also, that it is sometimes called St Stephen's Stone is an odd coincidence in view of the fact that Jasper wonders whether Durdles's nickname (Stony Durdles) stands for 'Stephen' in chapter 4 (see King, 1865, 201–11).

Tope] The prototype of Tope is reported to have been William Miles (1815–1909), a verger in Rochester Cathedral who was personally known to Dickens. Miles joined the staff of the Cathedral in 1824 and for seventy-five years was successively chorister, lay clerk, under-verger and verger (Walters, 1912, xxxiv). Tope was originally named 'Peptune'; this was revised in chapter 5. The word 'tope' does exist as a surname, but the definition of the word as a verb suggests perhaps that the verger makes free with communion wine. Alternatively, 'tope' used as a noun is a provincial name for the wren.

"And when and how

Mr. Crisparkle] The name reflects his Muscular Christianity (see note below, p. 38), and hints at 'Christ' (Bleiler, 1984, 137).

"Why, sir

Mr. Jasper was that breathed] Shortness of breath is a withdrawal symptom. Coleridge mentions that taking opium 'in the day-time increases the puffing' (*Notebooks* 2.1977). Withdrawal symptoms usually appear within twelve to fourteen hours of the last dose, which Jasper would have taken at the opium den that morning.

They all three

an old stone Gate House] There are three gate houses near the Cathedral and all have features in common with Jasper's home. College Gate (also known as College Yard Gate, Cemetery Gate and Chertsey Gate) is a picturesque weather-boarded structure with stone arching. It abuts on to the High Street, about a hundred yards to the north of the Cathedral front (see Map). It is too small to have provided the accommodation that Jasper has. To the east, and adjoining the Cathedral, beside the small burial-ground attached to it, is the ten-roomed Deanery Gate House. More suitable as to size, it, too, has an archway leading to the old Deanery. To the south of the Cathedral, Prior's Gate, or the 'Priory Gate House', is a castellated stone structure having a winding staircase or 'postern stair'. But, like College Gate, Prior's Gate is too small in actuality to have been Jasper's home, being merely a single medieval room with unplastered stone walls and an open fireplace (Arnold, 1961, 110). On the other hand, the location of Prior's Gate within the Cathedral precincts (the 'eerie Precincts'), away from the well-lighted High Street, would agree with Dickens's description of Jasper's Gate House as like a lighthouse in a sea of darkness.

A quest to identify Jasper's Gate House motivated W. R. Hughes to write to Luke Fildes in 1890. Fildes replied:

> The background of the drawing of 'Durdles cautioning Sapsea,' I believe I sketched from what you call . . . The College Gate. I am almost certain it was not taken from . . . the Prior's.
>
> The room in the drawing, 'On dangerous ground,' is imaginary.
>
> I do not believe I entered any of the Gatehouses.
>
> The resemblance you see in the drawing to the room in the Deanery Gatehouse . . . might not be gained by actual observation of the *interior*.

> In many instances an artist can well judge what the interior may be from studying the *outside*. I only throw this out to show that the artist may not have seen a thing even when a strong resemblance occurs. I am sorry to leave any doubt on the subject, though personally I feel none.
>
> You see I never felt the necessity or propriety of being locally accurate to Rochester or its buildings. Dickens, of course, meant Rochester; yet, at the same time, he chose to be obscure on that point, and I took my cue from him. I always thought it was one of his most artistic pieces of work; the vague, dreamy description of the Cathedral in the opening chapter of the book. So definite in one sense, yet so locally vague. (Hughes, 1891, 128–9)

strikes the hour] Evensong would be from four to four-thirty in the afternoon, so the hour is now five.

pile close at hand.] Perhaps the ruined castle, not mentioned elsewhere in the novel but prominent in Fildes's vignette for the title-page.

"Is Mr. Jasper's

Mr. Jasper's nephew] The prevalence and significance of uncles and nephews in Dickens's works has been discussed by Harry Levin (1975). There are many instances of comparison between *MED* and Wilkie Collins's novels, in particular *The Moonstone* (see Introduction, pp. 2, 5). An interesting likeness has been suggested between the relationship of Jasper with his nephew and Dickens and his protégé, Collins, from whom he was estranged at the time of writing the novel (Lonoff, 1980, 161–3).

"Well, well

Mr. Jasper's heart may not be too much set upon his nephew.] Job 7.17: 'What is man, that thou shouldest magnify him? and that thou shouldest set thine heart upon him?'

Our affections . . . in this transitory world] An echo of the Communion Service:

> And we most humbly beseech thee of thy goodness, O Lord, to comfort and succour all them, who in this transitory life are in trouble, sorrow, need, sickness, or any other adversity.

With a pleasant air

his quaint hat] The dean's hat is shown in the illustration, 'Durdles Cautions Mr. Sapsea against Boasting'; it has a lower crown than the top hats worn by the others, and has strings on each side between the crown and brim.

the snug old red-brick house] The Deanery at Rochester lies beside the ruins of the old chapter house at the east end of the Cathedral. The Deanery extends back into gracious gardens.

"in residence"] The Ecclesiastical Commissioner's Act of 1841 required a dean to be resident eight months out of the year:

> it is expected, of course, that a dean should show himself in his own cathedral. Let him reside and show himself, and the city which he graces by his presence will hardly demand from him other services.
>
> ('The Normal Dean of the Present Day', 33)

Mr. Crisparkle

Minor Canon] Periods of residence for canons were often brief so that greater responsibility fell to the minor canons, usually chosen by the dean and chapter for their ability to sing the services. Trollope's Mr Harding at Barchester had 'a fine voice and a taste for sacred music' which 'decided the position in which he was to exercise his calling, and for many years he performed the easy but not highly paid duties of a minor canon' (*The Warden*, 1855).

perpetually pitching himself head-foremost into all the deep running water] These words are underlined in Fildes's copy of the proofs (Cardwell, 1972, 269). Crisparkle's virtues of physical prowess, manliness, self-reliance and cheerfulness identify him as a 'Muscular Christian', the ideal type of manhood espoused by Charles Kingsley. At Rugby, Kingsley's admiration for Dr Arnold and Thomas Hughes, a noted school athlete, inspired him to develop his philosophy of a healthy and manly Christianity. Crisparkle resembles the heroes of Kingsley's *Westward Ho!* (1855) and *Two Years Ago* (1857). Amyas Leigh and Tom Thurnall are spirited, tough, confident and enterprising. But they are also godly, gentlemanly and, above all, pure. The probable source of the term 'Muscular Christianity' was an anonymous review of *Two Years Ago* which defined Kingsley's heroic type:

> We all know by this time what is the task that Mr Kingsley has made specially his own – it is that of spreading the knowledge and fostering the love of muscular Christianity. His ideal is a man who fears God and can walk a thousand miles in a thousand hours – who, in the language which Mr Kingsley has made popular, breathes God's free air on God's rich earth, and at the same time can hit a woodcock, doctor a horse, and twist a poker round his fingers.
>
> (*Saturday Review*, 3 (21 February 1857, 176)

Dickens revealed a humorous sympathy with Muscular Christianity when proposing a toast at a dinner for the University College Hospital (12 April 1864), to

> the Volunteers, of whose Muscular Christianity I avow myself a devoted admirer – holding, as I do, that muscular development of anything that is good is strong presumptive proof of soundness of condition. (*Speeches* 326)

early riser] The recommended habit of early rising was typical of some Victorian medical theories based more on fashions in morality than on science:

> The faculty of remaining asleep longer than is necessary cannot be indulged in without impairing the strength both of the body and mind. The continued depression of the nervous system and excessive transpiration occasion physical debility, while the intellectual faculties, from constantly slumbering in a state of inactivity, become gradually enfeebled. Valengin relates the case of a young man, who, in consequence of too much sleep, became lethargic, and died at the age of twenty-three years.
>
> ('Sleep', *HW* 2.472)

his early tea.] Crisparkle probably dined at midday. The distinction drawn between several kinds of evening meal reflects the habits of different classes. In chapter 3, Jasper and Edwin have dinner; in chapter 12, 'the Dean withdraws to his dinner, Mr Tope to his tea'.

"More good than

and I don't love doctors, or doctors' stuff."] The irony is that opium was very much 'doctors' stuff'. As the only effective painkiller, it was used for a variety of complaints in spite of uncertainty over its action.

Mr. Jasper is

six-and-twenty] The same age as Bradley Headstone, the would-be murderer in *OMF* (2.1).

the unfinished picture of a blooming schoolgirl] Perhaps Dickens preferred to be imprecise about her age: 'of sixteen at the utmost' is the MS reading. If the portrait is about a year old, Rosa is now celebrating her 17th birthday. Though a commonplace to have such portraits of handsome women, this may allude to the portrait of Matilda in Matthew Lewis's *The Monk* (1796). The portrait is revered by the initially saintly but latterly depraved Ambrosio, who is, like Jasper, a man of the church.

"We shall miss you

'Alternate Musical Wednesdays'] Fortnightly musical evenings, probably shared by the Cathedral community and other interested residents of Cloisterham.

'Tell me, shep-herds te-e-ell me] A snatch from 'The Wreath', a pastoral glee for three voices by J. Mazzinghi (1765–1844), favoured by choirs and singing classes in the last century:

> Ye, shepherds, tell me have you seen
> My Flora pass this way?
> In shape and feature beauty's Queen,
> In pastoral array.

Chorus
Shepherds, tell me, have you seen
  My Flora pass this way?
A wreath around her head she wore
  Carnation, lily, rose,
And in her hand a crook she bore,
  And sweets her breath compose.

The beauteous wreath that decks her head,
  Forms her description true.
Hands lily white, lips crimson red,
  And cheeks of rosy hue.

Septimus] MS shows that, until chapter 6, Crisparkle's name was 'Joe'; 'Arthur' was also an alternative.

"My dear Edwin!"

Edwin] The name was fashionable among High Church circles in the nineteenth century and so would be appropriate for the nephew of a cathedral choirmaster. But Dickens undoubtedly had in mind the ballad in Goldsmith's *The Vicar of Wakefield* (1766). Edwin is the beloved of the fickle Angelina, who drives her impoverished lover away. Realizing her folly, she seeks the protection of a hermit (her lover in disguise) and tells him her tale. She declares that she will die for Edwin, who died for her, whereupon the hermit 'clasped her to his breast . . . 'Twas Edwin's self that pressed!' Realizing that he is loved, he assures her that he is 'Thine own, thy long-lost Edwin here,/Restored to love and thee'. If Edwin Drood does not die, the theme of the return from the dead in this ballad is incentive to believe it to be Dickens's source for the name (Jacobson, 1975, 50–1).

"Get off your greatcoat

bright boy] Perhaps alluding to Horace, *Epistles* 2.2.4: 'candidus et . . . pulcher' ('a bright and beautiful boy').

"My dear Jack

moddley-coddley] A variant of 'molly coddle'. This would seem to be the first example of the usage in the sense of 'to coddle or cocker up' (*OED*).

With the check

Once for all, a look of intentness and intensity] Jasper's look has attracted various interpretations: Jasper's supposed mesmeric powers (Kaplan, 1975, 128–33); the much spying and watching throughout the novel (Dyson, 1969, 142); Jasper's devotion (Wright, 1935, 175–6); Jasper's innocence (Aylmer, 1964, 8). G. K. Chesterton comments that 'nothing . . . could be cleverer': this is not 'morbid affection but morbid antagonism' (1909, ix). As with Bradley Headstone's interest in Eugene Wrayburn, Jasper is 'more interested in Drood than in Rosa' (Cox, 1962, 35).

"What a jolly old

"What a jolly old Jack it is!"] Edwin may be thinking of 'The Sailor's Consolation' (1791) by Charles Dibdin:

> Spanking Jack was so comely, so pleasant, so jolly,
>   Though winds blew great guns, still he'd whistle and sing;
> Jack lov'd his friend, and was true to his Molly,
>   And if honour gives greatness, was great as a king.

whose birthday is it?"] Rosa's birthday, at the beginning of the novel, may have been intended to be important at the end, particularly if the time-scheme was designed to run through the passage of a year. Wilkie Collins had used Rachel's birthday in *The Moonstone* as the impulse of the story: the Moonstone diamond is a birthday gift to her, and the plot is structured around its theft on one birthday and restoration on the next.

"Not mine

Pussy's] Formerly a term of contempt or reproach, in the nineteenth century the name became a playful familiar term of endearment. Sometimes the name connotes shyness, but Edwin uses it patronizingly.

As the boy

Marseillaise-wise] In the manner customary when singing the 'Marseillaise': the singers put their arms round each other's shoulders.

"As a rule?

a difference in age of half a dozen years or so?] MS reads 'less than half a dozen years'; Edwin is six years younger than Jasper and will come of age in the spring.

"Because if it was

Begone dull care that turned a young man grey] From the popular song by John Playford published in *The Musical Companion* (1667). The first verse begins:

> Begone, dull Care, I prithee begone from me,
> Begone, dull Care, you and I shall never agree.

The second verse continues:

> Too much care will make a young man grey,
> And too much care will turn an old man to clay.
> My wife shall dance
> And I will sing
> So merrily pass the day.

These last words Edwin quotes again at the end of the chapter.

"Asks why not

"Asks why not, on Pussy's birthday] Alongside this passage in his proof copy Fildes wrote the word 'Brothers'. As Cardwell says, this is enigmatic (1972, 269); there are no brothers in this novel. Perhaps Fildes made a slip, as he must mean Jasper and Edwin, who are uncle and nephew, but of an age where they could be brothers.

"Hip, hip, hip

"Hip, hip, hip, and nine times nine, and one to finish with] In *Confessions of a Thug* (1839) Taylor observes that Ameer Ali longs to 'ask more about British drinking scenes, and the meaning of the words, Hip! hip! hip!', which he believes are of mystic significance. The popular cheer occurs in Thomas Hood, 'Sniffing a Birthday', 14:

> No flummery then from flowery lips,
> No three times three and hip-hip-hips,
> Because I'm ripe and full of pips –
> I like a little green.
> To put me on my solemn oath,
> If sweep-like I could stop my growth
> I would remain, and nothing loath,
> A boy – about nineteen.

Mr. Jasper's

again includes the portrait] A small slip: the portrait is in the other room.

"In point of fact

Miss Scornful Pert] 'Independence' has been replaced in MS by 'Pert' (not in Cardwell). Edwin calls her 'Little Miss Independence' at the end of the chapter.

"That's what

My dead and gone father and Pussy's dead and gone father must needs marry us together by anticipation.] In 1854 *HW* published a story about two children who are bound by their parents at birth, as in the Eastern custom, 'The Betrothed Children' (10.124). The betrothal of Edwin and Rosa may owe something to Tennyson's *Maud*, published the following year. The narrator and Maud are betrothed before her birth by their fathers:

> Men were drinking together,
> Drinking and talking of me;
> 'Well, if it prove a girl, the boy
> Will have plenty: so let it be.' (1.7.289–92)

This passage was inspired by a story from the *Arabian Nights* (Paden, 1942, 161). Maud later explains how her mother learnt of the pledge:

> How strange was what she said,
> When only Maud and the brother
> Hung over her dying bed –
> That Maud's dark father and mine
> Had bound us one to the other,
> Betrothed us over their wine,
> On the day when Maud was born;
> Seal'd her mine from her first sweet breath.
> Mine, mine by a right, from birth till death.
> Mine, mine – our fathers have sworn. (1.19.717–26)

Wilkie Collins had used the idea in *The Woman in White* (1860), in which 'an engagement of honour, not of love' was sanctioned on the deathbed of the heroine's father. In *OMF*, Bella resents her betrothal to John Harmon and complains of the husband she has not yet met: ' "how *could* I like him, left to him in a will, like a dozen of spoons, with everything cut and dried beforehand, like orange chips. Talk of orange flowers indeed!" ' (1.37).

The story of the engaged orphan in *MED* was suggested by Dickens to Forster in July 1869, in a letter which inquired: 'What should you think of the idea of a story beginning in this way? (*Nonesuch* 3.732). Forster quotes the letter and adds his own edited version of an entry in the *Book of Memoranda* (16):

> The idea of a story beginning in this; – two people – boy and girl, or very young – going apart from one another, pledged to be married after many years – at the end of the book. The interest to arise out of the tracing of their separate ways, and the impossibility of telling what will be done with that impending Fate.

'This was laid aside', Forster continues, 'but it left a marked trace on the story as afterwards designed, in the position of Edwin Drood and his betrothed' (3.18.425). Dickens drew on several entries from the *Book of Memoranda* for *MED*, and it is clear that the idea of engaged orphans was noted down before 1861, although not necessarily, of course, with this novel in mind. Kaplan's note on the entry mentioned by Forster summarizes the debate over the dating of the novel, a debate which Kaplan's edition of the *Book of Memoranda* resolves (97).

"Good Heaven, Jack

There's a strange film come over your eyes.] This also happens to Obenreizer in 'No Thoroughfare': 'a certain nameless film would come over his eyes – apparently by the action of his own will' (*CS*). The phenomenon is recorded by Wilkie Collins, in *The Moonstone*: of Jennings it is said that 'the sublime intoxication of opium . . . gleamed in his eyes' (2.4).

With a scared face

With a scared face] Edwin's distressed reaction is similar to that of Franklin Blake's concern for Ezra Jennings in *The Moonstone* when the

> grip of some terrible emotion seemed to have seized him, and shaken him to the soul. His gipsy complexion had altered to a livid greyish paleness; his eyes had suddenly become wild and glittering; his voice had dropped to a tone – low, stern, and resolute – which I now heard for the first time. (2.3)

with thick drops standing on his forehead] Collins described 'the dew of a stealthy perspiration' in *The Moonstone* (2.4). De Quincey had mocked Coleridge for 'the sweaty shine on his face when an exceptionally large dose incapacitated him' (Hayter, 1971, 12).

thus addresses him] A passage in a different tone was deleted in MS at this point (Cardwell, 1972, 10–11):

> "<I have been taking> opium for a pain – an agony – [I] sometimes have. Its effects steal over me like a blight or a cloud, and pass. <There is no cause for alarm> You see them in the act of passing. Put those knives out at the door – both of them!"
>
> "My dear Jack, why?"
>
> "It's going to lighten; they may attract the lightning; put them <away> in the dark."
>
> With a scared and confounded face, the younger man complies. No <lightning> flash ensues, nor was there, for a moment, any passing likelihood of a thunder storm. He gently and assiduously tends his kinsman who by slow degrees recovers and clears away that cloud or blight. When he, (Jasper) – is quite himself and is as it were once more all resolved into that concentrated look, he lays a tender hand upon his nephew's shoulder and thus addresses him

This scene might have been suggested by Macbeth's hallucination of the dagger (2.1.33–47). The reference to Edwin as 'kinsman' recalls two projected titles for the novel: 'A Kinsman's Devotion' and 'Two Kinsmen'.

"Upon my life

even in Pussy's house – if she had one – and in mine – if I had one——"] G. K. Chesterton wondered whether the mystery might not predate the beginning of the novel, to the period of Grewgious's love for Rosa's mother, and of a feud taken up by the Princess Puffer, relating to the apparently Asiatic past of Jasper:

> In any case, I am almost certain that the story would have worked backwards as well as forwards. Otherwise I cannot see why Dickens dragged in so many things requiring retrospective explanation, such as the opium hag's hatred of Jasper. An idea occurs to me even in connection with the pact of Edwin and Rosa: the idea of some substitute or false relationship. All this is intentionally hazy; but it has the advantage that it might make a mystery that was a mystery of Edwin Drood, and not a mystery of Dick Datchery or even of John Jasper . . . Suppose he were not detecting his own death but his own birth. Suppose the real mystery began before the story. (1928, 228–9)

"I really was

Lay Precentor, or Lay Clerk] The precentor is responsible for the direction of choral services in a cathedral. Lay clerks execute minor ecclesiastical functions. It is interesting to note that several characters are artistic in a professional, or amateurish, way. Apart from Jasper himself, Crisparkle is a musician, Edwin draws, Bazzard is a frustrated playwright, Sapsea has written an epitaph, and even Durdles sees himself as a creator (see Hark, 1977, 159).

"I hate it

"I hate it. The cramped monotony of my existence grinds me away] The monotony of life in a cathedral town, is touched upon in *DC*: ' "It may be a sacrifice," said Mrs. Micawber, "to immure one's-self in a Cathedral town; but surely, Mr. Copperfield, if it is a sacrifice in me, it is much more a sacrifice in a man of Mr. Micawber's abilities" ' (36).

Dickens understood the meaning of the drudging round; a speech delivered in September 1869 confesses: 'My own invention and imagination, such as it is, I can most truthfully assure you, would never have served me as it has, but for the habit of commonplace, humble, patient, daily, toiling, drudging attention' (*Speeches* 406). Perhaps Jasper portrays much that Dickens endured. Three months before he made public his separation from his wife, he wrote to Forster insisting on the proposed reading tours, explaining: 'I must do *something*, or I shall wear my heart away' (March 1858, *Nonesuch* 3.14). In his last years Dickens began to loathe residence in London, preferring the rural Gad's Hill. If Jasper is indeed a vehicle for Dickens's personal anxieties, it is significant, as Angus Wilson has observed, that in the winter before he died Dickens was drawn to the bustle of London: 'so it is in the novel: the good characters . . . are more and more collected in London [and] have fled from the petty meanness of Cloisterham' (1974, 27). There is evidence in the novels that during the 1860s Dickens was restless and pessimistic. This emerges in the irony of Venus's statements about the trophies of his art which have ruined his chances of love (*OMF* 1.7), and in the debilitating effect the daily routine of the schoolroom has upon Bradley Headstone.

"It often sounds

"It often sounds to me quite devilish.] De Quincey observed that music could oppress the opium-eater as being 'too sensual and gross. He naturally seeks solitude and silence' ('The Pleasures of Opium', *Confessions*).

carving demons out of the stalls and seats and desks.] As is usual in cathedrals, at Rochester the stalls, misericords (brackets on the underside of hinged choirstall seats), and front desks of the choir are decorated with carvings which include grotesque human and animal heads and monsters. The choirstalls at Rochester date from the thirteenth century and are probably the oldest work of the kind in England, but they were badly restored around 1870.

"Anyhow, my dear

"I must subdue myself to my vocation] Shakespeare, *Sonnets* 111:

> And almost thence my nature is subdu'd
> To what it works in, like the dyer's hand.
> Pity me then, and wish I were renew'd.

Mr. Jasper's steadiness

so marvellous that his breathing seems to have stopped.] The import of these warnings is obscure, although perhaps Jasper's sudden immobility results from the fear that he has said too much. The last line of the chapter, 'Mr. Jasper dissolves his attitude, and they go out together', comes when he is assured that Edwin has not taken fright. Edwin's claim that Jasper has been 'very unlike [his] usual self', and the suggestion that he has sacrificed himself, would be disturbing if Jasper was uncertain of what he might have revealed during his seizure. When he receives the required answer, he is able to relax.

"No; don't put

I shall then go engineering into the East] Engineering in Egypt was a topical subject because the Suez Canal was opened on 17 November 1869. Steamships had operated from the Suez from the 1830s, and the Overland Route, as it was called, was soon after established through the enterprising efforts of Thomas Waghorn. It became the main route from Britain to India. The Peninsular and Oriental Steamship Company took over the route in the 1840s. Thackeray travelled by P & O to Cairo in 1844 (as the guest of Sir James Emerson Tennent, incidentally) and discovered there 'tall factory chimneys . . . there are foundries and steam-engine manufactories' (*Notes of a Journey from Cornhill to Grand Cairo*, 1846, 15). A railway line from Alexandria to Cairo and Suez was built by an English company employing English surveyors between 1851 and 1853. Another Englishman, General Francis Rawdon Chesney, had surveyed the canal route in 1830, but, owing to government opposition to the idea of a canal,

5 The choir in Rochester Cathedral

led by Lord Palmerston, the building of the Suez Canal was left to a French engineer, Ferdinand de Lesseps. De Lesseps had visited England in 1855 and 1857 to publicize the idea and had won widespread public support, but the undertaking was finally financed by a French company. The building of the canal, with the ports at each end and the accompanying systems of signals and lighthouses, was one of the great engineering achievements of the age. Despite the fact that it was built and financed by the French, it effectively became a British canal: over 75 per cent of the traffic within the first few years of its opening was British. The introduction to Egypt of commerce and European influence was widely predicted to be a benefit to the country and, in particular, to bring an end to slavery (see Hoskins, 1966, passim). Engineers and inventors appear as heroes in a number of mid-Victorian novels: for example, Mrs Gaskell's *Mary Barton* (1848) and *LD*. Engineers and inventors such as Robert Stephenson are prominent among the models included in Samuel Smiles's influential *Self-Help* (1859), and his *Lives of the Engineers, with an Account of Their Principal Works* (3 vols, 1861–2) heroically depicts the lives of numerous eminent British engineers. Smiles observes that only in comparatively modern times have the British ceased to depend on foreigners for their engineering works: 'Instead of borrowing engineers from abroad, we now send them to all parts of the world' (Preface, v).

"Shall we go

"Shall we go and walk in the churchyard?"] In chapter 23, Jasper tells the opium-woman that he dreams of a journey with a companion; the churchyard may be significant in terms of this journey.

"By all means

Only gloves for Pussy] 'Nothing was more common in the way of present-making than gloves' ('Gloves', *AYR* 9.425).

Mr. Jasper, still

'Nothing half so sweet in life'] From 'Love's Young Dream', by Thomas Moore, *Irish Melodies* (1807–35):

> But there's nothing half so sweet in life
> As love's young dream:
> No, there's nothing half so sweet in life
> As love's young dream.

Chapter 3

THE NUNS' HOUSE.

For sufficient reasons

For sufficient reasons which this narrative will itself unfold . . . a fictitious name] 'Cloisterham' is nowhere identified, but many topographical allusions can be explained by reference to Rochester. The city recurs in the works: in *GE* disguised as 'Great Winglebury'; in *SB* as 'Mudfog'; and in *UT* as 'Dullborough'. It appears anonymously as Scrooge's birthplace, and Bleak House was originally to have been situated in Rochester.

The city belongs both to Dickens's maturity and to his youth. His father had been stationed at Chatham from 1817 to 1823, years during which the young Dickens doubtless came to know Rochester as well as Deputy knows Cloisterham. That he later saw the city as a refuge is evident in a letter he wrote to Miss Coutts from Broadstairs (23 October 1850) when he had just finished *DC*, and had 'an idea of wandering somewhere for a day or two – to Rochester, I think, where I was a small boy – to get all this fortnight's work out of my head' (*Nonesuch* 2.241). His affection for the city increased when he came to live at Gad's Hill, from where he would arrange excursion parties to show off its charms. A letter to James T. Fields, who had himself enjoyed such an excursion with Dickens, reports that a group of friends, including Forster and the American poet, Longfellow, went with their host 'to look at the old houses in Rochester, and the old cathedral, and the old castle, and the house for the six poor travellers' (7 July 1868, *Nonesuch* 3.657).

An excursion to Rochester in *PP* (2) discovers Mr Jingle surveying the old city:

> 'Ah! fine place . . . glorious pile – frowning walls – tottering arches – dark nooks – crumbling staircases – Old cathedral too – earthy smell – pilgrims' feet worn away the old steps – little Saxon doors – confessionals like money-takers' boxes at theatres – queer customers those monks – Popes, and Lord Treasurers, and all sorts of old fellows, with great red faces, and broken noses, turning up every day – buff jerkins too – match-locks – Sarcophagus – fine place – old legends too – strange stories: capital.'

Closer to the actual details of Cloisterham is a description of Rochester in a *HW* article which Dickens co-authored. 'Seen in the distance, rising from among corn-fields, pastures, orchards, gardens, woods, the river', is the bridge and 'the roofs of ancient houses' with the ruins of abbey or castle beside the 'venerable Cathedral spires' looking 'like a solemn historical presence, above the city'. Inside the Cathedral, the visitor notices 'the long perspectives of pillars and arches' and the 'earthy smell, preaching . . . the common doom'. The mellowing effect of the stained-glass windows, the carvings on the stalls, and the influence of the monks settle beside effigies of archbishops and bishops 'found built up in the walls'.

Long gleams of light slant into the crypt, ivy twines about the graves, and bells ring in the tower. The Cathedral Close has red-brick houses and 'staid gardens', and the footsteps of visitors echo as they do outside Minor Canon Corner in chapter 6. Significantly, the organ 'fills all that space, and all the space it opens in the charmed imagination' while the 'shivering choristers . . . [huddle] on their gowns as they drowsily go to scamper through their work' in company with 'the drawling voice without a heart, that drearily pursues the dull routine' (2.1).

as Cloisterham] Behind the name, aside from an allusion to the cloisters which no longer survive on the south side of the Cathedral, there may be a memory of De Quincey's *Klosterheim, or, The Masque* (1832).

It was once possibly known to the Druids by another name] Rochester has had different names during its history. *Murray's Handbook for Travellers in Kent and Sussex* (1858, 35), a volume that Dickens would probably have had on hand to give guests at Gad's Hill, explains that Rochester must always have held a position of importance:

> . . . the name of the Roman Castrum here, *Durobrivæ* (*Dwr* – water, and the Celtic term *briva*, always found in connection with similar river ferries), seems to imply that a British stronghold had still earlier been fixed at this place. Its Saxon name, *Hrofeceastre* (Rochester), retains, according to Bede, that of *Hrof*, the Saxon chieftain, who first settled here (Hrof's ceastre or castle).

'The Seven Poor Travellers' (*CS*) recalls the history of Rochester, the High Street of which is 'oddly garnished with a queer old clock':

> as if Time carried on business there, and hung out his sign. Sooth to say, he did an active stroke of work in Rochester, in the old days of the Romans, and the Saxons, and the Normans; and down to the times of King John, when the rugged castle – and I will not undertake to say how many hundreds of years old then – was abandoned to the centuries of weather which have so defaced the dark apertures in its walls, that the ruin looks as if the rooks and daws have pecked its eyes out. (1)

An ancient city

Cathedral crypt] The crypt (Plate 2) is one of the largest, most beautiful and best preserved in England. It boasts a carefully worked specimen of Early English groining. The two western bays, which date from about 1200, are of Gundulf's early Norman work. The ancient glass in the east windows was probably a gift from Canterbury; on the vault above are the remains of many fine frescoes (Hope, 1900, 41).

monastic graves] Bishops, patrons and minor ecclesiastics were buried in the Cathedral, but most of the ancient gravestones have been displaced or broken up.

small salad] Mustard and cress used in the seed leaf as salad herbs.

dirt-pies] In a *HW* article, which unfavourably compared English education with the Prussian system, under which all children attended school, Dickens had observed that one could 'search all the gutters, and there's not an innocent disporting himself – there's not a mud-pie made in the whole district' (2.314).

every ploughman in its outlying fields renders to once puissant Lord Treasurers . . . the attention] Compare *Hamlet* 5.1.207–10:

> Imperious Caesar, dead and turn'd to clay,
> Might stop a hole to keep the wind away,
> O, that that earth which kept the world in awe,
> Should patch a wall t'expel the winter's flaw!

The idea alludes to one of the minor issues in the public debate on interment in churchyards and cemeteries which began in the early 1840s. Several revolutionary suggestions were proposed by the landscape gardener and horticultural writer J. C. Loudon in his important book, *On the Laying out, Planting, and Managing of Cemeteries, and on the Improvement of Churchyards* (1843). He suggested that temporary cemeteries could be created from fields rented on a twenty-one-year lease. After fourteen years they would be completely filled with graves, and seven years later the fields would revert to the landlord to be cultivated, planted or laid down in grass. Loudon also suggested that Union workhouses should use a portion of their garden as a cemetery, which would be restored to cultivation after a period of time. These proposals were criticized by the *Quarterly Review* (73, 1844, 451).

the Ogre in the story-book desired to render to his unbidden visitor, and grinds their bones to make his bread.] In 'Jack and the Beanstalk' (or 'Jack the Giant-Killer'), the hero climbs a beanstalk into the sky where he encounters an Ogre who eats broiled boys and whose keen sense of smell, reported in the well-known rhyme, assists him in pursuing his fancy:

> Fee, fau, fum,
> I smell the blood of an English man,
> Be he alive, or be he dead,
> I'll grind his bones to make my bread.

A drowsy city

sun-browned tramps] Forster comments that, although Dickens enjoyed his dogs as pets, 'with his high road traversed as frequently as any in England by tramps and wayfarers of a singularly undesirable description, they were also a necessity' (3.8.191). David Copperfield, on the road from London to Dover, which passes through Rochester, was filled with dread of the 'ferocious-looking ruffians, who stared at me as I went by; and stopped, perhaps, and called after me to come back and speak to them, and when I took to my heels, stoned me' (13).

a paved Quaker settlement] Although Quakers (the Society of Friends) were enjoined to live according to the principles of simplicity and plainness in their homes as well as with regard to their dress and speech, they were not inclined to live separately in such settlements as described here. Interestingly, there were very few Quakers in Kent. The corner of the Cathedral Close seems to be described in this way not because of any actual association with Quakers but merely because of its appearance. By 1860 the Quakers' peculiarity of dress and speech (the collarless coat and broad-brimmed hat for men, the dark prim Quakeress's bonnet for women, and the use of the archaic 'thee' and 'thou') had become optional, so that Dickens's reference is to a passing custom which had become quaint. John Bright, the original of Mr Honeythunder, was customarily depicted by *Punch* in Quaker dress, although after entering public life he no longer wore it (Isichei, 1970, 144–59).

In a word

Fragments of old wall] With the foundation of the church by Ethelbert in 604, the city was enclosed on the south by the Roman wall, as it is still on the east and north; the north and south walls diverge westwards, so that the section on which the church and monastery were built was a wedge-shaped area (Hope, 1900, 137).

saint's chapel] Perhaps a reference to the chapel built as the shrine of St William of Perth, a Scottish baker who was murdered near Rochester in 1201 while on pilgrimage to the Holy Land. He was buried in the Cathedral by the monks, who were probably mindful of the growing fame of the miracles wrought at the tomb of St Thomas of Canterbury (Hope, 1900, 40).

chapter-house, convent, and monastery] Ruins of twelfth-century constructions.

its drooping and despondent little theatre] The old Rochester Theatre Royal, also known as the Lyceum Theatre, was built in 1791, at the foot of Star Hill. A wooden structure with a handsomely ornamented plastered front, it was remembered by Dickens as the sanctuary where he had come to know 'the many wondrous secrets of Nature'. In later years, poor patronage caused it to fall into a

> bad and declining way. A dealer in wine and bottled beer had already squeezed his trade into the box-office, and the theatrical money was taken – when it came – in a kind of meat-safe in the passage . . . It was To Let, and hopelessly so . . . No, there was no comfort in the Theatre. It was mysteriously gone, like my own youth. ('Dullborough Town', *UT*).

foul fiend, when he ducks from its stage] The devil in pantomimes would make his entrances and exits through the trap-door on the stage leading into the garden.

In the midst of

the Nuns' House] At the east end of the High Street stands Eastgate House (see Map); the illustration 'Good-Bye, Rosebud, Darling!' is a faithful depiction of the entrance and gate that still stand; behind the building, the sunken garden and its sundial are seen in 'Jasper's Sacrifices'. Eastgate House was never a convent, nor does it stand on the site of a convent, but at the time Dickens was writing *MED* it accommodated a school for young ladies. On an interior beam is carved the date 1591, and the house is rich in oak and panel-work, carved ornament, and elaborate ceilings. Built by Sir Peter Bucke, it is a three-storeyed red-brick house, quaint in its many juttings, leaded-light windows and extensions. The same house served as the model for the ladies' seminary, 'Westgate House', in *PP*, where Mr Pickwick is captured by the inmates.

resplendent brass plate] The two large brass plates reading 'Eastgate House' and 'Ladies College' which adorned the wooden gates in Dickens's time now survive in Eastgate House Museum.

Miss Twinkleton] An early study of Miss Twinkleton is Miss Pupford of 'Tom Tiddler's Ground', who kept an 'establishment for six young ladies of tender years' (*CS*). As John Beer has noticed, her name recalls Miss Pinkerton, the head of the school attended by Becky and Amelia in *Vanity Fair* (1984, 188).

Whether the nuns of yore

a stiff-necked generation] Derives from Exodus 33.5: 'Ye are a stiffnecked people.'

the many chambers of their House] Reminiscent of 'in my Father's house are many mansions' (John 14.2).

whether they were ever walled up alive] This traditional punishment features in Matthew G. Lewis, *The Monk* (1796), when Agnes is walled up alive beneath the abbey of Saint Claire. And Walter Scott's *Marmion* (1808), set in 1513, tells of Constance de Beverley, a perjured nun whose fickle lover is killed in the battle of Flodden. Constance is punished in this manner:

> And now that blind old Abbot rose,
> To speak the Chapter's doom,
> On those the wall was to enclose,
> Alive, within the tomb. (2.25)

Scott commented on these lines:

> It is well known that the religious, who broke their vows of chastity, were subjected to the same penalty as the Roman vestals in a similar case. A small niche, sufficient to enclose their bodies, was made in the massive wall of the convent; a slender pittance of food and water was deposited in it, and the awful words, *VADE IN PACE*, were the signal for immuring the criminal. It is not likely that, in latter times, this punishment was often resorted to; but among the ruins of the Abbey of Coldingham were some years ago discovered the remains of a female skeleton, which, from the shape of the niche, and position of the figure, seemed to be that of an immured nun.

Although Dickens would have been familiar with Lewis and Scott, his particular source was surely the ghost of the nun in Charlotte Brontë, *Villette* (1853). The house in the rue Fossette, run as a school by Madame Beck, 'had in old days been a convent . . . before the city had overspread this quarter and when it was tilled ground'. Lucy Snowe records that 'a vague tale went of a black and white nun, sometimes, on some night or nights of the year, seen in some part of this vicinage'. In the grounds were 'certain convent-relics, in the shape of old and huge fruit trees'; at the foot of one could be seen 'a glimpse of slab, smooth, hard, and black':

> The legend went, unconfirmed and unaccredited, but still propagated, that this was the portal of a vault, imprisoning deep beneath the ground, on whose surface grass grew and flowers bloomed, the bones of a girl whom a monkish conclave of the drear middle ages had here buried alive for some sin against her vow. Her shadow it was that tremblers had feared, through long generations after her poor frame was dust; her black robe and white veil that, for timid eyes, moonlight and shade had mocked, as they fluctuated in the night-wind through the garden-thicket. (12)

such unprofitable questions] The phrase is biblical: 'But avoid foolish questions, and genealogies, and contentions, and strivings about the law; for they are unprofitable and vain' (Titus 3.9).

As, in some cases

As, in some cases of drunkenness, and in others of animal magnetism, there are two states of consciousness which never clash] 'Animal magnetism' is the process derived from the theories of the Austrian, Franz Anton Mesmer (1734–1815). A showman and confidence trickster, he found favour in the French court where he set up his extraordinary practice. In mid-nineteenth-century England animal magnetism attracted the attention of Dickens and other writers such as Elizabeth Barrett Browning, Harriet Martineau, Kingsley, Rogers and Thackeray. Dickens's own knowledge of mesmerism was influenced by his acquaintance with the eminent physician and surgeon, John Elliotson (1791–1868), who had pioneered the treatment of medical disorders by mesmerism and described it in his *Human Physiology* (1840), a copy of which he presented to Dickens. 'By certain processes', Elliotson wrote,

> such as passing the points of the fingers at a short distance from a person in a direction from the face down the arms, trunks, and legs, with a degree of energy, the state of sleep, or sleep-waking, may actually, we are told, be induced. It is then termed *magnetic*, and the whole phenomena *animal magnetism*. The patient becomes insensible to all around, but may have the inward senses augmented as in common ecstasis . . . A delightful feeling of ease and lightness is experienced, the body grows warmer, and perspires freely, though sometimes anxiety, palpitation, slight convulsions, and wandering pains take place . . . On coming out of the sleep-waking, the person is

> unconscious of all that has occurred; but, when thrown into it again, recollects the whole and converses on it. The magnetiser can put an end to this state at pleasure: and, when he is a good magnetiser and the patient very susceptible, a single movement of the hand may instantly magnetise, and even knock down and kill; a look may magnetise: and we are told that all these effects may sometimes be produced at great distances by the mere volition of the magnetiser. (27.660–1)

During the 1840s Dickens himself practised mesmerism, on his wife and sister-in-law occasionally, but notably on Madame de la Rue, whom he met in Genoa in 1844. His fascination with the case was still evident years later, for he described it in a letter on 24 November 1869:

> I confided to her husband that I had found myself to possess some rather exceptional power of animal magnetism (of which I had tested the efficacy in nervous disorders), and that I would gladly try her. She never developed any of the ordinarily-related phenomena, but after a month began to sleep at night – which she had not done for years, and to change, amazingly to her own mother, in appearance . . . From that time, wheresoever I travelled in Italy, she and her husband travelled with me, and every day I magnetized her; sometimes under olive trees, sometimes in vineyards, sometimes in the travelling carriage, sometimes at wayside inns during the mid-day halt. Her husband called me up to her, one night at Rome, when she was rolled into an apparently impossible ball, by tic in the brain, and I only knew where her head was by following her long hair to its source. (*Nonesuch* 3.752)

During the 1840s pamphlets and books on mesmerism were widely read and reviewed, but by the end of the decade, and certainly by 1869, it was no longer taken seriously, and Elliotson himself was pressured to resign his position on account of a public scandal (see Kaplan, 1974, passim). As mesmerism had fallen into disrepute, it is unlikely that Dickens would have shown Jasper to be a mesmerist. Whereas the opium theme is explicit in the novel, mesmerism is only implied. Interest would be more likely to centre on Jasper's psyche than upon the magnetic fluids in which, no doubt, Dickens was no longer interested. But there are several instances where the mesmeric influence could be said to be at work: the scene at the piano in Minor Canon Corner in chapter 5; that in the Gate House in chapter 7; Jasper's eavesdropping on the conversation between Crisparkle and Neville in chapter 12; the waylaying of Neville in chapter 15; Crisparkle's going to the Weir, seemingly involuntarily, in chapter 16; and the encounter of Jasper with Rosa beside the sundial in chapter 19.

thus if I hide my watch when I am drunk, I must be drunk again before I can remember where] In his section on 'Sleep-Waking', Dr Elliotson cites the case of an Irish porter

> who forgot, when sober, what he had done when drunk: but, being drunk, again recollected the transactions of his former state of intoxication. On one occasion, being drunk, he had lost a parcel of some value, and in his sober

> moments could give no account of it. Next time he was intoxicated, he recollected that he had left the parcel at a certain house, and there being no address on it, it had remained there safely, and was got on his calling for it. (27.646)

In *The Moonstone* Ezra Jennings reads this passage from Elliotson to Franklin Blake and then explains his plan to reconstruct the environment in which the Moonstone diamond has been stolen in order to discover the thief. It has been suggested that Dickens's reference to Elliotson may be a critical aside to Wilkie Collins 'intimating that he was proposing to do something better in his own mystery story' (Forsyte, 1980, 49).

a certain season at Tunbridge Wells] An inland watering-place owing its popularity to its chalybeate spring and beautiful situation among wooded hills in Kent. The wells are beside the Parade, or Pantile, a walk associated with fashion from the time it was paved with pantiles during the reign of Queen Anne, for whom the town was a favourite resort before her accession to the throne. Tunbridge retained its eminence as a fashionable resort throughout the mid-nineteenth century. Thackeray sketched it humorously in *The Virginians* (1859). In *BH* Esther notices a cheap memento, 'a mug, with "A Present from Tunbridge Wells" on it' in Mrs Jellyby's house (4). And in *LD* Flora Finching was proposed to by Mr F ' " on a donkey at Tunbridge Wells" ' (1.24).

a certain finished gentleman (compassionately called by Miss Twinkleton . . . "Foolish Mr. Porters")] 'Finished gentleman' applies to a man of accomplished and consummate qualities. Miss Twinkleton is like her predecessor, Miss Pupford, whose young ladies have a notion

> that Miss Pupford was once in love, and that the beloved object still moves upon this ball. Also, that he is a public character, and a personage of vast consequence . . . On the whole, it is suspected by the pupil-mind that G is a short chubby old gentleman, with little black sealing-wax boots up to his knees, whom a sharply observant pupil, Miss Linx, when she once went to Tunbridge Wells with Miss Pupford for the holidays, reported on her return (privately and confidentially) to have seen come capering up to Miss Pupford on the Promenade, and to have detected in the act of squeezing Miss Pupford's hand, and to have heard pronounce the words, "Cruel Euphemia, ever thine!" – or something like that. ('Tom Tiddler's Ground', *CS*)

Miss Pupford also betrays the romanticism sharply perceived by the pupils of Miss Twinkleton, 'and would own to the possession of a great deal of sentiment if she considered it quite reconcilable with her duty to parents'.

Mrs. Tisher] In 'Tom Tiddler's Ground', Miss Pupford also has in her assistant a companion and confidante, 'and it is thought by pupils that, after pupils are gone to bed, they even call one another by their christian names in the quiet little parlour'.

she has seen better days.] An expression current since the sixteenth century; see *As You Like It* 2.7.120–1:

> True it is that we have seen better days,
> And have with holy bell been knoll'd to church.

the departed Tisher was a hairdresser.] That is, a barber and wigmaker. 'Barbarous Torture' in *HW* comments that in 'the present degenerate days' hairdressing is 'a branch of the fine arts', which is 'almost extinct' (12.247).

The pet pupil

The pet pupil] Kitty Kimmeens in 'Tom Tiddler's Ground' was also 'the pet of the whole house'.

Miss Rosa Bud, of course called Rosebud] Dickens wrote 'Bella' in MS and corrected it to read 'Rosa' (not in Cardwell). Bella Wilfer appears in *OMF*, the novel preceding *MED*.

by affecting to shake her head over it] In 'Tom Tiddler's Ground', Miss Pupford greets the news of a former pupil's engagement 'with an air of gentle melancholy, as if marriage were (as indeed it exceptionally has been) rather a calamity'.

The Nuns' House

instantly taken up and transported.] Transportation from England to Botany Bay had been a mode of penal sentence since the seventeenth century. The last shipment to Botany Bay was in 1840, and to Tasmania in 1864. Magwitch, in *GE*, was transported to New South Wales.

as briskly as the bottle at a convivial party in the last century.] The drunkenness of men's parties in the eighteenth century had become a byword.

Mr. Edwin Drood

a terrestrial and a celestial globe] Pairs of globes, one showing the earth and the other the heavens, were essential in every schoolroom. Miss Pupford 'is half supposed to hint' that ' "she came into the world, completely up in . . . the use of the globes" '.

Wandering Jewess] The Wandering Jew, a legendary Jew doomed to wander until the second coming of Christ because he had taunted Jesus bearing the cross.

The last new maid

a little silk apron thrown over its head] Other of Dickens's women characters throw their aprons over their heads in moments of confusion, notably Affery Flintwinch in *LD*.

"The whole thing is

the girls and the servants scuttling about after one, like mice in the wainscot] Perhaps a reminiscence of Tennyson, *Maud* (1855): 'I hear the dead at midday moan,/And the shrieking rush of the wainscot mouse' (1.6.259–60).

It is the custom

Tweezers] A case of small instruments which ladies wore attached to their waistband by a cord or chain.

"Well, that's something

And how did you pass your birthday, Pussy?"] This question and the next forty-two lines of dialogue, down to 'He checks the look, and asks' are not in MS, not even on an interpolated sheet. Dickens complained in a letter to Forster (22 December 1869) that the first two numbers of the novel were '*twelve printed pages too short!!!*' (*Nonesuch* 3.754). The account of Rosa's birthday party, which serves to underline the delicacy of her relationship with Edwin, was inserted (Cardwell, 1969, 221).

She nods her head again

quaintly bursts out with: "You know we must be married] In *The Merchant of Venice*, Portia expresses the same resignation: 'I may neither choose who I would nor refuse who I dislike; so is the will of a living daughter curb'd by the will of a dead father' (1.2.21).

Through a fortuitous

rustling through the room like the legendary ghost of a Dowager in silken skirts] The Dowager has not been identified. The inclusion in the proofs of the word 'legendary', which is not in MS, might suggest that Dickens had a particular tale in mind, but it is possible that he was merely referring to the preponderance of this sort of ghost in tales of the supernatural. Alternatively, the Dowager may simply be an image, as when 'rustling' is used to describe Guster, the Snagsbys' servant in *BH* who comes 'rustling and scratching down the little staircase like a popular ghost' (19). Betsey Trotwood in *DC* is also likened to a ghost 'in a long flannel wrapper in which she looked seven feet high' and 'appeared, like a disturbed ghost, in my room' (35).

"Don't be foolish

polished leather boots] Patent leather boots for men were a current fashion.

That discreet lady

work-table] A small table with a drawer for scissors, buttons, threads and so on. Suspended from a frame which slides out from underneath a drawer was often a large fabric pouch to hold wool and pieces of needlework.

Rosa replies

Lumps-of-Delight] Turkish Delight, a sweetmeat. Amusingly, Rosa is eating Turkish Delight during their tiff over tiresome old Eastern customs.

"A red nose?

to be sure she can always powder it."] A 'recognisable use of rouge had now become a symbol of dubious morals and the more flagrant perfumes were banned; it was ladylike however to employ pearl-powder, lavender water or eau-de-Cologne' (Cunnington, 1970, 460).

"Yes. She takes

an undeveloped country] For British engineering in Egypt and the opening-up of the country to European influence, see note to chapter 2, pp. 46–8.

"Ah! you should hear

"Ah! you should hear Miss Twinkleton] Miss Twinkleton would have had a wide choice of books from which to learn about Egypt. The country had caught the imagination of the British public in the 1820s and retained its fascination throughout the century, partly because of the discovery of antiquities, some of which were exhibited in London, and partly through association with both the Bible and the exotic tales of the *Arabian Nights.* The discovery in the 1830s of the Overland Route to India, via Egypt, made Egypt a new attraction for the intrepid (and wealthy) English tourist, and added to the number of books written about the country. The explorer and Egyptologist, Sir John Gardner Wilkinson (1797–1875), wrote a popular work, *The Topography of Thebes and General Survey of Egypt* (1835), which was partly intended as a practical guide for travellers. His most important work, *Manners and Customs of the Ancient Egyptians* (3 vols, 1837) was followed by an abridged version, *A Popular Account of the Ancient Egyptians* (1854), and by many other volumes on the subject, including the early editions of Murray's *Handbook for Travellers in Egypt.* Wilkinson's researches inspired the Egyptologist, Samuel Sharpe (1799–1881); Sharpe's great work, *The History of Egypt* (1846), went into many editions. An important influence on the attitudes of the Victorian public towards Egypt was E. W. Lane's *Manners and Customs of the Modern Egyptians* (1836). Other popular sources of information on Egypt were the Egyptian Hall at the Crystal Palace at Sydenham, and the many panoramas which depicted journeys down the Nile or along the Overland Route.

Tiresome old burying grounds!] The Valley of Kings at Luxor, the burial-ground of the pharaohs of ancient Egypt.

Isises, and Ibises, and Cheopses] In Egyptian mythology, Isis is the wife of Osiris and mother of Horus. The sacred ibis was the bird venerated by the ancient Egyptians. Cheops was the king who built the Great Pyramid.

And then there was Belzoni] Giovanni Battista Belzoni (1778–1823), engineer and excavator of Egyptian antiquities. The son of a poor barber of Padua, he studied hydraulics in Rome until the invasion of Napoleon forced him to flee to England, where he found a devoted wife but no interest in hydraulics. Instead, he put his extraordinary size and strength to use as a strong man in Astley's circus and at Sadler's Wells. In 1815, while travelling in Malta with his wife, he met an agent of the Egyptian Pasha, Mohamed Ali, and so found his way to Egypt to put his knowledge of hydraulic engineering into use. The British consul-general, Henry Salt, also employed Belzoni: first as an engineer to transport the huge head of Rameses II up the Nile, and then as the excavator of the sites at Abu Simbel, the Valley of Kings, and the Pyramids. As financier of the operations, Henry Salt became the owner of most of the movable discoveries, transported many of them to England, and sold them to the British Museum during the years 1818–21. Their exhibition attracted huge crowds. The serene smile of the colossal red granite bust of Rameses II fascinated the Romantic writers, who took it to be Memnon, around whom there is a complex of legend: De Quincey, Shelley (in 'Ozymandias') and Keats (in 'Fall of Hyperion') all make use of the legend. Belzoni himself opened his own exhibition of antiquities, drawings and facsimile models in the Egyptian Hall, Piccadilly, during 1821–2. Thousands of visitors paid to see it. In 1820, John Murray published Belzoni's *Narrative of the Operations and Recent Discoveries within the Pyramids, Temples, Tombs, and Excavations of Egypt and Nubia*, complete with an atlas of forty-four plates. As the first contribution to English research on Egypt, it was a great success and quickly went into several editions. Belzoni himself set off in 1823 to trace the source of the Niger but died of dysentery *en route.* Dickens often alludes to Belzoni and published an article about him in *HW* ('The Story of Giovanni Belzoni', 2.548–52).

dragged out by the legs, half choked with bats and dust.] Belzoni's *Narrative . . .* gives several accounts of excavations where, at Beban-al-Malook, for example, 'we found a great quantity of bat's-dung which choked up the way, so that we could go no further without digging' (1.357). His description of the mummy-pits complains of the 'vast quantity of dust' so fine that 'it requires great power of lungs to resist it and the strong effluvia of the mummies' (1.242).

"Why, I thought

you Egyptian boys could look into a hand and see all sorts of phantoms?] The palm-reading gypsies were believed to be Egyptians; 'gypsy' and 'Egyptian' were interchangeable. The reference recalls an incident in *The*

Moonstone, coincidentally also at the end of the third chapter. Three Indians in search of the diamond use a boy endowed with psychic qualities to discover the whereabouts of Franklin Blake. A dark ink-like liquid is poured into the boy's palm and he reads there the information they require. In *Human Physiology*, Dr Elliotson gives an account of the 'tricks performed by Asiatic and African jugglers', who cause 'unblemished boys or women, or pregnant women, to see in ink the figure of any dead or absent individual that a third person may name' (1840, 27.670). The practice is described in two *HW* articles of 1850, explaining that 'in Egypt, the Divining Glass is superseded by putting a blot of thick black fluid into the palm of a boy's hand, and commanding him to see various people and things' ('The Magic Crystal', 2.285). But the magical powers ascribed to a blot of ink are derided in 'The Irish Use of the Globe' (2.55). George Eliot used the notion metaphorically in *Adam Bede* (1859):

> With a single drop of ink for a mirror, the Egyptian sorcerer undertakes to reveal to any chance comer far-reaching visions of the past. This is what I undertake to do for you, reader. With this drop of ink at the end of my pen, I will show you the roomy workshop of Mr Jonathan Burge. (1.1)

Chapter 4

MR. SAPSEA.

Accepting the Jackass

Mr. Thomas Sapsea, Auctioneer] The prototype of Mr Sapsea is reported to have been a former mayor of Rochester who was a member of the city council and an auctioneer by trade (Cuming Walters, 1912, xxxiii). The name 'Sapsea' appears in the list of 'Available Names' in the *Book of Memoranda*, where it has been ticked as used (22).

Mr. Sapsea "dresses at"

Mr. Sapsea "dresses at" the Dean] Dickens had been amused before by the assumption of the appearance of a clergyman, as when the waiter at the wedding breakfast of Bella in *OMF* 'looked much more like a clergyman than *the* clergyman, and seemed to have mounted a great deal higher in the church: not to say, scaled the steeple' (4.4).

Mr. Sapsea has

Much nearer sixty years of age than fifty] A recollection of Falstaff's description of himself as a

> goodly portly man, i' faith, and a corpulent; of a cheerful look, a pleasing eye,

and a most noble carriage; and, as I think, his age some fifty, or, by 'r lady, inclining to three-score. (*1 Henry IV* 2.4.408)

and society?] MS reads 'to himself, to the Constitution, and to society'. The idea of Sapsea's faith in the Constitution is introduced in chapter 6.

Mr. Sapsea's premises

Mr. Sapsea's premises are in the High Street] The building described is a block of three half-timbered houses in Rochester High Street, opposite Eastgate House but built slightly later (see Map). Three massive gables and bay windows project over the pavement supported by carved brackets. They are described in *GE* as the home of Pumblechook, the seed merchant (8).

Fever and the Plague] Typhus, typhoid and cholera struck Britain in major, devastating epidemics from the 1830s onwards. These were exacerbated by the overcrowded, unventilated and unsanitary housing conditions of the urban poor, crushed into the cities during the Industrial Revolution. Sanitary reform, one of the major social issues of the mid-nineteenth century, was a subject in which Dickens took a life-long and active interest, as evidenced in his novels, journalism and speeches.

The chastity of the idea] The eighteenth-century custom of dressing statues in Roman costume and contemporary wigs had come to seem absurd by the mid-nineteenth century. 'Chastity' was an eighteenth-century aesthetic term applied to the 'purity' of classical style. In *MC* Mr Pecksniff uses it to describe the beauties of the home of Ruth Pinch's employer: ' "I could not leave this very chaste mansion, without adding my humble tribute, as an Architect, to the correctness and elegance of the owner's taste" ' (9).

By Mr. Sapsea's side

"Ethelinda"] A novelistic name: in 1790, Mrs Charlotte Smith published *Ethelinde; or, The Recluse of the Lake*, and 'Ethelinda' is the name of a heroine in 'Morton Hall', a short story by Mrs Gaskell in *HW* (8.265–72). Dickens included the name in the list of girls' names in the *Book of Memoranda*, where it is spelt 'Ethlynida' (23).

"And I, sir, have long

"When the French come over,/May we meet them at Dover!"] A toast recalling the time of the Napoleonic encampment at Boulogne in 1804 when England was threatened by invasion from France.

This was a patriotic toast

appropriate to any subsequent era.] Nostalgia for the 'good old times' infuriated Dickens. He wrote to Douglas Jerrold on 3 May 1843, for example: 'If ever I destroy myself, it will be in the bitterness of hearing those infernal and damnably good old times, extolled' (*Letters* 3.481).

"Your reputation for that knowledge

"Your reputation . . . has always interested and surprised me] Jasper's public manner resembles that of the hypocrite in 'Hunted Down' (*RP*), who wears his hair parted down the middle, as does Jasper in Fildes's illustration, 'On Dangerous Ground':

> I listened to his talk at dinner, and observed how readily other men responded to it, and with what a graceful instinct he adapted his subjects to the knowledge and habits of those he talked with. As, in talking with me, he had easily started the subject I might be supposed to understand best, and to be the most interested in, so, in talking with others, he guided himself by the same rule... He knew just as much of each man's pursuit as made him agreeable to that man in reference to it, and just as little as made it natural in him to seek modestly for information when the theme was broached. (2)

"If I have not gone

"If I have not gone to foreign countries . . . foreign countries have come to me.] The proverb is: 'If the Mountain will not come to Mahomet, Mahomet will go to the mountain.'

I instantly lay my finger on him and say 'Paris!'] Since the word 'Paris' would probably be on the clock face, this may not be such a remarkable achievement, any more than the recognition of Chinese ceramics, or that bamboo and sandalwood come from the East Indies and Eskimo spears from the North Pole.

'Pekin, Nankin, and Canton'] Sapsea is probably referring to eighteenth-century armorial china, designed to suit European taste, the product of the great porcelain works at King-te-chen and Canton which flourished until the growth of the porcelain works in Europe and England during the nineteenth century.

bamboo and sandal-wood] Bamboo was imported into Europe for basket-making, furniture, and umbrellas and walking-sticks. Sandalwood from India and the Pacific islands was used in the manufacture of boxes, fans and similar ornamental objects.

'Spear of Esquimaux make] The MS reads 'Bow and arrow'. Eskimos hunt with spears, not bows and arrows.

"We were, sir

fever of the brow] A cliché with literary pretensions.

now dead three quarters of a year."] Mrs Sapsea would have died last Christmas, at about the same time as Durdles had been woken from a drunken sleep by the 'ghost of one terrific shriek' (chapter 12); the coincidence is interesting, as is the curiosity Jasper shows in her tomb.

"Half a dozen years

it is not good for man to be alone."] A plagiarism from Genesis 2.18: 'And the Lord God said, it is not good that man should be alone; I will make him an help meet for him.'

"Miss Brobity at that time

"Miss Brobity] Towards the end of the *Book of Memoranda* Dickens listed: ' "Then I'll give up snuff"./Brobity/An Alarming Sacrifice/Mr Brobity's Snuff box./The pawnbroker's account of it?' (25). Forster thought that since

> 'Brobity' is the name of one of the people in his unfinished story . . . the suggestion may have been meant for some incident in it. If so, it is the only passage in the volume which can be in any way connected with the piece of writing on which he was last engaged. Some names were taken for it from the lists, but there is otherwise nothing to recall *Edwin Drood*. (3.12.266)

There are, however, a number of entries in the *Book of Memoranda* which are relevant to the novel; Kaplan has shown how Forster's account 'has been somewhat controversial' (106).

the finger of scorn] An echo of *Othello* (4.2.54–6):

> but, alas, to make me
> The fixed figure for the time of scorn
> To point his slow unmoving finger at!

"I have been since

wasting my evening conversation on the desert air.] From Gray, 'Elegy Written in a Country Churchyard' (55–6):

> Full many a flower is born to blush unseen,
> And waste its sweetness on the desert air.

Mr. Jasper complying

ETHELINDA] The nature of inscriptions on tombstones and funereal monuments was a religious and aesthetic issue in the larger public discussions on interment in churchyards and cemeteries which began in the 1840s. The arbiters of taste were such writers as A. W. Pugin (*An Apology for the Revival of Christian Architecture in England*, 1843), J. C. Loudon (*On . . . Cemeteries . . .*, 1843), J. H. Markland (*Remarks on English Churches, and on the Expediency of Rendering Sepulchral Memorials Subservient to Pious and Christian Uses*, 1843) and George Blair (*Biographic and Descriptive Sketches of Glasgow Necropolis*, 1857). Journals such as the *Ecclesiologist, Quarterly Review* (73, 1844, 438–77) and *HW* helped to popularize the campaign for a reform of the current standards of epitaphs (see Morley, 1971, 52–62).

In general, the reformers urged 'enlightened and chastened taste', and a rejection of clichés and of 'vulgar extravagancies' (*Quarterly Review*, 465, 466). On these points, and according to the contemporary trend towards asceticism, Mr Sapsea's epitaph for his wife violates all the rules of decorum. Epitaphs should be brief, humble, and free of such 'paganisms' as irrelevant information, mention of occupation, and latinate expressions (of which 'STRANGER PAUSE' is a variant). Moreover, capital letters were considered appropriate only for the initial letters of the names of the deceased, and all lines should be of uniform length. Above all, epitaphs should never be set out in the shape of an altar or urn, as Mrs Sapsea's is – a particular point of pride for her husband, who cautions Jasper: ' "The setting out of the lines requires to be followed with the eye, as well as the contents with the mind." '

A genuine epitaph as indecorous as Ethelinda's was published in *HW*, 1.168:

HERE LIES THE BODY
OF
LADY O'LOONEY,
GREAT NIECE OF BURKE,
COMMONLY CALLED THE SUBLIME.
SHE WAS
BLAND, PASSIONATE, AND DEEPLY RELIGIOUS;
ALSO, SHE PAINTED
IN WATER-COLOURS,
AND SENT SEVERAL PICTURES
TO THE EXHIBITION.
SHE WAS FIRST COUSIN
TO LADY JONES;
AND OF SUCH
IS THE KINGDOM OF HEAVEN

In regard to his own epitaph, Dickens left instructions in his will:

> I DIRECT that my name be inscribed in plain English letters on my tomb, without the addition of "Mr." or "Esquire". I conjure my friends on no account to make me the subject of any monument, memorial, or testimonial whatever. I rest my claims to the remembrance of my country upon my published works, and to the remembrance of my friends upon their experience of me in addition thereto. (Forster 3. Appendix. 517)

The dark slab covering the grave of Dickens in Westminster Abbey bears only the inscription: 'Charles Dickens, Born February the Seventh, 1812. Died June the Ninth, 1870.'

AUCTIONEER, VALUER, ESTATE AGENT] A *HW* writer agrees with contemporary reformers in denouncing 'pagan' epitaphs and in urging modesty and humility. He objects to:

> a statement of common-place matter, such as the survivor's address, profession, or trade. The mention that the deceased was the son, or wife, &c. of John So-and-so, 'Pork Butcher in Smith Street,' is intolerable. What business has an advertisement in such a place? (6.109)

STRANGER PAUSE] From the 'Siste, Viator' ('Stop, Traveller') of Roman inscriptions. The use of the expression in English epitaphs was ridiculed by Sir Thomas Browne and Dr Johnson. The *HW* writer quotes Johnson and agrees with him: 'We depart from Nature when we imitate the Romans, and so miss all due effect altogether' (6.109).

WITH A BLUSH RETIRE] A reminiscence of Sterne, *Tristram Shandy* (1760–7):

> Ten times in a day has Yorick's ghost the consolation to hear his monumental inscription read over with such a variety of plaintive tones, as denote a general pity and esteem for him . . . not a passenger goes by without stopping to cast a look upon it, – and sighing he walks on, Alas, poor YORICK! (1)

Durdles is a stonemason

Durdles is a stonemason] The prototype of Durdles is reported to have been a German, or a man of German origin, who carved figures out of fragments of stone in the crypt of Rochester Cathedral. He carried his carvings in a coloured handkerchief and hawked them around Rochester. He lodged at the inn called the Fortune of War (Cuming Walters, 1912, xxxiv). These connections seem tenuous. The name Durdles probably derives from 'Duddles', which appears in the list of 'Available Names' in the *Book of Memoranda* (22).

He is the chartered libertine of the place.] *Henry V* 1.1.48: 'when he speaks,/The air, a charter'd libertine, is still'.

Fame trumpets him a wonderful workman] The personification of Fame as a female figure was known in classical antiquity, but her trumpet is an invariable addition of Renaissance and later art.

a wonderful sot] The unpleasant nature of their work meant that sextons and gravediggers were inevitably drunkards of a low, degraded type. This was one of the abuses condemned in Edwin Chadwick's *Supplementary Report on the Results of a Special Inquiry into the Practice of Interment in Towns* (1843), one of the several parliamentary reports of the early 1840s on metropolitan burial-grounds. In an article on the *Supplementary Report*, the *Quarterly Review* (73, 1844, 458–9) commented that the class of sextons and gravediggers has 'notoriously become one of the most demoralized and shameless . . . The evidence given of the habits of the metropolitan grave-diggers is too sickening to repeat.' A witness examined by the inquiry testified:

> It is a frequent thing that a gravedigger, who smells strongly of liquor, will ask the widow or mourners for something to drink, and, if not given, he will follow them to the gates and outside the gates, murmuring and uttering reproaches.

seen strange sights.] A revision of the MS reading, 'a strange sight or so'; the phrase is traditional, as in Donne, 'Song': 'If thou be'st born to strange sights,/Things invisible to see'. Also compare *The Winter's Tale* (4.4.806): 'We must to the King and show our strange sights'; and *Julius Caesar* (1.3.138): 'There's two or three of us have seen strange sights'.

And then he turned to powder."] The rapid disintegration of corpses into powder after exposure to the air was a phenomenon which fascinated Dickens. In *PP* Jingle comments on the 'old fellows, with great red faces, and broken noses, turning up every day' (2) (see Jingle's apostrophe to Rochester, quoted in note to chapter 3, p. 49). In *GE* the boy Pip remembers how he had been 'taken to one of our old marsh churches to see a skeleton in the ashes of a rich dress, that had been dug out of a vault under the church pavement'. He associates Miss Havisham with this memory: 'she must have looked as if the admission of the natural light of day would have struck her to dust' (8).

Similar comparisons are made in *BH* (29) and *TTC* (1.3). There is a romantic tale in *HW* about a tomb discovered in the Via Appia, supposed to be the burial-place of Cicero's daughter Tullia. In the middle of the sixteenth century the body of a woman was found there,

> with her hair done up in tresses, and tied with a golden thread; also a lighted lamp, which if the story were true, must have been burning for at least one thousand five hundred and fifty years. But this admirable spectacle did not last long . . . and the body – fading like a ghost before the eyes of the beholders – fell into a heap of formless dust. (8.185)

One of the most celebrated of the stories about the opening of graves and one likely to have been known to Dickens is that of Francis Lovell, a trusted friend of Richard III, and referred to as 'Lovell that dog' in the verse of the time. After the accession of Henry Tudor, Lovell escaped to his home and probably died of starvation in the vault in which he was hiding. In 1708 a new chimney was built in the house and a vault was discovered in which the skeleton of a man seated at a table crumbled to dust minutes after air was admitted (*DNB*). Dickens would also have known the opening stanza of Tennyson, 'Aylmer's Field' (1864):

> Dust are our frames; and, gilded dust, our pride
> Looks only for a moment whole and sound;
> Like that long-buried body of the king,
> Found lying with his urns and ornaments,
> Which at a touch of light, and air of heaven,
> Slipt into ashes, and was found no more.

Tennyson noted: 'This happened on opening an Etruscan tomb at the city of Tarquinii in Italy'; and his son added: 'The warrior was seen for a moment stretched on the couch of stone, and then vanished as soon as the air touched him' (Tennyson, 1907–8, 2.357).

But perhaps the most immediate literary connection is with Victor Hugo, *The Hunchback of Notre-Dame* (1831), of which there are many echoes in *MED*. A few years after the execution of Esmerelda, during which time nothing has been seen of Quasimodo, the skeleton of a man was found embracing that of a young woman:

> There was no rupture of the vertebrae at the nape of the neck, whence it was evident that he had not been hanged. Hence it was inferred that the man must have come thither of himself and died there. When they strove to detach this skeleton from the one it was embracing, it fell to dust. (54)

In a suit

Bench of Justices] The seat where magistrates sit in court, hence the place where justice is administered.

a little antiquated hole of a house that was never finished] The suggested original was a detached one-roomed house 'lit by a window that looked as if it had been part of some ecclesiastical edifice'; it also had 'a door of monkish origin', and the floor was made from 'fragments of tombstone taken from the nave of the Cathedral when it was repaved' (Harris, 1931, 82).

the city wall.] Proximity to the churchyard, according to Percy Carden, explains how 'it was possible for Jasper to carry the quick-lime from Durdles's yard to the Drood sarcophagus without attracting observation' (1920, 31).

a petrified grove of tombstones] Perhaps Dickens had in mind the famous so-called 'Petrified Forest' in the Eastern Desert near the old road from Cairo to Suez, described by Harriet Martineau (*Eastern Life, Past and Present*, 1848):

> We began to note some odd-looking stones lying about in the sand, and among ordinary looking pebbles . . . Fragments of palm trunks, approaching to the size of logs, were perhaps the commonest kind: but there were several kinds of wood; even the bamboo was there, with its joints distinctly visible. (2)

mechanical figures emblematical of Time and Death.] Figures made of wood or of wax and moved by clockwork had been popular subjects in exhibitions in London since the eighteenth century. Sometimes nearly life-size, the figures represented a wide variety of allegorical, fictional and historical characters. They derived from the clock jacks which existed in England from the fourteenth century and were often arranged in elaborate theatrical scenes to give their clockwork performances. A pair of clock jacks which was a favourite of Dickens and which had been well known in London since the 1670s was that at St Dunstan's in the West, Fleet Street. These were life-size wooden figures of savages, each holding a club in his right hand which struck the quarters on two suspended bells (Altick, 1978, 57).

"No, I don't

as the Catechism says, a walking in the same all the days of your life] This is the answer to the third question in the Catechism about the promises of godparents, that 'thirdly . . . I should keep God's holy will and commandments, and walk in the same all the days of my life'. Perhaps the most charming of Dickens's many jokes about this response is in *GE* (7) when the young Pip understands it literally, and supposes that his

> declaration that I was to 'walk in the same all the days of my life,' laid me under an obligation always to go through the village from our house in one particular direction, and never to vary it by turning down by the wheelwright's or up by the mill.

Mr. Sapsea rises

Mr. Sapsea rises, takes a key from a drawer, unlocks an iron safe] Dickens makes something of the finding and placing of the key, in the case of both Sapsea and Durdles; and Jasper observes everything. In the number plan 'Jasper and the Keys' is noted, and in the chapter plan is 'The Keys' (see pp. 16–17).

"By-the-bye

as he idly examines the keys] Jasper is listening to the sounds the keys make as they rub against each other so that he will be able to distinguish them by the sound they make and by their weight.

But the stony one

as though he were an Ostrich, and liked to dine off cold iron] A traditional belief, as in *2 Henry VI* 4.10.25: 'I'll make thee eat iron like an ostrich and swallow my sword like a great pin ere thou and I part.'

deigning no word of answer.] In order to smooth the transposition of chapter 5 from the second to the first number, Dickens rewrote and added the paragraph which ends here.

Chapter 5

MR. DURDLES AND FRIEND.

In MS this was chapter 8 but was moved forward to make up the length of number 1. Dickens made many minor changes in the chapter to suit its new position.

John Jasper, on his way

John Jasper, on his way home through the Close] This chapter had originally followed on from the party at Minor Canon Corner, so that Jasper would have crossed the Close to return to the Gate House in the High Street.

the iron railing of the burial-ground] Dickens was probably thinking of the small area on the north side of the Cathedral which is a burial-ground, and which once may have been railed (see Map). This would be the one that Durdles and Jasper look down upon from the Cathedral tower in chapter 12.

the old cloister-arches] The arches in the cloister garth are all that remain of the old cloisters built by Ernulph; the effects of fire can be seen in the stonework.

"Mulled agin!"] A term in athletics meaning to fail; for example, mulling a pass in rugby, or mulling a catch in a ball game.

"Making a cock-shy

"Making a cock-shy of him] The diversion of throwing at cocks originated at the Shrovetide fairs; later, living birds were replaced by toys made in the shape of cocks, on large stands of lead at which the boys could throw. He who could overturn the toy claimed it as a reward for his adroitness. The custom had virtually died out by 1865.

"He gives me

chants, like a little savage, half stumbling and half dancing] In the *Book of Memoranda* is a note that may relate to this scene: 'The father and boy, as I dramatically see them. Opening with the wild dance, I have in my mind' (20).

"Widdy widdy wen!] In the game of 'Warning', otherwise known as 'Widdy', a player stands behind a line and delivers the following challenge or caution:

> Warning once, warning twice, warning three times over;
> A bushel of wheat, a bushel of rye,
> When the cock crows, out jump I!
> Cock-a-doodle-doo! – Warning!

The crier runs out and touches the first he can overtake; these two return to bounds and together try to touch another until the whole group is touched. The London version of the cry is closer to Deputy's: 'Whiddy, whiddy, way, If you don't come, I won't play' and 'Whiddy, whiddy, wake-cock. Warning!' (Opie, 1969, 92; Wright, 1898, 6.486).

This would seem

a poetical note of preparation] An echo of *Henry V* (Chorus, 4.10–14):

> Steed threatens steed, in high and boastful neighs
> Piercing the night's dull ear; and from the tents
> The armourers, accomplishing the knights,
> With busy hammers closing rivets up,
> Give dreadful note of preparation.

"Do you know this thing

"Do you know this thing, this child?"] Deputy is similar to the boy in *HM* who disturbs the conscience of Redlaw: 'A baby savage, a young monster, a child who had never been a child, a creature who might live to take the outward form of man, but who, within, would live and perish a mere beast' (1). This boy also struggles to be let free and, when asked his name, declares that he has ' "Got none" '. To the question, ' "Where do you live?" ' he replies, ' "Live! What's that?" ' (1).

"I'm man-servant

Travellers' Twopenny] This is reputed to be modelled on Kitt's Lodging House, known as the Fourpenny Lodging House, located just off Rochester High Street (see Map). Kitt's seems to be the place David Copperfield remarks on when passing through Rochester:

> One or two little houses, with the notice, 'Lodgings for Travellers', hanging out, had tempted me; but I was afraid of spending the few pence I had, and was even more afraid of the vicious looks of the trampers I had met or overtaken. (13)

Common lodging houses sheltered anyone who could pay a few pence. Mayhew describes one in London which would keep a fire for lodgers to cook their own food. The accommodation comprised five rows of bunks, twenty-four deep:

> The sanitary state of these houses is very bad. Not only do the lodgers generally swarm with vermin, but there is little or no ventilation to the sleeping-rooms, in which 60 persons, of the foulest habits, usually sleep every night. There are no proper washing utensils, neither towels nor basins, nor wooden bowls . . . The lodgers never think of washing themselves. The cleanliest among them will do so in the bucket, and then wipe themselves with their pocket-handkerchiefs, or the tails of their shirts. (3.315)

Accompanied by friends and protected by the police, Dickens visited such a house in the summer of 1869, the period when his ideas for the novel were taking shape. One of his friends, James T. Fields, who also visited the opium den with Dickens (see note to chapter 1 above, pp. 22–3), recalled Dickens's reaction to the lodging-house inmates:

> At the door of one of the penny lodging-houses (it was growing toward morning, and the raw air almost cut one to the bone), I saw him snatch a little child out of its poor drunken mother's arms, and bear it in, filthy as it was, that it might be warmed and cared for. I noticed that whenever he entered one of these wretched rooms he had a word of cheer for its inmates, and that when he left the apartment he always had a pleasant 'Good night' or 'God bless you' to bestow upon them. (1900; reprinted 1970, 203)

Gas Works Garding] Gas Works Garden.

"All us man-servants at Travellers' Lodgings is named Deputy.] Wilkie Collins's 'Gooseberry' in *The Moonstone* plays a minor but essential role in the denouement, as Deputy may have been intended to do. Only the detective, Cuff, who might be assumed to be playing the same role as Datchery in this novel, calls Gooseberry by his real name. In Dickens's visits to London's seamier parts with Inspector Charles Field, the landlords of several lodging houses sent their Deputies to show them round:

> Deputy is heard to stumble out of bed. Deputy lights a candle, draws back a bolt or two, and appears at the door. Deputy is a shivering shirt and trousers by no means clean, a yawning face, a shock head much confused externally and internally. We want to look for someone. You may go up with the light, and take 'em all, if you like, says Deputy, resigning it, and sitting down upon a bench in the kitchen with his ten fingers sleepily twisting in his hair. ('On Duty with Inspector Field', *HW* 3.269).

"Not on any account

Your own brother-in-law] What association does Jasper's family have with Cloisterham so that Edwin's father would be buried here? We do not know where Jasper's sister, who is Edwin's mother, is buried. We also have no knowledge of Jasper's relationship with his sister, who must have been some years older than he.

broken column . . . a vase and towel, standing on what might represent the cake of soap . . . extinguished torch.] The reformers of ecclesiastical art considered such classical motifs to be heathen emblems unbecoming to Christian cemeteries (see note on 'ETHELINDA' in chapter 4, pp. 64–5). All the writers agreed with Pugin:

> There is not, in fact, the least practical difficulty in reviving at the present time consistent and Christian monuments for all classes of persons, and at the same cost now bestowed on pagan abominations . . . Surely the Cross must be the

> most appropriate emblem on the tombs of those who profess to believe in God crucified for the redemption of man; and it is almost incredible, that . . . the types of all modern sepulchral monuments should be essentially pagan; and urns, broken pillars, extinguished lamps, inverted torches, and sarcophagi, should have been substituted for recumbent effigies, angels, and emblems of mercy and redemption. (*An Apology for the Revival of Christian Architecture in England*, 1843, 37)

(See also [F. E. Paget], *A Tract upon Tomb-Stones . . .*, 1843, 20–1; John Armstrong, *A Paper on Monuments*, 1844; 'Graves and Epitaphs', *HW* 6.108.)

the common folk that is merely bundled up in turf and brambles] Under the Metropolitan Interments Act of 1842, portions of ground in cemeteries both consecrated and unconsecrated (for denominations other than Anglican) were required to be set apart for paupers and the poor. This class of person could not afford monuments for their graves (*Westminster Review*, 40 (1843), 149–82 passim).

"Own brother, sir

Peter the Wild Boy] Peter the Wild Boy was caught in woods outside Hamelin in 1724 and became an instant celebrity. He was brought to England by order of George I in the following year and was put into the care of Dr Arbuthnot, who wanted to study the efficacy of educating a child found walking on all fours and subsisting on the bark of trees, leaves and berries. It was established that Peter had run away from home when his widowed father remarried. Although there appeared to be no defect in the boy's speech organs, he could not be taught to speak: denied human contact as an infant and child, he never recovered the ability to communicate. Dr Arbuthnot's project failed, therefore, and Peter was placed under the care of a Hertfordshire farmer, with whom he lived until his death in 1785.

The condition of Peter the Wild Boy fascinated scientists and philosophers. A favourite thesis was that presented by Daniel Defoe in *Mere Nature Delineated* (1726). Defoe discredited rumours of the squirrel-like running on all fours, but claimed that because the boy was devoid of language he was necessarily devoid of a soul, and thereby of intellect, emotion, passion and desire. Such a view, favoured among eighteenth-century empiricists, was taken up by Wordsworth. His Peter Bell (1819), a 'wild and woodland rover' with a hardness of cheek and of eye denoting his psychological and moral limitations, is in many respects a model for Deputy (Bewell, 1983, 321–46).

"That's it, sir

Short terms in Cloisterham Jail.] Mayhew ascertained that thirty-four out of the fifty-five inhabitants of one of the lodging houses he visited 'had been in gaol, once or oftener' (3.316).

"He has plenty

a sort of a – scheme of a – National Education?"] The National Education movement evolved out of the demands made by education reformers from the 1840s onwards for governmental support first of the 'ragged schools' (established for slum children and run on a voluntary basis), and then of reformatory schools as a solution to juvenile delinquency and destitution. Dickens had long advocated the responsibility of the state to provide education for all, and he encouraged the aims of the ragged school movement, but he criticized its bias towards voluntarism and evangelicalism. For other reasons as well, his support was less than wholehearted. In praising the work of the Duck Lane Ragged School, he commented:

> Our readers will distinctly understand that, in advocating the cause of such an establishment, we do so, only as it tends to mitigate a monstrous evil already in existence. To endow such Institutions, and leave the question of National Education in its present shameful state, would be to maintain a cruel absurdity to which we are most strongly opposed. The compulsory industrial education of neglected children, and the severe punishment of neglectful and unnatural parents, are reforms to which we *must* come, doubt it who may. (*HW* 3.41–2)

Many other articles in *HW*, several by Dickens himself, manifest his continuing interest in national education (see, for example: 'The Schoolmaster at Home and Abroad', 1.82–4; 'Mr Bendigo Buster on Our National Defences Against Education', 2.313–19; 'The Metropolitan Protectives', 3.97–105; and 'Boys to Mend', 5.597–602). The agitation of the reformers culminated in the Education Act of 1870.

So they go on

a rear rank of one, taking open order] Military terms: the rear ranks are the men at the back of the army or camp; and open order is the formation in which individual men are set three or more yards apart.

"Well! Inasmuch as

than in mine.] After 'mine' MS has a paragraph on Durdles:

> As the mental state of Durdles, and of all his sodden tribe, is one hardly susceptible of astonishment in itself, so it is one hardly susceptible of any reasonable interpretation by other minds. But it happens to fall out tonight – just as it might have happened to fall out quite the other way – that Durdles rather likes his position in the dialogue, and chuckles over it.

"I have even

hanged by the neck, on his evidence, until they are dead] The words of the death sentence: 'The sentence of the Court upon you is, that you be taken from this place to a lawful prison and thence to a place of execution and that you be hanged by the neck until you be dead.'

"Not really

"Not really Mrs. Sapsea?"] This scene is important to those who believe that Edwin is dead and that Jasper uses Mrs Sapsea's tomb in which to secrete the body. But this is not Mrs Sapsea's tomb, as the repetition of ' "say Mrs. Sapsea" ' makes clear (see Lang, 1905, 22; Carden, 1920, 16–38; Baker, 1951, 61–2).

They have but

the vineyard] The 'Vines' is a tree-lined walk lying to the south of the Cathedral and beyond Minor Canon Row (see Map).

The semblance of an inn

conventional red curtaining] An old custom; all Dickens's inns are thus decorated.

feeble lights of rush or cotton dip] A rush candle, or rush light, is made by dipping the pith of a rush in tallow or other grease. A dip candle is made by repeatedly dipping a wick into melted tallow.

As Durdles and Jasper come near . . . All is silent] In place of these paragraphs, MS reads:

> As Durdles and Jasper come near, a woman is seen crouching and smoking in the cold night air on a seat just outside the door, which stands ajar.
>
> Of a sudden, Jasper stops, and looks at this woman – the lighter-colored figure of Durdles being between himself and her – very keenly.
>
> "Is that Deputy?" she croaks out in a whimpering and feeble way; "where have you been, you young good for nothing wretch?"
>
> "Out for my Elth," returns the hideous sprite.
>
> "I'll claw you," retorts the woman, "when I can lay my fingers on you. I'll be bad for your Elth! (O me, o me, my breath is very short!) I wanted my pipe and my little spoon, and ye'd been and put 'Em on a shelf I couldn't find."
>
> "Wot did yer go to bed for then?" retorts Deputy, quite unabashed. "Who ha' thought yer wos going to get up agin?"
>
> "You. You might ha' known I was like to do it."
>
> "Yer lie!" says Deputy, in his only form of contradiction.
>
> Jasper, touching Durdles on the shoulder, and laying his finger on his lips when that worthy looks round, leads the way onward gingerly enough. He more than once or twice looks back, but utters no word until they have reached the corner of the lane; then he casually remarks in a subdued voice that he is well

> out of any unseemly quarrel or discussion in such a place, and glances back again. All is still.

It is possible to assume some connection between Deputy and the Princess Puffer, though some of the suggestions (that she is Deputy's mother, for example) are a little wild. Dickens's omission of the passage from the published text must indicate that if Jasper were to have known that the opium-woman was in Cloisterham his suspicions would be aroused. This must not happen, or the effectiveness of chapter 23 would be spoiled.

an inscribed paper lantern over the door, setting forth the purport of the house.] According to a contemporary witness, this was in fact a gas street-lamp on which was painted 'Good Beds, 4d and 6d' (Edwin Harris, cited in Oliver, 1978, 109–10).

This remonstrance

according to a custom of late years comfortably established among the police regulations of our English communities, where Christians are stoned on all sides] In 'The Ruffian' (*UT*), Dickens had complained that members of the public were not sufficiently protected by the police from roughs:

> The throwing of stones in the streets has become a dangerous and destructive offence, which surely could have got to no greater height though we had had no Police but our own riding-whips and walking-sticks – the Police to which I myself appeal on these occasions.

the days of Saint Stephen] Stephen, the first Christian martyr, was accused of blasphemy and stoned to death: 'And thou shalt stone him with stones, that he die; because he hath sought to thrust thee away from the Lord thy God' (Deuteronomy 13.10).

At the corner

a stone came rattling at his hat] MS reads 'and knocking it off', but perhaps this is not an appropriate place to have Jasper look foolish.

a crow, as from some infernally-hatched Chanticleer] Somewhat reminiscent of *Hamlet* 1.1.149–52:

> I have heard
> The cock, that is the trumpet to the morn,
> Doth with his lofty and shrill-sounding throat
> Awake the god of day.

John Jasper returns

a peculiar-looking pipe] See note to chapter 1, p. 27.

His nephew lies asleep

John Jasper stands looking down upon him] The moment recalls the man who murders his nephew in *MHC*. He is fascinated by his victim and sometimes 'would steal upstairs and watch him as he slept'.

Chapter 6

Second monthly number
May 1870

PHILANTHROPY IN MINOR CANON CORNER.

The title has been inserted in a balloon in MS.

The Reverend Septimus

Reverend Septimus Crisparkle] 'Septimus' was chosen after some deliberation over 'Arthur' (already given to the hero of *LD*) and 'Joe', which was later bestowed on the omnibus-driver.

six weak little rushlights] These were old-fashioned candles made with reeds dipped into hot grease. They were dim and flickered, and were often used in a perforated tin as a night light.

having broken the thin morning ice near Cloisterham Weir] For Crisparkle as a type of Muscular Christian, modelled on Charles Kingsley, see note to chapter 2, p. 38. The nearest weir to Rochester is Snodland Weir at Allington, about eight miles away. It has been suggested that this is the weir Dickens had in mind (Hughes, 1893, 135).

boxing-gloves] John Broughton, champion until 1750, is said to have introduced boxing-gloves for practice.

It was scarcely

waiting for the urn.] Before breakfast the housemaid would place the heater of the tea-urn on the hottest part of the kitchen fire; when breakfast was served, she filled the urn with hot water.

'Neither, please God

Here's wind] A sporting phrase referring to easy or regular breathing.

Bring in the other young couple. Yes

Neville and Olympia Heyridge – or Heyfort?

Neville and Helena Landless

Mixture of Oriental blood – or imperceptibly acquired nature – in them. Yes

(Mystery of Edwin Drood. – No. II.)

Chapter V.

Philanthropy in Minor-Canon Corner

old Mrs Crisparkle

The Blusterous Philanthropist — China Shepherdess

Mr Honeythunder

Minor Canon Corner

Chapter VI.

More Confidences than One.

Neville's to Mr Crisparkle.

Rosa's to Helena

Piano scene with
Jasper. She singing;
he following her lips.

Chapter VII

Daggers Drawn.

Quarrel (Fomented by Jasper). Goblet. And then

confession to Mr Crisparkle

Jasper lays his ground

Chapter VIII

Mr Durdles and friend

Deputy engaged to stone Durdles nightly

No — Carry through the woman of the 1st chapter

Carry through Durdles's calling – and the
bundle & the Keys

John Jasper looks at Edwin asleep.

In a concluding round

into Chancery] A term deriving from the tenacity and control with which the court of Chancery holds cases, where there was certainty of high costs and loss of property. Here it means that the head is held under the left arm and severely pummelled, the victim meanwhile unable to retaliate effectively.

he being within five years of forty] This would make Crisparkle about fifteen years older than Helena, with whom it is suggested he forms a romantic attachment.

They were a good pair

Minor Canon Corner] Minor Canon Row in Rochester consists of six houses built between 1721 and 1723 and a seventh at the east end for the organist built in 1735 (Hope, 1900, 210). They are described in 'The Seven Poor Travellers' as 'a wonderfully quaint row of red-brick tenements' that had 'odd little porches over the doors, like sounding-boards over old pulpits' (*CS*). Crisparkle occupies the corner house at the west end (actually 1 Minor Canon Row), next to Prior's Gate (see Map).

Swaggering fighting men . . . beaten serfs . . . powerful monks] Rochester had a turbulent history, dating back to the ancient British stronghold that occupied the site. The Romans succeeded, and then the Saxons. In the years following Ethelbert's building of the wall (600–4), Rochester suffered from fire and sword as Ethelred plundered and the Danes attacked, though driven off by Alfred in 888. The Normans brought order, but medieval Rochester suffered battles, and its largely wooden buildings were set on fire. King John seized the castle from the barons, but Louis the Dauphin retook it the following year (1216). In 1264, Simon de Montfort laid siege to the castle after capturing the city and, in 1668, Rochester was ravaged by plague. Thereafter it was disrupted no more. For Dickens's opinions on the feudal system ('beaten serfs'), see *CHE* 9, 19. The 'powerful monks' were Benedictines who, under Gundulph, began in 1077 to build the new cathedral.

that serenely romantic state of the mind – productive for the most part of pity and forbearance – which is engendered by a sorrowful story that is all told, or a pathetic play that is played out.] An allusion to the theory of catharsis, from Aristotle's *Poetics*, that the essential function of tragedy is to purge the emotions of the audience through pity and fear. For the effect Dickens intends, see the opening description of the ancient battlefield in *BL*.

"It's from Mr. Honeythunder

Mr. Honeythunder] Dickens had considered 'Mr Honeyblast' as an alternative in his Manuscript List of Projected Names and Titles.

"Of course

"Haven of Philanthropy] The many philanthropic movements that flourished in the mid-nineteenth century, particularly those run by evangelicals, were targets of Dickens's satire from his earliest novels. Although he himself collaborated in various charitable schemes with prominent evangelical philanthropists, he did not hesitate to criticize the pretence of piety, the sanctimonious hypocrisy and spiritual arrogance which the movement seemed to engender in its adherents. In 'A Handful of Humbugs', for instance, an *AYR* article of 1863, he attacked what might be described as a 'haven of philanthropy', Exeter Hall, the 'Temple' of philanthropy with its 'votaries' and 'priesthood' (10.57).

In particular, it has been suggested that Honeythunder embodies the harsh attitudes of the Charity Organization Society, established in 1869 partly to systematize charitable resources and their distribution and partly to vindicate the rigorous notion that no charity at all was preferable to indiscriminate charity (see Pope, 1978, 20–35, 244–6). The biblical quotations with which evangelicals and nonconformists laced their language are evident in 'the apple of their eye' (Psalms 17.8; Proverbs 7.2), 'the face of the earth' (Genesis 1.2), and 'to love your brother as yourself' (Leviticus 19.18; Matthew 19.19) in the passage summarizing Honeythunder's philosophy near the end of the chapter. In the same passage, the references to 'you were to do nothing in private . . . and were evermore to live upon a platform' allude to the evangelicals' penchant for proselytizing oratory from public platforms such as Exeter Hall.

Collins's *The Moonstone* also has a philanthropist, Godfrey Ablewhite, but there the parody is different. Ablewhite is young and attractive, exerting an insidious allure to benefit ladies' charities as well as his own vanity.

' "Denouncing a public

Neville and Helena Landless] Dickens considered 'Heyridge' and 'Heyfort' as surnames, and Helena was originally given another Greek name, 'Olympia'. 'Helena Landless' sounds so much like the name of the actress whom Dickens met in 1857 and on whose account he separated from his wife in 1858, Ellen Lawless Ternan, that Ellen in some way must have inspired the naming and characterization. (For further comment, see notes to chapter 19, p. 157.) In the characterization of the Landlesses as dark, gypsy-like and 'untamed', it has been suggested that Dickens was influenced by the orientalism of *The Moonstone* (Cuming Walters, 1912, xxxiv). Moreover, Cuming Walters notes the evidence that Dickens was attracted to the type of beauty Helena represents: in Paris in 1856, he had seen a woman resembling Helena (in some respects) at a dance frequented by prostitutes. He described them to Wilkie Collins:

> Some pretty faces, but all of two classes – wicked and coldly calculating, or haggard and wretched in their worn beauty. Among the latter was a woman of thirty or so, in an Indian shawl . . . Handsome, regardless, brooding, and yet

> with some nobler qualities in her forehead. I mean to walk about to-night and look for her. I didn't speak to her there, but I have a fancy that I should like to know more about her. Never shall, I suppose. (22 April, *Nonesuch* 2.763)

For the connection of the Landlesses with Ceylon, see note to chapter 7, pp. 86–7.

"And it is another

bumping them into the paths of peace.] Proverbs 3.17: 'Her ways are ways of pleasantness, and all her paths are peace.'

Therefore, dear Madam

to be read with] Many clergymen took in pupils in this way; it was an alternative education to public school.

Your affectionate brother (In Philanthropy)] A parody of the term used by the clergy: 'brother in Christ'.

"I should call him

"but that his voice is so much larger."] In *BH*, Mr Jarndyce makes the remark that 'there were two classes of charitable people: one, the people who did a little and made a great deal of noise; the other, the people who did a great deal and made no noise at all' (8).

"Hah!" said Septimus

Superior Family Souchong] One of the finer varieties of black China tea. A *HW* article explains that 'Souchong' means 'small or scarce sort' and that it is 'the best black tea of the second crop' (3.328).

Mrs. Crisparkle's sister

Corporation preferment in London City.] An appointment which gives social or pecuniary advancement and is chiefly an ecclesiastical post.

"I am sure you will agree

the fairy bride that is to be] From 'The Mistletoe Bough', a 'celebrated English ditty of the olden time' (with words by T. H. Bayley). The song tells of a young bride who, during games at Christmas, hides in an oak chest. Years later, her skeleton is discovered. The lyrics suggest sinister overtones with regard to the ending of the novel; the third verse reads:

They sought her that night, and they sought her next day,
And they sought her in vain, when a week pass'd away,
In the highest, the lowest, the loneliest spot,
Young Lovell sought wildly, but found her not.
And years flew by, and their grief at last
Was told as a sorrowful tale long past.
And when Lovell appear'd the children cried,
'See, the old man weeps for his fairy bride.'
Oh! the mistletoe bough,
Oh! the mistletoe bough.

(The allusion was identified by Longley, 1981, 105.) There may be another allusion to the song when David Copperfield describes Emily as 'the fairy little woman' (10). A play based on the song was frequently performed in the nineteenth century: *Fairy of the Missletoe Bough.*

In those days

there was no railway to Cloisterham] In a letter to the American poet Bayard Taylor, who visited him at Gad's Hill, Dickens explained that his home could be reached 'either by North Kent Railway from Charing Cross, for Higham Station, the next beyond Gravesend – a mile from here; or by London Chatham and Dover Railway to Strood (Rochester Bridge) Station, two miles and a half distant' (*Nonesuch* 3.663). But this was in August 1868; it had not been until 1853 that the line to Strood, adjoining Rochester, was opened. A fragment of main line to Maidstone had been completed in 1844; Maidstone Road Station was the nearest (twenty-one miles) to Rochester.

The Railway Chronicle Travelling Chart (1846) explains that the South-Eastern Line

> instead of pursuing the old coach-road through Rochester and Canterbury, as was proposed, was compelled by the benighted, and now repentant, opposition of the inhabitants of North Kent to make a circuitous route through the Weald of Kent.

Up to the 1850s, then, travellers rode from London to Maidstone (opened 1844) and an omnibus took them to Rochester. By the time Dickens was writing *MED* there was a line from Victoria to Chatham, which he used. Here he suggests the older route from London Bridge Station, and *Bradshaw* (no. 34, 1 September 1844) shows that the journey took just over two hours: a train leaving at 2.55 p.m. would arrive at 5.00 p.m.

For many Victorians, the railway boom of the 1840s and 1850s marked the end of an age. Thackeray observes that 'Gunpowder and printing tended to modernise the world . . . but your railroad starts the new era, and we of a certain age belong to the new time and the old one' ('De Juventute', from *The Roundabout Papers*, 1860–3).

Mr. Sapsea said there never would be.] This dispute may refer to the tussle for the occupation of Kent between the East Kent Company and the South Eastern companies. The South East were determined to be the purveyors of railway transport for the county, and then the North Kent Company proposed a shorter line, alleging that the inhabitants of Rochester were in their favour and that the wardens would contribute to their proposed road and rail bridge over the Medway. There is opposition to the railway at Staggs's Gardens in *DS*, where the population is confident of 'long outliving any such ridiculous inventions'. But, far from being 'a sacred grove not to be withered by railroads', the Gardens are swept away (6).

deserting the high road . . . by a back stable-way] Passengers for Rochester, having to alight at Maidstone Road Station, continued their journey by omnibus, entering the city by Crow Lane, now Maidstone Road. The approach to a town is often 'by all the back lanes where the pigs lived: which, although not a magnificent or even savoury approach, was, as is usual in such cases, the legitimate highway' (*HT* 3.7).

To this ignominious

a short squat omnibus] Omnibuses were established in London in 1829 and quickly spread to other cities.

like a little Elephant with infinitely too much Castle] The Elephant and Castle is a celebrated tavern (mentioned as early as the sixteenth century) situated on the south bank about a mile and a half distant from Westminster, Waterloo and Blackfriars bridges. It stands at the meeting-point of the Kennington, Walworth and New Kent roads, 'that ganglion of roads from Kent and Surrey, and of streets from the bridges of London' (*BH* 27). During coaching days the tavern was a popular halting station for travellers journeying south from London.

seated on the box] The seat beside the driver.

"Reverend Mr. Septimus

a double eye-glass] A pince-nez.

Mrs. Crisparkle had need

very large and very loud excrescence] The suggested original of Honeythunder is John Bright (1811–89), the radical Quaker politician. He was known to be rude and brusque in manner, although admirers would describe him as candid. A prominent member of the Peace Society, he was notorious for denouncing war in a pugnacious manner and was often caricatured in *Punch* as a prizefighter or as having a clenched fist (see Fielding, 1952, 1084). Bright has been described as a 'hard-hitter' in politics, strong in expression, rich in voice, and imposing in appearance. At a dinner party, he did most of the talking, usually about matters most interesting to himself:

> It must have been some reform of the criminal law which the Judges opposed, that excited him, for at the end of dinner, over the wine, he took possession of the table in his old way, and ended with a superb denunciation of the Bench, spoken in his massive manner, as though every word were a hammer, smashing what it struck: –
> "For two hundred years, the Judges of England sat on the Bench, condemning to the penalty of death every man, woman, and child who stole property to the value of five shillings; and, during all that time, not one Judge ever remonstrated against the law. We English are a nation of brutes, and ought to be exterminated to the last man." (Adams, 1907; reprinted 1918, 190–1)

Although Dickens had criticized Bright ('my worthy friend John Bates') and the Peace Society in a *HW* article ('Whole Hogs', 3.505–7), the depiction of Honeythunder may well be informed by Tennyson's satiric portrait of Bright in *Maud* (1855, 1.10.3):

> Last week came one to the county town,
> To preach our poor little army down . . .
> This broad-brimm'd hawker of holy things . . .
> This huckster put down war!

For further discussion of Honeythunder and John Bright, see notes to chapter 17, pp. 145–6.

his philanthropy was of that gunpowderous sort] *OED* cites 1868 as the earliest use of 'gunpowder' as an adjective. Except for the usage here, the examples cited are 'gunpowdery'.

You were to abolish military force, but you were first to bring all commanding officers who had done their duty, to trial by court martial] An allusion to the role of the philanthropic and missionary societies in one of the major political controversies of the late 1860s, the Governor Eyre case. In October 1865, Edward Eyre, the English governor of Jamaica, had violently suppressed a riotous insurrection against British rule during which some police and Europeans were killed. Martial law, imprisonments, floggings and nearly five hundred executions effected the suppression. George William Gordon, a Baptist leader of the rebellion, was removed from Jamaica, where he had been safe from martial law, to Morant Bay, where a military court condemned him to death. When the news was received in England, public opinion was divided. Eyre's actions were condemned as repressive and precipitant by liberals, abolitionists, missionaries and philanthropists. Determined to bring Eyre to justice, they formed the Jamaica Committee and appointed J. S. Mill as chairman. Among the members was John Bright. In opposition to the Jamaica Committee, leading conservatives formed the Eyre Defence Fund, maintaining that Eyre had acted decisively in the face of incipient revolution. Popular sentiment also supported Eyre, and this contributed to his being exonerated from prosecution before a grand jury in 1867. Dickens himself supported Eyre, as did such other writers as Carlyle, Froude, Kingsley, Ruskin and Tennyson.

The dinner was

lapsed into a sort of gelatinous state] Mr Dombey's celebration of his son's christening is similar: 'The party seemed to get colder and colder, and to be gradually resolving itself into a congealed and gelid state, like the colation round which it was assembled' (5).

Chapter 7

MORE CONFIDENCES THAN ONE.

This was chapter 6 in MS.

"To be *my guardian?*

we come (my sister and I) from Ceylon?"] Dickens's choice of Ceylon as the home of the Landlesses was influenced by his close friendship with Sir James Emerson Tennent (1804–69), to whom he dedicated *OMF*. A distinguished traveller, politician and writer, Tennent was civil secretary to the colonial government of Ceylon from 1845–50. His *Ceylon: An Account of the Island, Physical, Historical, and Topographical* ... (2 vols, 1859) proved so popular that it was reprinted several times within the first eight months. He presented a copy to Dickens, and the work provided material for a number of articles in *AYR*.

Tennent gives accounts of the savage wars between the native races of the island and of its violent colonization by first the Portuguese and then the Dutch before British rule began in 1796. A boom in coffee and tea plantations in the 1820s attracted hordes of European speculators (among them 'the very *worst* class of Englishmen', in the words of a colonial governor, Lord Torrington) and enticed the island's officials, judges and clergymen to neglect their duties in an attempt to make their fortunes. The rapid appropriation of land led to a Sinhalese rising in 1848 (2.6.1–3).

In chapter 8, Neville speaks of the 'Heathens' among whom he was raised. The predominant religion in Ceylon was Buddhism, of which Tennent gives a sympathetic account. He argues, nevertheless, that, unlike Christianity, Buddhism is insufficient 'to arrest man in his career of passion and pursuit', his evidence being the widespread practice of demon worship. And yet he is forced to admit that Christianity had made little headway in Ceylon (1.4.11). This was an experience that missionaries had shared throughout the east, and by the middle of the nineteenth century the colonizing motive of conversion had largely been abandoned. Dickens's juxtaposition of the Christian church in Cloisterham with the exotic east and the demonic in man (as represented by the passionate nature of the Landlesses) reflects this new relativism which was often expressed as the confirmation of an essential depravity in man (see Hyam, 1976, passim).

The rumour spread about Neville in chapter 16, 'Before coming to England he had caused to be whipped to death sundry "Natives" ', is not, of course, intended as an allusion to the actual relations in Ceylon between Europeans and non-whites (see note to chapter 16, p. 137). Such relations were easier in Ceylon than in British India for several reasons. Partly, Europeans found they could deal with Buddhism better than with Hinduism or Islam. Partly, the Christian community of Eurasians, a legacy of the Portuguese and the Dutch, enjoyed a higher status than did the Eurasians in India and had become one of the most westernized communities in the east. Finally, the minority Tamil group readily adopted the English language, and many were employed in government service (Kiernan, 1969, 76–7).

"I wonder at that

Our mother died there] It may be significant that Neville says nothing of his father; like Rosa and Edwin, the Landlesses, as their name suggests, are orphans.

for no better reason that I know of] Perhaps another reason, and a better one, was to have emerged later, if Honeythunder's role was to have been developed. Philanthropists were among the advocates of the numerous and controversial schemes which promoted emigration to the colonies for poor people, reformed criminals, and ragged school graduates (see Pope, 1978, 185–7).

"Quite lately

"Quite lately] Avoidance of specific time: where the Landlesses have been since may be important.

"I have had, sir

I have been stinted of education] Neville's complaint echoes that of Orlando in *As You Like It* (1.1.66–74):

> My father charg'd you in his will to give me good education: you have train'd me like a peasant, obscuring and hiding from me all gentleman-like qualities. The spirit of my father grows strong in me, and I will no longer endure it; therefore allow me such exercises as may become a gentleman, or give me the poor allottery my father left me by testament; with that I will go buy my fortunes.

"In a last word

Each time she dressed as a boy] Her past experience of dressing as a boy is the basis of the belief that Helena would adopt the role of Datchery (Cuming

Walters, 1912, 237, and Nicoll, 1912, 153). Cardwell points out (1969, 130) that Helena's disguise borrows details from the notorious case of Constance Kent, an account of which is given by William Roughead, who also believes that the disappearance of the 13-year-old girl and her brother in 1857 is the likely source for this episode.

The similarity with Helena begins when Constance disguises herself in old clothes of her brother's, and cuts off her hair. Hand in hand the pair walked ten miles to Bath and asked for accommodation at the Greyhound Hotel, where the landlady was suspicious; the little boy broke down and confessed, but Constance, in spite of a night in a prison cell, and after she returned to her father's house, remained doggedly silent. She declared only that she ' "wished to be independent" and meant to make for Bristol, with a view to leaving England'. Three years later, in 1860, a young half-brother was found with his head almost entirely severed from his body. Constance admitted her guilt in 1878 when the eminent authority on mental illness, Dr J. C. Bucknill, interviewed her in prison and concluded that her motive was revenge: her mother had died after years of insanity (though still bearing her husband's children), and Mr Kent married the governess soon after (Roughead, 1926, 51–2, 82–3).

Wilkie Collins adapted aspects of the case in *The Moonstone.* Dickens may also be recalling the more immediate experience of acting in 'No Thoroughfare' on which he collaborated with Collins: brave Marguerite climbs over a cliff to save the wounded Vendale.

we were seven years old when we first decamped] If they ran away 'four times in six years' and were seven when they 'first decamped', that gives them thirteen years; but where they have been and what they have been doing, or how old they are, we are not told. Neville must be at least 18 or much the same age as Edwin, who is about to come of age. This would concur with the intimation, through her protectiveness, that Helena is a few years older than Rosa.

how desperately she tried to tear it out, or bite it off.] Those who believe Helena to be Datchery point to her long hair as the reason why Datchery's large head of white hair must be a wig. But if she had intended, under stress, to cut off her hair at an earlier age she could as easily cut it off now. Furthermore, this is not necessarily a manly action, but one born of despair.

"Of that, Mr. Neville

I will not repay your confidence with a sermon.] 'Not that I have any curiosity to hear powerful preachers,' Dickens writes during his tour of London churches in *UT*. 'Time was, when I was dragged by the hair of my head, as one might say, to hear too many'.

"You don't know, sir

what a complete understanding can exist between my sister and me] This bond is unexplained, but may be a type of mesmerism corresponding to Jasper's hypnotic powers. This telepathy may be important to the plot, as far as that goes, but if Neville had been guilty Helena would have known, so that her conviction of his innocence clears him of suspicion.

A similar *rapport* occurs in Dion Boucicault's *The Corsican Brothers*, first performed at the Princess's Theatre on 24 February 1852, with Charles Kean playing the double part of the Franchi brothers. Similar in concept, though not directly based on Dumas's tale of the same name, Boucicault's play portrays telepathic knowledge that passes between the brothers. Fabian explains that 'there is a strange, mysterious sympathy between us; no matter what space divides us, we are still one in body, in feeling, in soul. Any powerful impression which the one experiences is instantly conveyed by some invisible agency to the senses of the other' (1.1). Boucicault was almost certainly influenced by current interests in animal magnetism.

Mr. Jasper was seated at the piano

Mr. Jasper was seated at the piano] On Fildes's copy of the proofs, he has drawn a line alongside this passage (Cardwell, 1972, 269), indicating his intention to illustrate the dinner guests grouped around the piano.

he followed her lips most attentively] This moment is pointed to in the work plans: 'Piano scene with Jasper. She singing; he following her lips.'

Miss Twinkleton's fan] Fashionable throughout the nineteenth century, folding fans had a particular resurgence of popularity in the 1860s and 1870s when Whistler introduced the Japanese influence from Paris.

that sort of exhibitor's proprietorship] In *GE* Magwitch would ask Pip to read to him: 'While I complied he . . . would stand before the fire surveying me with the air of an Exhibitor' (40).

"Not under any circumstances

"Not under any circumstances," returned Helena.] This affirmation, possibly important for the unravelling of the plot, is recalled when Rosa confides her hatred of Jasper to Helena later in the chapter.

Miss Twinkleton now opining

the future wives and mothers of England] Mrs Sarah Ellis, author of a trilogy of advice to women, entitled *The Mothers of England* (1843), *The Wives of England* (1845) and *The Daughters of England* (1845), has a style not unlike that of Miss Twinkleton, who shares her unimaginative view of women's roles. Although Mrs Ellis had noticed that it seemed 'to be the peculiar taste of the present day to write, and to read, on the subject of woman', she has no revolutionary advice to offer. Rather, her preaching accords with that of Miss Twinkleton, who would have been brought up with the conviction that

> while the character of the daughter, the wife, and the mother, are so beautifully exemplified in connection with the dignity of a British Queen, it is the privilege of the humblest, as well as the most exalted of her subjects, to know that the heart of woman, in all her tenderest and holiest feelings, is the same beneath the shelter of a cottage, as under the canopy of a throne. (Preface, *The Daughters of England*)

"Oh, don't, don't, don't!"

I feel as if he could pass in through the wall] This may be influenced by Dickens's memories of Dr Elliotson's claims that he had conducted experiments across miles and through walls. If so, Dickens was impressed enough to repeat the idea here after having caused Bradley Headstone, also pressing unwelcome attentions upon the heroine, to insist that ' "if I were shut up in a strong prison, you would draw me out. I should break through the wall to come to you" ' (*OMF* 2.15).

"He has made

frightful sort of dream] Has Dickens calculated that Rosa should use words which typify the opium addict's world? In *The Moonstone* Ezra Jennings records in his journal the harrowing experience of 'the vengeance of yesterday's opium, pursuing me through a series of frightful dreams' (2.4). Glazed eyes define the effects of opium, either as here or, as in chapter 2, as a 'film' over the eyes.

The lustrous gipsy-face

The lustrous gipsy-face drooped over the clinging arms and bosom] With such promise as is laid down here, Helena deserves a romantic and noble fate. It seems a shame to dress her up in a tight blue surtout to lounge about Cloisterham as an idle old buffer hoodwinking Sapsea and tossing coins to Deputy. G. K. Chesterton comments that 'we might almost as easily imagine Edith Dombey dressing up as Major Bagstock. We might almost as easily imagine Rebecca in *Ivanhoe* dressing up as Isaac of York' (1909, xiii). Cardwell agrees that 'Helena cannot be Datchery as the notion is aesthetically so absurd' (1969, 179).

Chapter 8

DAGGERS DRAWN.

This was chapter 7 in MS.

"Not this time

to-morrow] MS reads 'tomorrow morning'. Edwin would have left Cloisterham by the time the rumours that distress Rosa reach the Nuns' House.

until next Midsummer] When Edwin will come of age, receive his patrimony and marry. The time-span within the novel would by then have run through four seasons, and would perhaps end, as it begins, in the autumn.

"Going to wake up Egypt

"Going to wake up Egypt] An allusion to Leigh Hunt's sonnet, 'To the Nile' (1816):

> It flows through old hush'd Egypt and its sands,
> Like some grave mighty thought threading a dream,
> And times and things, as in that vision, seem
> Keeping along it their eternal stands, –
> Caves, pillars, pyramids, the shepherd bands
> That roamed through the young world, the glory extreme
> Of high Sesostris, and that southern beam,
> The laughing queen that caught the world's great hands.

The British, *c.*1869 and after, were encouraged to be involved with the development of Egypt by the Khedive Ismail. Their presence was welcomed (see note to chapter 2, pp. 46–8).

"Reading!" repeats Edwin Drood

"Reading!" repeats Edwin Drood, with a touch of contempt.] Edwin's retort is the standard one of a 'man of action', recurring with embarrassment in Pip when he tells Miss Havisham that he is reading with Mr Pocket, and makes 'the admission with reluctance, for it seems to have a boyish look' (*GE* 29).

Doing, working, engineering.] See note to chapter 2, pp. 46–8.

my guardian and trustee.] One to whom property is entrusted for administration on behalf of another – an important fact in the light of theories that claim money to be Jasper's motive for murdering Edwin. The circumstances of the elder Drood's death are vague: we only know that he is buried in

Cloisterham (chapter 5) and chose Jasper as Edwin's guardian, a macabre irony if the guardian does murder his nephew. Drood would have died after Jasper's own coming of age five years ago, so Edwin would have some memory of his father.

"It does not seem

my ideas of civility were formed among Heathens."] For Buddhism as the prevailing religion in Ceylon, see note to chapter 7, pp. 86–7.

"All over then!

not a stone's throw from Minor Canon Corner.] The Priory Gate is nearer Minor Canon Row than College Gate; the location of the Gate House is discussed in chapter 2, pp. 36–7.

you are up and away to-morrow.] MS reads 'tomorrow morning early'; Dickens has again altered Edwin's departure to a less definite time.

a stirrup-cup] A cup of wine or other alcoholic beverage handed to a huntsman before the hunt or to a man on horseback setting out on a journey.

Mr. Jasper, still walking in the centre

beautifully turns the refrain of a drinking-song] The theme of Jasper's musicianship, particularly his strange propensity to be at his best musically when he is at his most evil morally, runs throughout the novel. Possibly the climax of this macabre theme is achieved in chapter 14, which devotes a paragraph to his perfect performance in services: 'Mr. Jasper is in beautiful voice this day'. Edwin and Neville dine with him and after that evening Edwin is not seen again. If Jasper intended to commit murder that night, his temperament was perfectly pitched.

The air of leisurely patronage

and turns his back to mix a jug of mulled wine at the fire. It seems to require much mixing and compounding.] 'Mulled wine' is a sweetened and spiced hot wine sometimes thickened with beaten egg-yolk. Work plans read 'Quarrel (Fomented by Jasper)'; surely 'fomented' is significant. 'Much mixing and compounding' suggests that something has been added. The question is what is in the goblet that produces such startling effects. Dyson believes the wine is drugged to intensify the efficacy of the mesmerism Jasper is practising (144). Hayter suggests that 'very strong drink, to which he was not accustomed, and Jasper's subtle egging-on, were quite enough to account for Landless's response' (letter to the author, 30 December 1973). Alternatively, Jasper's use of opium suggests the reasonable assumption that the fomenting is done with opium. A *HW* article had noted that opium

> acts either as a stimulant or a sedative, according to the quantity taken, the frequency of repetition, and the state of the system when it is administered . . . to persons unaccustomed to its use, the eating of less than a grain of opium generally produces a stimulant action. (16.105)

Neville's reaction is similar to that of John Harmon, drugged with an unidentified compound in *OMF*:

> 'I had drunk some coffee, when to my sense of sight he began to swell immensely, and something urged me to rush at him. We had a struggle near the door. He got from me, through my not knowing where to strike, in the whirling round of the room, and the flashing of flames of fire between us. I dropped down. Lying helpless on the ground, I was turned over by a foot . . . I was trodden upon and fallen over. I heard a noise of blows, and thought it was a wood-cutter cutting down a tree. I could not have said that my name was John Harmon – I could not have thought it – I didn't know it – but when I heard the blows, I thought of the wood-cutter and his axe, and had some dead idea that I was lying in a forest.' (2.13)

"That's your misfortune

Juno, Minerva, Diana, and Venus] Classical goddesses whose combined attributes included beauty, wisdom, power and love.

"Look at him!"

The world is all before him where to choose.] The expulsion of Adam and Eve in *Paradise Lost* (12.641–9):

> They looking back, all th' eastern side beheld
> Of Paradise, so late their happie seat,
> Wav'd over by that flaming Brand, the Gate
> With dreadful Faces throngd and fierie Armes:
> Some natural tears they dropd, but wip'd them soon;
> The World was all before them, where to choose
> Thir place of rest, and Providence thir guide:
> They hand in hand with wandring steps and slow,
> Through *Eden* took their solitary way.

"See how little

to pluck the golden fruit that hangs ripe on the tree] The golden apples of the Hesperides were given to Jupiter by Juno on the day of their nuptials. They were guarded by three nymphs, daughters of Hesperus, in a garden abounding in delicious fruits. The garden itself was guarded by a dragon which never slept. One of the labours of Hercules was to procure some of the apples.

His speech has become

His speech has become thick and indistinct.] Typical of one in his cups, but this could be from drugging.

looks to Neville] Jasper's eye movements in this section may suggest a mesmeric control of dialogue.

"Pooh, pooh," says Edwin

You may know a black common fellow] Although Crisparkle has alluded to the dark gypsy appearance of the Landlesses, this is the first indication that they may have coloured blood: it is mere presumption that their mother was Sinhalese, or partly so; their father's name suggests that he was English. The origin of these two remains one of the mysteries of the novel. (See Plate 6.)

It is Mr. Crisparkle's custom

practising his favorite parts in concerted vocal music.] That is, music arranged in parts for a number of voices.

The south wind that goes where it lists] John 3.8: 'The wind bloweth where it listeth, and thou hearest the sound thereof, but canst not tell whence it cometh, and whither it goeth: so is everyone that is born of the Spirit.'

The Minor Canon props him

strictly scientific manner] Reference is to the skills of the science of pugilism (see notes to chapter 17, pp. 141–5).

book-room] Not a library, but a study in which Crisparkle would work and keep his books.

"I am afraid I am not

I can satisfy you at another time that I have had very little indeed to drink] In what way can and does Neville give this assurance? When John Harmon had been drugged, he recalls the attempt upon his life, and explains to Pleasant Riderhood that ' "I was muddled, but not with fair drinking. I had not been drinking, you understand. A mouthful did it" ' (*OMF* 2.12). Both Harmon and Neville realize that one glass has had an unusual effect.

Scooping his hand

as skilfully as a Police Expert] A hammer-lock.

reading-table] A small square table, often with a splayed spindle-gallery, which occasionally has an adjustable top, and a drawer, as in a small modern desk.

6 **Study for the head of Neville Landless, by Sir Luke Fildes.** From F. G. Kitton, *Dickens and His Illustrators*, 1899

The phrase

The phrase smites home. "Ah!" thinks Mr. Crisparkle] Jasper eavesdrops three times: here; earlier in this chapter before overtaking Edwin and Neville; and when he listens to Crisparkle and Neville's conversation when he and Durdles are on their way to the Cathedral in chapter 13. It has been suggested that Dickens goes out of his way to show that sounds could be heard from inside and outside the Minor Canon's house: Neville hears Crisparkle playing the piano before entering the house and his soft knock is immediately answered (Baker, 1951, 56–9).

"You, my dear sir

"even you, have accepted a dangerous charge."] The MS continues at this point: 'You must sometimes – no doubt, often – have to put yourself in opposition to this fierce nature and suppress it. After what I have seen tonight, I am fearful even for you.'

Chapter 9

BIRDS IN THE BUSH.

The chapter was added to number 2 to make up its length after Dickens had begun number 3; the introduction of Grewgious had been intended for the third number.

Rosa, having no relation

Rosa, having no relation that she knew of in the world, had . . . known no home but the Nuns' House, and no mother] An echo of the ballad, 'The Poor Peasant Boy':

> Thrown on the wide world, doom'd to wander and roam,
> Bereft of his parents, bereft of a home,
> A stranger to pleasure, to comfort and joy,
> Behold little Edmund, the poor peasant boy.

The ballad is quoted in *BH* (31) and *OMF* (1.15).

from the seventh year of her age] Rosa's present age is not precisely given; perhaps she is 17.

drowned . . . Every fold and color in the pretty summer dress, and even the long wet hair, with scattered petals of ruined flowers still clinging to it] The image in Rosa's memory seems to derive from the painting, 'Ophelia' (1852), by Sir John Everett Millais (Plate 7). It was Millais who recommended Sir Luke Fildes to Dickens as the illustrator of *MED*.

7 **'Ophelia' (1852), by Sir John Everett Millais** (see p. 96)

on the first anniversary of that hard day.] Rosa was aged 5 when her mother died. Her father died a year later, at which time she was placed in the care of Grewgious, who brought her to Miss Twinkleton. Edwin's father also died, but we are not told how much longer after the death of Rosa's father. Edwin is three or four years older than Rosa, and would have been 9 or 10 when she came to Cloisterham, and Jasper would have been 15.

By what means

By what means the news that there had been a quarrel] A reminiscence of Sterne, *The Life and Opinions of Tristram Shandy* (1760–7), when Susannah 'instantly imparted' the family secret 'by signs to Jonathan':

> and Jonathan by tokens to the cook, as she was basting a loin of mutton; the cook sold it with some kitchen-fat to the postillion for a groat, who trucked it with the dairy maid for something of about the same value – and though whispered in the hay-loft, FAME caught the notes with her brazen trumpet, and sounded them upon the house-top – In a word, not an old woman in the village or five miles round, who did not understand the difficulties of my uncle Toby's siege, and what were the secret articles which had delayed the surrender. (9.32)

the adulteration of his milk] The sale of adulterated foods and beverages was a widespread scandal during the 1850s and 1860s. The extent of the abuse was brought home to the public through the analyses by microscope of Dr Arthur Hill Hassall, the results of which were published in the *Lancet* from 1851 to 1854 and collected as a book, *Food and Its Adulterations* (1855). Articles in the popular press, including *HW* and *AYR*, supplemented and disseminated the findings of Hassall. For example, an article entitled 'Milk' in *AYR* (13.126–31) explains that milk could be thinned with water, then thickened with starch and coloured with egg-yolk and saffron. Diluted milk could also be whitened and thickened with substances such as chalk and plaster of Paris. The cost of milk was such that 'if one competitive milkman will supply the article required, other milkmen follow the example, and the quality of the milk is deteriorated' (129).

sacrificing to the Graces.] In Greek mythology, the Graces were the personification of grace, charm and beauty, usually spoken of as three in number: Aglaia, Thalia and Euphrosyne.

As in the governing

Peter Piper, alleged to have picked the peck of pickled pepper]

> Peter Piper picked a peck of pickled pepper;
> A peck of pickled pepper Peter Piper picked;
> If Peter Piper picked a peck of pickled pepper,
> Where's the peck of pickled pepper Peter Piper picked?
> (*Peter Piper's Practical Principles of Plain and Perfect Pronunciation*, 1819)

It was reserved

Queen Elizabeth's first historical female friend at Tilbury Fort.] In *CHE* (31), Dickens describes Elizabeth's review of her troops at Tilbury on 8 August 1588:

> So, with all England firing up like one strong angry man, and with both sides of the Thames fortified, and with the soldiers under arms, and with the sailors in their ships, the country waited for the coming of the proud Spanish fleet, which was called THE INVINCIBLE ARMADA. The Queen herself, riding in armour on a white horse, and the Earl of Essex and the Earl of Leicester holding her bridle rein, made a brave speech to the troops at Tilbury Fort opposite Gravesend, which was received with such enthusiasm as is seldom known.

Queen Elizabeth had no 'historical female friend', and certainly not at Tilbury Fort, where, though Dickens has her flanked by the two foremost earls of the land, in all the illustrations of the event the Queen is alone while she assures her men that she has the heart of a king. Miss Twinkleton, in the person of the great queen, is given a 'historical' friend for the first time: her second-in-command at the Nuns' House, Mrs Tisher. In chapter 13, Mrs Tisher is referred to as the 'deputy High Priest'.

the Bard of Avon] Alludes to Jonson, 'To the Memory of my Beloved, the Author, Mr William Shakespeare':

> Sweet Swan of *Avon*! what a sight it were
> To see thee in our waters yet appeare,
> And make those flights upon the bankes of *Thames*,
> That so did take Eliza, and our James!

Jonson employs the metaphor in his elegy in accordance with the belief mentioned below that the swan sings at its death.

the immortal SHAKESPEARE] Compare Dr Johnson's use of 'immortal Shakespeare' in 'Prologue at the Opening of the Theatre in Drury Lane' (1747); and also Pope, *Epistles and Satires of Horace Imitated, To Augustus* (69–72): 'Shakespeare . . . grew Immortal in his own despight'.

the ancient superstition that the bird of graceful plumage . . . sang sweetly on the approach of death] The eighteenth century and nineteenth century poured scorn upon the notion accepted in earlier times. Shakespeare refers to the belief in *Othello*: 'I will play the swan,/And die in music' (5.2.250–1), and in *The Merchant of Venice* (3.2.43–5):

> Let music sound while he doth make his choice;
> Then, if he lose, he makes a swan-like end,
> Fading in music.

Rumour . . . had been represented by that bard . . . as painted full of tongues.] The stage direction for the induction in *2 Henry IV* reads: '*Enter* RUMOUR, *painted full of tongues.*' 'Rumour' was traditionally personified as a figure adorned with tongues and also with eyes. Virgil's Fama was perhaps the source; she has many eyes, tongues and ears, and sings of truth and falsehood alike (*Aeneid* 4.181–90). Dickens uses the image in *BH* (10).

"who drew/The celebrated Jew"] The lines, ascribed to both Pope and Johnson on witnessing Macklin's performance of Shylock in 1741, are 'This is the Jew/That Shakespeare drew'.

our vivacious neighbour, Monsieur La Fontaine)] Jean de La Fontaine (1621–95), best-known for his poetical versions of Aesop's *Fables* which were used as texts for learning French.

"airy nothings"] The phrase from *A Midsummer Night's Dream* (5.1.14–17) was by this time something of a cliché:

> And as imagination bodies forth
> The forms of things unknown, the poet's pen
> Turns them to shapes, and gives to airy nothing
> A local habitation and a name.

(whose name and date of birth] The name of the poet is Shakespeare who, according to tradition, was born on 23 April 1564.

But the subject

clapping on a paper moustache] The sketch by Charles Collins for the wrapper of the monthly parts shows Edwin wearing a moustache, but Fildes has him clean-shaven, as is Neville, whom the girls would not yet have had a chance to see. This chapter was written before the appointment of Fildes.

With too great length

what is called a near sight] Dickens has made a slip: in chapter 17, Grewgious watches from his window in Staple Inn and can see over to 'yonder house' where he recognizes 'a slinking individual' to be Jasper.

some strange capacity in him of making on the whole an agreeable impression.] Mr Grewgious is in the tradition of those characters, headed by Newman Noggs of *NN* who, Forster writes, ushered in for Dickens 'that class of the creatures of his fancy in which he took himself perhaps the most delight'. They were:

> gentlemen by nature, however shocking bad their hats or ungenteel their dialects; philosophers of modest endurance, and needy but most respectable coats; a sort of humble angels of sympathy and self-denial, though without a particle of splendour or even good looks about them, except what an eye as fine as their own feelings might discern. (1.9.145–6)

"My visits," said

"My visits . . . are, like those of the angels . . . few and far between.] The simile is from Robert Blair, 'The Grave' (1743):

> The good he scorn'd
> Stalk'd off reluctant, like an ill-us'd ghost,
> Not to return; or, if it did, its visits,
> Like those of angels, short, and far between.

Thomas Campbell imitated Blair in the use of the phrase in *The Pleasures of Hope* (1799):

> What though my wingèd hours of bliss have been,
> Like angel-visits, few and far between? (2.377–8)

This point, again

the Celestial Nine] In Greek mythology, the goddesses of creative inspiration in poetry, song and the other arts.

" 'Marriage.' Hem!"

as if I was a bear – with the cramp – in a youthful Cotillon."] Dancing bears led round the streets by itinerants and street-musicians were common well into the eighteenth century, but the amusement survived into Dickens's time. At Gad's Hill in the summer of 1869 he broke up a scuffle caused by some roughs who attempted to dance with two muzzled bears owned by strolling Savoyards (Fields, 1900; reprinted 1970, 213–14). The cotillon, or cotillion, is the name of several dances, chiefly of French origin, consisting of a variety of steps and figures, and usually danced by four or eight people who advance and retire.

"I do particularly

"I don't like Mr. Jasper to come between us] It is sometimes thought that Jasper's motives for murder could be connected with the will, the contents of which are known only to Grewgious and the two young people.

"I mean," he explained

I seem to have come into existence a chip.] Dickens published a series of brief articles in *HW* entitled 'Chips'. The introductory article of the series discusses the meanings of the word; perhaps Grewgious's description involves all of them:

> There is a saying that a good workman is known by his chips. Such a prodigious accumulation of chips takes place in our Manufactory, that we infer we must have some first-rate workmen about us.

> There is also a figure of speech, concerning a chip of the old block . . . There is a popular simile – an awkward one in this connexion – founded on the dryness of a chip. This has almost deterred us from our intention of bundling a few chips together now and then. But, reflection on the natural lightness of the article has reassured us; and we here present a few to our readers, – and shall continue to do so from time to time. (1.350–1)

an annuity of two hundred and fifty pounds.] A sum that would enable Rosa to live in comfort and security.

"Why, certainly, certainly

a Norfolk farmer] Norfolk turkeys are celebrated:

> The best species of poultry in France, with reference both to the eye and the palate, are, first, the turkeys, which are excellent, being pure types of the genuine old black Norfolk breed. (*HW* 11.399)

"Ah, Mr. Grewgious

Miss Twinkleton might have said a pen-and-ink-ubus] Forster naïvely cited Dickens's use of this old pun as an example of his conversational wit: ' "I call him an Incubus!" said a non-literary friend, at a loss to express the boredom inflicted on him by a popular author. "Pen-and-ink-ubus, you mean," interposed Dickens' (3.19.481). But Forster's source is probably the *Book of Memoranda* (18).

As he held it

the great western folding-door of the Cathedral] The west front of Rochester Cathedral, of late Norman work, is considered one of the most beautiful and elaborate in England. The recessed doorway is the most striking feature of the exterior.

"Dear me," said

"it's like looking down the throat of Old Time."] Grewgious conflates the figure of Father Time with representations of the mouth of Hell.

Old Time heaved

the river, the green pastures, and the brown arable lands] The same scene is described in *PP* (5):

> On either side, the banks of the Medway, covered with cornfields and pastures, with here and there a windmill, or a distant church, stretched away as far as the eye could see, presenting a rich and varied landscape, rendered more beautiful by the changing shadows which passed swiftly across it, as the thin and half

formed clouds skimmed away in the light of the morning sun. The river, reflecting the clear blue of the sky, glistened and sparkled as it flowed noiselessly on; and the oars of the fishermen dipped into the water with a clear and liquid sound, as the heavy but picturesque boats glided slowly down the stream.

all became grey, murky, and sepulchral] The substitution of 'murky' for the MS reading, 'dusky', perhaps recalls *Macbeth* 5.1.35: 'Hell is murky.'

Mr. Grewgious answered

Mr. Grewgious answered somewhat sharply] In the MS reading of this passage, Grewgious is amiable, not merely polite. Perhaps his attitude towards Jasper was moderated in order to give his later obvious dislike more credibility.

"So, you settled

"I see! Mr. Grewgious . . . between my nephew and me, that] These words were substituted in the proofs for a passage in MS of small-talk and quibbling between Jasper and Grewgious.

preparations for May] The month of Edwin's coming of age, and of his intended marriage.

Chapter 10 Third monthly number June 1870

SMOOTHING THE WAY.

Dickens's note in the work plans explains the title.

"Too late, indeed

He was still as pale as gentlemanly ashes] One of the effects of opium is to leave the subject with a livid colour.

As, whenever the Reverend

a glass of Constantia] A red Cape wine of fine flavour produced on Constantia farm near Cape Town. *HW* observes:

Pursue Edwin Drood and Rosa?

Lead on to final scene between them in No. V? IV?

Yes

How many more scenes between them?

Way to be paved for their marriage –

——— and parting instead. Yes.

Miss Twinkleton's ? No. Next No.

Rosa's Guardian? Done in No. II.

Mr Sapsea? Yes. Last chapter

Neville Landless at Mr Crisparkle's

Yes

And Helena?

Neville admires Rosa. That comes out from himself

(Mystery of Edwin Drood. – No. III.)

Chapter <I> X[1]

Smoothing The Way

That is, for Jasper's plan, through Mr Crisparkle: who takes new ground on Neville's new confidence.

Minor Canon Corner. The closet I remember there as a child

Edwin's appointment for Xmas Eve

Chapter X[1]

A Picture and a Ring

P

J T

1747

Dinner in chambers

Bazzard the clerk

The two waiters

Mr Grewgious's past story

"A ring of diamonds and rubies delicately set in gold.

Edwin takes it

Chapter XI[1]

A Night with Durdles

Lay the ground for the manner of the Murder, to come out at last.

Keep the boy suspended

Night picture of the Cathedral.

1. Cardwell notes that Dickens had already written these figures as 'IX', 'X' and 'XI', and had to alter them to allow for the new chapter 9 in number 2.

> few people who even touch at the Cape fail to visit the Constantia wine farms, producing the delicious sweet wine of that name . . . There are many varieties of it. And, oh, how seductive that same Constantia is! Who can resist it in all its delicious varieties? (1.590)

Constantia had long been known for its curative powers, as in Jane Austen, *Sense and Sensibility* (1811): 'My poor husband! how fond he was of it! Whenever he had a touch of his old cholicky gout, he said it did him more good than anything else in the world' (30).

It was a most wonderful closet] Mrs Crisparkle's dining-room closet and medicinal herb closet integrate metaphorically the oriental and domestic aspects of the novel. The pickles, wine and spices suggest trade with the East and with Africa during Britain's growth of Empire, while fruits, vegetables, preserves and fruit cordials affirm the unchanging traditions of an English cathedral town.

a portrait of Handel in a flowing wig] Of the numerous portraits of Handel, this is perhaps an engraving by Harding (1799) of the portrait by Balthasar Denner which was exhibited in London in 1868. The name of Handel is affectionately given by Herbert to Pip in *GE* (22).

continuations] Gaiters, continuous with shorts or knee-breeches, as worn by senior clergy.

a mighty japanned sugar-box] The papier maché box would be varnished to a high gloss in imitation of the oriental lacquerwork imported since the seventeenth century.

slender ladies' fingers, to be dipped into sweet wine and kissed.] Compare Keats, *Cap and Bells* (1848): 'Steep some lady's fingers nice in candy wine' (48).

The Reverend Septimus

like the highly-popular lamb who has so long and unresistingly been led to the slaughter] Isaiah 53.7: 'He was oppressed, and he was afflicted, yet he opened not his mouth: he is brought as a lamb to the slaughter, and as a sheep before her shearers is dumb, so he openeth not his mouth.' A correspondent wrote to Dickens objecting to this figure of speech on the grounds of its being taken from the Bible. In one of his last letters, Dickens justified the usage:

> It would be quite inconceivable to me – but for your letter – that any reasonable reader could possibly attach a scriptural reference to a passage in a book of mine, reproducing a much abused social figure of speech . . . I am truly shocked to find that any reader can make the mistake.
>
> I have always striven in my writings to express veneration for the life and lessons of Our Saviour; because I feel it . . .
>
> But I have never made proclamation of this from the house tops. (8 June 1870, *Nonesuch* 3.784)

as Lady Macbeth was hopeless of those of all the seas that roll.] A conflation of speeches by Macbeth and Lady Macbeth: 'Will all great Neptune's ocean wash this blood/Clean from my hand?' (2.2.59–60); and 'All the perfumes of Arabia will not sweeten this little hand' (5.1.48).

"I have never yet

I should feel that I had an injury against him on hers."] Neville's jealousy of Edwin possibly bears on the resolution of the novel. It has been suggested that Neville may be so much of the scapegoat as to have been led to murder Edwin, without knowing it, and that this resolution would be the 'curious idea' mentioned by Dickens to Forster as being 'difficult to work' (Cardwell, 1969, 125–6). Other proposals are that Neville will help to uncover Jasper's guilt (he has been thought to be the figure pointing upwards at the top of the spiral stairway on the cover design), and that he will die in a struggle with the murderer.

"Mr. Neville, Mr. Neville

the Searcher of all hearts] Romans 8.27: 'And he that searcheth the hearts knoweth what is the mind of the Spirit, because he maketh intercession for the saints according to the will of God.'

"Tut!" said the Minor Canon

"I am much overpaid!"] Fildes's illustration of this scene, 'Mr. Crisparkle is Overpaid', shows Neville holding a walking-stick which in fact he was not to have purchased until Christmas Eve (chapter 14).

Jasper was lying asleep

"What is the matter? Who did it?"] An echo of Macbeth's cry when he sees the ghost of Banquo: 'Which of you have done this?' (3.4.49).

"I was dreaming

"I was dreaming at a great rate] Perhaps Dickens had in mind the theories explained in a *HW* essay, 'Dreams':

> We can, however, readily conceive that, when the mind is oppressed, or disturbed by the recollection of some event it dreads to dwell upon, it may be disturbed by the most terrific and ghastly images. A guilty conscience, too, will unquestionably produce restlessness, agitation, and awe-inspiring dreams. Hence Manfred, in pacing restlessly his lonely Gothic gallery at midnight, pictures to himself the terrors of Sleep:

> "The lamp must be replenish'd, but even then It will not burn so long as I must watch:
> My slumbers – if I slumber – are not sleep,
> But a continuance of enduring thought,
> Which then I can resist not: in my heart
> There is a vigil, and these eyes but close To look within."

> Contrition and remorse oppose his rest. If we remember right, it was Bishop Newton, who remarked that the sleep of innocence differed essentially from the sleep of guilt. (2.568–9; quotation from *Manfred* emended)

an indigestive after-dinner sleep.] Compare *Measure for Measure* 3.1.32–4: 'Thou hast nor youth nor age,/But, as it were, an after-dinner's sleep/Dreaming on both.' De Quincey describes withdrawal as 'a state of unutterable irritation of stomach (which surely is not much like dejection), accompanied by intense perspirations' ('The Pains of Opium', *Confessions*). Elsewhere, he explains that, under the influence of opium, 'when it reaches its maximum in diseasing the liver and deranging the digestive functions, all exertion whatever is revolting in excess' ('Recollections of Charles Lamb', 1834).

Chapter 11

A PICTURE AND A RING.

Behind the most ancient

Holborn, London] London is introduced, like Cloisterham, as being 'ancient'; it became a well-fortified and well-organized town during the Roman occupation, and High Holborn existed then as one of the principal roads to the west.

certain gabled houses] The row of timbered Tudor buildings situated at Holborn Bar in front of Staple Inn. A general description of this style of architecture as surviving in Holborn appears in a *HW* essay, 'Left Behind':

> The beetling cavernous stories – the small, diamond-paned windows – the grotesque faces leering like jubilant goblins from timber brackets and supports – the carved roses, fleur-de-lis, and other heraldic devices . . . the projecting leaden spouts, and slanting roofs. (9.545)

the Old Bourne that has long run dry] 'Holborn' derives from 'burne' meaning 'stream in the hollow'. The stream that 'once ran right down the middle of Holborn' (*BH* 10) vanished out of sight to flow underground in a brick culvert still joining the Thames near Blackfriars Bridge.

two irregular quadrangles, called Staple Inn.] One of the Inns of Court and of Chancery established during the Middle Ages as unchartered societies with the exclusive right of calling barristers to the English Bar. Today only Lincoln's Inn and Gray's Inn obtain as establishments within the practice of law; the Inns of Chancery, of which Staple Inn was one, have disappeared. The old buildings remain, however. Staple Hall is the furthest of two connecting quadrangles.

a few smoky sparrows twitter in smoky trees] The smoky atmosphere in London resulted from the burning of coal, which produces more smoke and soot than any other fuel.

a few feet of garden mould] The little pastoral refuge within the city offering 'visions of the country' (*OCS* 1) is an incongruity that fascinated Dickens (see Robison, 1978).

legal nooks] Such as those described in *PP* (31):

> Scattered about, in various holes and corners of the Temple, are certain dark and dirty chambers, in and out of which, all the morning in Vacation, and half the evening too in Term time, there may be seen constantly hurrying with bundles of papers under their arms, and protruding from their pockets, an almost uninterrupted succession of Lawyers' Clerks.

a little Hall, with a little lantern in its roof] Staple Hall was built by Richard Champion in 1581, with an open timber roof into which is set a louvre or lantern which is windowed and domed.

In the days when

as menacing that sensitive Constitution, the property of us Britons] Reminiscent of Mr Podsnap, who refers, 'with a sense of meritorious proprietorship, "to Our Constitution, Sir. We Englishmen are Very Proud of our Constitution, Sir. It Was Bestowed Upon Us By Providence. No Other Country is so Favoured as This Country" ' (*OMF* 1.11). Wilkie Collins deals with the Tory-Jackass attitude in a similarly cynical tone in *The Moonstone*: the Verinder family retainer is taken aback by the foreign influences that invade 'our quiet English house' in the form of a 'devilish Indian diamond' given to Rachel Verinder by her vagabondish uncle: 'who ever heard the like of it – in the nineteenth century, mind; in an age of progress, and in a country which rejoices in the blessings of the British constitution?' (1.6).

no neighbouring architecture of lofty proportions had arisen] Perhaps the Patent Office, planned in 1843 and built soon after, and Birkbeck Buildings founded in 1851 (Aylmer, 1964, 37).

Neither wind nor sun

the mysterious inscription] The letters refer to John Thompson who was principal of Staple Inn for two terms in 1747, and whose arms appear in the oriel window, north of the Inn (Plate 8).

8 **Doorway in Staple Inn.** From Thornbury and Walford, *Old and New London*, 1873–8

Who could have told

"convey the wise it call," as Pistol says.] From *The Merry Wives of Windsor* (1.3.26–7):

> *Nym:* The good humour is to steal at a minute's rest.
> *Pistol:* 'Convey' the wise it call. 'Steal' foh! a fico for the phrase!

'Convey' is thieves' slang for 'steal'.

No. Coy Conveyancing would

being blown towards him by some unaccountable wind] Having just alluded to *The Merry Wives of Windsor*, Dickens may be recalling *2 Henry IV* (5.3.84–5):

> What wind blew you hither, Pistol?
> Not the ill wind which blows no man to good.

a pretty fat Receivership] A receiver is appointed by the court to receive money on behalf of others, frequently in regard to a deceased estate or a bankruptcy.

two rich estates] One is that of Rosa's father, but we know nothing about the second.

under the dry vine and fig-tree] Micah 4.4: 'But they shall sit every man under his vine and under his fig tree; and none shall make them afraid: for the mouth of the Lord of hosts hath spoken it', and also 1 Kings 4.25.

Many accounts

garnished Mr. Grewgious's rooms.] 'Garnish' is also a term in law meaning to serve notice on a debtor, or to summon a person to litigation already in progress.

There was no luxury

the hotel in Furnival's Inn] Grewgious lodges Rosa here in chapter 20 (see note p. 162). By the nineteenth century, Furnival's Inn was no longer an Inn of Chancery. It has been entirely rebuilt in 1818 and was let in chambers and partly occupied by the hotel. Dickens leased a set of rooms in Furnival's Inn from 1834 until 1837 when (now with a wife, child and sister-in-law) he moved to Doughty Street.

As Mr. Grewgious

clerk of Mr. Grewgious] Although 'Bazzard the clerk' is noted in the work plans, his introduction at this point may have been in order to fill out the number, whereupon a purpose in the denouement may have been found for him (Cardwell, 1969, 254). This purpose has most usually been thought to be that Datchery is Bazzard in disguise. If any of the protagonists in the novel is indeed Datchery, then Bazzard is the most likely contender, not because of his Thespian proclivities, or because other solicitors' clerks have played leading roles in Dickens's novels, but, rather, because we know so little about him that there is less to argue against the proposition.

like a fabulous Familiar] The genie, in the tale of Aladdin in the *Arabian Nights.*

that baleful tree of Java has given shelter to more lies] The bark of the upas tree (*Antiaris toxicaria*) yields a poisonous gum used to douse the points of arrow heads. The legends surrounding the destructive powers of the tree were introduced to Europe in the seventeenth century, and later absorbed and embroidered by poets such as Blake, Southey and Byron. 'From that accursed venom springs/The Upas Tree of Death,' writes Southey in 'Thalaba' (1801); beneath Blake's 'tree of mystery' men die after eating of its fruit ('The Poison Tree', *Songs of Experience*, 1789–94); and Byron writes of 'trees whose gums are poison' in canto 4 of *Childe Harold's Pilgrimage* (1818). In 1820, Francis Danby (1793–1861) excited London when he exhibited his huge painting of the upas tree (Grigson, 1947, 56–63).

"Now, Bazzard

Bazzard] The name is still current, but Dickens may have remembered that Bazard was the name of the author of a play performed in Brussels on which he reported in *HW* (1.602). A possible source for the name is an incident in *The Moonstone* which might have struck Dickens's fancy. Betteredge, the crusty old family retainer, is unwillingly taking instructions from Ezra Jennings to rearrange the Verinder house and explains that the hall cannot be furnished exactly as it was last year ' "Because there was a stuffed buzzard, Mr Jennings, in the hall last year. When the family left, the buzzard was put away with the other things. When the buzzard was put away – he burst" ' (2.4).

"Dear me!" said Mr. Grewgious

his pair of office candles.] Cheap tallow candles were made from mutton fat.

"I wonder where he

collected his skirts for easy conversation.] Necessary, to prevent the frock-coat's being scorched. The stance would also increase the warming effects of the fire.

It was like

Circumlocutional Department] The name coined by Dickens for the dilatory government office which practises the skills of doing nothing in *LD*.

As the fog had been

a zest far surpassing Doctor Kitchener's.] William Kitchiner, MD (1775?–1827), was the author of *The Cook's Oracle* (1817), *The Art of Invigorating and Prolonging Life* (1821), *The Housekeeper's Ledger* (1825) and many other works. An epicure, he was convinced that health depends upon the proper preparation of food, and he was renowned for his lunches, dinners and conversaziones attended by the famous. Thomas Hood commemorated him in 'Ode to W. Kitchener [sic] MD' (1825):

> Oh, hast thou still those Conversazioni,
> Where learned visitors discoursed – and fed?
> There came Belzoni,
> Fresh from the ashes of Egyptian dead –

a condiment of a profounder flavor than Harvey.] Harvey's Sauce was specially compounded by Peter Harvey, an innkeeper, for travellers who frequented his inn. In 1776 the recipe was given to his sister Elizabeth, who married the head of a firm of London grocers. After her husband died, she devoted her energies to sauces and pickles. Long after her death, the concern was acquired by Crosse & Blackwell (Hill, 1945, 31).

like Macbeth's leg when accompanying him off the stage with reluctance to the assassination of Duncan.] Dickens is recalling Macready's performance as Macbeth, at the moment in which he stealthily crosses the stage to Duncan's chamber and hears the signal bell sounded twice. After delivering the lines: 'Hear it not Duncan, for it is a knell/That summons thee to heaven or to hell' (2.2.63–4), Macready would exit into Duncan's chamber. But 'his desire to over-elaborate made him pause, and when his body was actually off the stage his left foot and leg remained trembling in sight, it seemed, fully half a minute' (Coleman, 1889, 223). Other actors copied this piece of business, the use of which here was first noted by Crosse (1916, 25). Like Macbeth, Jasper may be the murderer of his kinsman and his guest, as Forsyte has noted (1980, 89).

"And May!" pursued

the thorn of anxiety] Grewgious alludes to the title of Bazzard's play (see notes to chapter 20, pp. 161–2). In another sense, roses and thorns have some relevance in view of the fact that the cover design for the wrapper of the monthly parts has a motif of rose branches forming a circle around the title and Dickens's name.

It was wonderful

a charity boy] Schools supported by charitable bequests or by voluntary contributions provided free or cheap education to children of the poor. Such schools were frequently condemned by Dickens for their inefficiency, and for the humiliation they forced upon their pupils through their conspicuous uniforms.

But not for long

like the carved image of some queer Joss] The pidgin-English name given to idols and deities worshipped in the East Indies, used adjectivally for many things connected with Eastern religious rites. The reference here may well be to the partly enamelled Chinese Joss figure which Dickens himself owned (see Stonehouse, 1935, 131).

"Mr. Edwin, this rose

ashes among ashes, and dust among dust] The words of the Burial Service: 'We therefore commit his body to the ground; earth to earth, ashes to ashes, dust to dust; in sure and certain hope of the Resurrection to eternal life.'

Chapter 12

A NIGHT WITH DURDLES.

Mr. Sapsea's importance

he has become Mayor of Cloisterham.] MS reads 'it is settled that he will be the next'; the revision accords with the movement in time.

the whole framework of society] *OED* cites 1816 as the first usage of this phrase.

Mayors have been knighted for "going up" with addresses] The words 'Rise, Sir ——' are spoken by the sovereign after having dubbed a man a knight. Mayors were frequently knighted and would 'go up' to London to deliver a loyal address to the monarch.

Of such is the salt of the earth.] A conflation of Matthew 5.13: 'Ye are the salt of the earth: but if the salt have lost his savour, wherewith shall it be salted?'; and Mark 10.14: 'of such is the kingdom of God'.

Mr. Sapsea has improved

no kickshaw ditties, favorites with national enemies, but gave him the genuine George the Third home-brewed . . . so small a nation of hearts of

oak] 'Kickshaw' (from 'quelque chose') here denotes 'frivolous, trifling', but also suggests the more frequent contemptuous application of the term to fancy French cookery, as opposed to familiar and substantial English dishes (*OED*). Sapsea derides the songs by Italian, German and French composers which dominated fashionable salon music. A revival of interest in traditional English airs was stimulated in 1838 by the publication of Chappell's *A Collection of National Airs, Consisting of Ancient Song, Ballad, and Dance Tunes* (2 vols). The work was the subject of a review article, 'Charles Dibdin, and National Song', published by Dickens in *Bentley's Miscellany* (4, 1838, 626–8) during the period of his editorship. The preface to Chappell's *Collection* laments that 'It has been too much the fashion with us to pay little attention to our own tunes' (iii), a point expanded by the reviewer in *Bentley's*:

> *Italian song* has within a few years become such a fashionable importation that very few home-bred musicians have *dared to have sense themselves.* The native growth, it is to be regretted, has been discouraged in the very quarters where it would most fondly look for support. Those who have written at all have abandoned their national style, (once the envy of our neighbours,) and contented themselves with . . . imitations of a "manner of music" totally foreign to their native land and sentiment. (627)

Chappell's *Collection* contains numerous anti-French and patriotic songs, among them: 'The British Grenadiers'; 'The British Sailor's Lament' ('In Georgy's day when war's alarms from shore to shore were bandied . . .'); 'Britons, Strike Home!'; and 'From Merciless Invaders'. In Dickens's library at Gad's Hill was a copy of Charles Dibdin's *Songs, Naval and National* (1841), a collection which contains further examples of the kind of song admired by Sapsea. Several include the patriotic image 'hearts of oak': for example, 'Stand to Your Guns, My Hearts of Oak'; 'Ye Free-Born Sons' (second stanza); and 'Hearts of Oak'.

and all continents, peninsulas, isthmuses, promontories, and other geographical forms of land soever] The parody is of the 'Question and Answer' schoolbook, such as *Chambers's Miscellaneous Questions* (1866, 14):

11. What is a portion of land nearly surrounded by water called? – A peninsula.
12. What is a point of land jutting out into the sea called? – A cape or promontory.
13. What is a bend of the sea into the land called? – A bay or gulf.
14. What is a narrow connecting portion of the sea called? – A strait or channel.
15. Mention some of the features of the land. – Mountains, hills, plains, and valleys.

(See Shatto, 1974.)

"How so, Mr. Mayor?"

Fetch] The apparition, double or wraith of a living person.

The lamplighter now

The lamplighter now dotting the quiet Close with specks of light, and running at a great rate up and down his little ladder with that object . . . which all Cloisterham would have stood aghast at the idea of abolishing] Street-lamps, fitted to burn oil or, latterly, gas, were lit by hand. The lamplighter carried a lightweight ladder to rest on a projecting arm of the lamp-post. He used a pole at the end of which was a small oil-lamp surrounded by a perforated cylinder which protected the flame; the lantern was protected by glass panels, one of which was pushed open to bring the pole-head in contact with the lantern, enabling the lamplighter to turn on the gas-tap (Brumleigh, 1942, 212). Cloisterham is still illuminated by oil lamps even though gas lighting was introduced to most streets in London in the 1820s. Provincial cities and towns were slower, or actually reluctant, to adopt the innovation; Dickens mocks Broadstairs, for example, in 'Our English Watering-Place', for bickering over 'the novel question of Gas': 'there was a great No Gas party' against which the Gas party

> took the high ground of proclaiming . . . that it was said Let there be light and there was light; and that not to have light (that is gas-light) in our watering-place, was to contravene the great decree.

Meanwhile the No Gas party chalk up scruffy marks on walls, war-whooping ' "No Gas!" and "Down with Gas!" '. Dickens celebrates the victory of the Gas party because 'we have had our handful of shops illuminated for the first time', whereas the No Gas party sulkily and stubbornly burn tallow in their shops, cutting off their noses to spite their faces by 'cutting off their gas to be revenged on their business' (*RP*).

Repairing to Durdles's

two skeleton journeymen out of the Dance of Death] A reference to the drawings by Holbein (1497?–1543) which represent Death as a skeleton dancing after all sorts and conditions of persons to the grave. Beginning with Adam and Eve, he follows the judge, the priest, the nun and the doctor, the bride, the beggar, the king and the infant. Dickens was also familiar with the Dance of Death by Rowlandson (1756–1827) but had known the version by Holbein since boyhood and purchased a copy for his own library in 1841 (*Letters* 2.229). Dickens's interest in the series is examined by Hill (1981, ch. 3); see also Hollington (1983).

Surely an unaccountable

stealing forth to climb, and dive, and wander] As Ariel does in *The Tempest* 1.2.189–92:

> I come
> To answer thy best pleasure; be't to fly,
> To swim, to dive into the fire, to ride
> On the curl'd clouds.

Mr. Jasper stops

"What you call quick-lime?"] The use of quicklime to hasten the decomposition of corpses was a controversial subject in the public discussions of the mid-century on cemetery reform. During the 1843 parliamentary inquiry into the practice of interment in towns, the question repeatedly put to witnesses was: 'Do you think there would be an objection to burying bodies with a certain quantity of quicklime?' Progressive, utilitarian authorities such as J. C. Loudon recommended its use as a solution to the problem of disposing of the greatest number of bodies at the least expense in a restricted area so as to accommodate more graves. The general public, however, considered the suggestion revolting and irreverent (*Westminster Review*, 40 (1843), 173–4; *Quarterly Review*, 73 (1844), 451; Loudon, *On . . . Cemeteries . . .*, 1843; Morley, 1971, 46). Jasper may have in mind the same plan as Orlick in *GE*. He warns Pip that when he has killed him and put his remains in the lime-kiln, ' "I won't have a rag of you, I won't have a bone of you, left on earth" ' (53).

The reference to lime may be significant in the chapter of which Dickens noted in the work plans: 'Lay the ground for the manner of the Murder, to come out at last.' Forster claims that he was told that Edwin's body was to be destroyed by quicklime but that the gold ring would resist 'the corrosive effects of the lime into which he [the murderer] had thrown the body'. The ring would provide evidence to identify the murderer and the murdered man (3.18.426).

They go on

the Monks' Vineyard] The tree-lined walk known as 'The Vines' in Rochester.

It is not until

and bursts into a fit of laughter.] This incident is strikingly similar to that in *The Hunchback of Notre-Dame* (1831), when Quasimodo has just witnessed the hanging of Esmerelda:

> at this most awful moment, a demon laugh, a laugh such as one only who has ceased to be human is capable of, burst forth upon the livid face of the priest. Quasimodo [who is deaf] heard not this laugh, but he saw it. The bell-ringer recoiled a few steps from the archdeacon. (52)

(For the influence of this novel on *MED*, see Introduction, p. 2).

Among those secluded

a mysterious lady, with a child in her arms and a rope dangling from her neck, has been seen flitting] Probably a fictional ghost created to precede Durdles's account of a more believable one. The story that Restoration House (opposite The Vines) is haunted was not published until 1880 (Langton 25). If the story was in circulation during Dickens's lifetime, there is no evidence that he knew about it.

the innate shrinking of dust with the breath of life in it] An echo of the Burial Service, quoted in the previous chapter by Mr Grewgious: 'We therefore commit his body to the ground; earth to earth, ashes to ashes, dust to dust; in sure and certain hope of the Resurrection to eternal life.'

"If the dead do, under any circumstances, become visible to the living] This brings to mind the cover design for the wrapper of the monthly parts: Fildes has drawn the figure of a man holding a lantern and opening a door which is probably the entrance to the crypt. By the light of his lamp, he sees the figure of another man standing inside. All commentators agree that the man with the lamp is John Jasper. If, as seems likely, the other man is Edwin Drood, whom Jasper believes to be murdered by his own hand, then the dead has 'become visible to the living' (for a discussion of this point, see Introduction, p. 6).

Hence, when Mr. Jasper

descending into the crypt by a small side door] The crypt (Plate 2) is entered from the south choir aisle near the medieval wooden vestry.

"Well, it would *lead*

"But do you think there may be ghosts of other things] Durdles asks the educated man about the supernatural, just as in *Hamlet* Bernardo and Marcello turn to Horatio for information about the ghost they have seen on the ramparts (1.1.42).

"What cries do you mean

"What cries do you mean? Chairs to mend?"] One of the traditional cries of the itinerant street-sellers who cried out their services and wares: 'Umbrellas to mend!'; 'Knives and scissors to grind, O!'; 'Dust-ho!'; 'Lily-white muffins!' and so on. By the 1850s the custom had largely died out or been banned by legislation against noise nuisance (see the *HW* articles, 'Old Clothes', 5.93–8, and 'Cries from the Past', 11.606).

"No. I mean screeches

This time last year . . . And what woke me? The ghost of a cry.] This strange incident has been dated, to the day, one year later, when another murder may be planned. Whose cry was it? Whose dog howled? This is not a 'manifestation of a prophetic gift' in Durdles (Aylmer, 1964, 64–6), and Mrs Sapsea (who must have died at about that time) is not likely to have shrieked thus – or the whole town would know about it. Once again, we do not know. The suggested source of this account is a play which Dickens may have seen or heard of during his visit to Paris in 1868, Erckmann's *Le Juif Polonaise* (1867). In the play Mathis murders a Polish Jew for his money; fifteen years later a Jew, alike in appearance, comes to the inn, and Mathis unwittingly reveals the truth of the murder. It had taken place on Christmas Eve, and the body, severely beaten, was disposed of in lime. The play betrays an interest in mesmerism and a pre-occupation with the return-from-the-dead motif, and hinges upon how the crime will be exposed in the end (Cardwell, 1969, 58–9).

the ghost of a howl of a dog] One of the sketches by Charles Collins shows the Dean with Sapsea and Tope. At Sapsea's feet is a small dog. Is this the dog that howled a year ago? Does Mrs Sapsea, dead 'three quarters of a year', have anything to do with Durdles's dream? Once again, we do not know.

Then they go up

Then they go up the winding staircase of the great tower . . . they emerge into level low-arched galleries, whence they can look down into the moonlit nave] Dickens and his illustrator use some licence in this scene. One cannot see into the nave from the triforium ('level low-arched galleries') of Rochester Cathedral, and the stairs depicted on the wrapper for the monthly parts differ from those in the actual tower, which are enclosed in a narrow stone well. The 'great tower' is that depicted in Jasper's dream in chapter 1, the central tower of the Cathedral, not Gundulph's Tower adjacent to the north transept.

they look down on Cloisterham, fair to see in the moonlight] Dickens elsewhere describes the vistas from church towers (*OCS* 53 and *CC* 2), but this seems to be based on the scene in *The Hunchback of Notre-Dame* in which Quasimodo looks down from a tower in Notre-Dame Cathedral:

> A few columns of smoke issued from different points of this vast surface of roofs, as from the fissure of an immense solfatera. The river which dashes its waters against the piers of so many bridges, and the points of so many islands, was streaked with lines of silver. Around the City, beyond the ramparts, the sight was lost in a wide circle of fleecy vapours, through which might be faintly discerned the indefinite line of the plains and the graceful swelling of the hills. All sorts of sounds floated confusedly over this half-awakened city. Towards the east the morning breeze drove across the sky a few white flakes rent from the mantle of mist that enwrapped the hills. (52)

Once again

and especially that stillest part of it which the Cathedral overshadows.] The 'ruined habitations and sanctuaries of the dead, at the tower's base' described in the previous paragraph. If a man were to be thrown from the Cathedral tower, he would fall to this graveyard.

Only by times

As aëronauts lighten the load they carry, when they wish to rise] The craze for ballooning which lasted well into the nineteenth century was initiated by the ascent from Versailles of the Montgolfier brothers in 1783 and subsequently by the flights of Vincenzo Lunardi from London in 1784. Balloon launches became a popular form of outdoor entertainment. Dickens describes a launch he witnessed at Vauxhall in 'Vauxhall Gardens by Day' (*SB*).

Snatches of sleep surprise him on his legs, and stop him in his talk. A mild fit of calenture seizes him] Calenture, a disease incident to sailors in the tropics, is a type of heat-stroke. The afflicted become delirious and believe the sea to be a green field into which they long to run. The delusion of Durdles, induced by the laudanum-spiked alcohol, is perhaps (or perhaps not) a hint that Dickens intended Jasper's victim to fall to his death.

"Two!" cries Durdles

"Two!" cries Durdles, scrambling up; "why didn't you try to wake me, Mister Jarsper?"] A rough estimate gives Jasper four or five hours on his own.

As Durdles recalls

Durdles recalls that touching something in his dream] If Durdles did not forget the earlier experience, he may have reason to remember this ghost-like dream as the novel unfolds.

"I should think

Durdles wouldn't go home till morning] From the song 'Billy Taylor' by John Baldwin Buckstone (1802–79). The tune of 'We Won't Go Home till Morning' is founded on an air which originated during the Duke of Marlborough's campaign, and is known as 'Malbrough', or 'Malbrook':

On such an occasion as this,
  All time and nonsense scorning,
Nothing shall come amiss,
  And we won't go home till morning.

The song is sung in *PP* (7) when

> the convocation of worthies of Dingley Dell and Muggleton were heard to sing, with great feeling and emphasis, the beautiful and pathetic national air of
>
> We won't go home 'till morning,
> We won't go home 'till morning,
> We won't go home 'till morning,
> 'Till daylight doth appear.

"What! Is that baby-devil

"What! Is that baby-devil on the watch there!"] Considering that Jasper has just passed four or five hours on his own in the Cathedral, it is interesting to speculate on what he suspects Deputy of having seen.

he is no sooner taken by the throat] It has been suggested that Deputy here enacts 'what Edwin Drood is to suffer at the gatehouse' when Jasper 'comes upon his nephew from behind, to throttle him with his great black scarf. Surely here is the "ground for the manner of the murder, to come out at last" ' (Baker, 1951, 137).

"I'll blind yer

bellows me!"] 'Bellows away!' or 'Bellows him well!' are adjurations to a boxer not to spare his opponent but to force him to pant for wind.

"Yer lie, I haven't

Kinfreederel] This pronunciation was decided upon after several deletions.

Deputy, with another

as everything comes to an end] The variants of the proverb are: 'Everything has an end' and 'Everything has an end and a pudding has two' – an odd proverb to have in this novel, which has been given so many endings!

Chapter 13

Fourth monthly number
July 1870

BOTH AT THEIR BEST.

Miss Twinkleton's establishment

what was now called, as being more elegant, and more strictly collegiate, "the term"] As at Dr Blimber's Academy in *DS*:

> Any such violent expression as "breaking up," would have been quite inapplicable to that polite establishment. The young gentlemen oozed away, semi-annually, to their own homes; but they never broke up. They would have scorned the action. (14)

'Recess', used chiefly of Parliament, began to be used of schools in the eighteenth century; similarly, by the 1860s 'term' began to apply to schools where it had previously applied to University and the law courts; the 'half' became current

Once more carry through Edwin and Rosa?

or, Last time?

<Last scene but one between them> Last time.

Then

Last Meeting of Rosa and Edwin <in> outside the Cathedral? Yes

Kiss at parting

"Jack.

Edwin goes to the dinner.

The Windy night.

The Surprise and Alarm

Jasper's failure in the one great object made known by Mr Grewgious

Jasper's Diary? Yes.

(Mystery of Edwin Drood. – No. IV.)

Chapter XIII

Both at their Best

The Last Interview And Parting

Chapter XIV

When shall these three meet again?

How each passes the day

Watch and shirt pin
all Edwin's jewellery

Neville
Edwin
Jasper

Watch to the
Jeweller

"And so he goes up the Postern stair"

Storms of wind

Chapter XV.

Impeached

Neville away early

Pursued and brought back

Mr Grewgious's communication:

And his scene with Jasper

Chapter XVI

Devoted

Jasper's artful use of the communication on his recovery.

Cloisterham Weir, Mr Crisparkle, and the Watch and pin.

Jasper's artful turn

The Dean. Neville cast out

Jasper's Diary. "I devote myself to his destruction"

after the school year was divided in 1865. Mr Grewgious has suggested that the Nuns' House is far from being a school, choosing 'College' instead (chapter 9), a delicacy made fun of in *HW*: 'where our benighted grandfathers had boys' and girls' schools, we have seminaries, academies, lyceums, and colleges' (5.6).

cowslip wine] A beverage of so low an alcoholic content that in *DC* Peggotty sends two bottles to David at school (7); and the ladies in Mrs Gaskell's *Cranford* (1851–3) drink 'a newly decanted bottle' (14). To make cowslip wine: boil honey in water and pour over halved lemons and cowslips. Leave to stand overnight. Stir in yeast and sweetbriar and leave the mixture to stand for three or four days. Strain, pour into a cask, and, after six months bottle it (Francatelli, *The Cook's Guide*, revised edition, 1888, 316).

little Rickitts (a junior of weakly constitution), took her steel drops daily.] Rickets, a vitamin-deficiency disease, was endemic in children of the poor, particularly those of industrial towns. The disease causes emaciation, and spinal and other deformities of the bones. Chalybeate medicines, especially iron chloride (steel drops), were prescribed as a tonic. Iron or steel filings were sometimes administered internally, as was water in which iron or steel had been quenched when red hot. Cod-liver oil was known from the 1840s to cure rickets, but it was not widely administered (Wohl, 1983, 56–7).

until suffocated in her own pillow by two flowing-haired executioners.] An allusion to the murder of the two princes in the Tower of London by order of Richard III. As *CHE* recounts, two hired murderers, described as 'those evil demons, John Dighton and Miles Forest, who smothered the two princes with the bed and pillows and carried their bodies down the stairs, and buried them under a great heap of stones at the staircase foot' (25).

Nor were these

golden youth of England expected to call, "at home"] From *Henry V* 2, Chorus, 1–2: 'Now all the youth of England are on fire,/And silken dalliance in the wardrobe lies'. The 'at home' (the words inscribed on the invitation) was an intimate gathering given by ladies either in the afternoon or the evening. The evening 'at home' was a more formal affair, and special entertainment, such as music, might be provided.

The concluding ceremony

held a Drawing-Room] The name of the reception given by the monarch at court several times a year.

revolving year] A poeticism; for example, Thomas Moore's translation of Anacreon, Ode 25, begins:

> Once in each revolving year,
> Gentle bird! We find thee here.

Also compare Shelley, *Adonais* (18, 53).

Mr. Addison's impressive tragedy] Addison's *Cato* (1713) opens with Portius speaking these lines. Once again Miss Twinkleton stops on the brink of saying something unseemly, for the words that follow are 'big with fate/Of Cato and of Rome'.

Not so. From horizon

the Spartan General, in words too trite for repetition, at the battle it were superfluous to specify] Leonidas was the Spartan general at the celebrated battle of Thermopylae (480 BC), when the Greeks learnt to despise the Persians, fighting under Xerxes, and to rely upon their own strength and intrepidity. Of the numerous accounts in English of the battle, a likely version for Miss Twinkleton to prescribe would be that in Goldsmith's *History of Greece* (1774), in which Leonidas addresses his men before battle, saying: 'Come, my fellow soldiers . . . let us dine cheerfully here, for to-night we shall sup with Pluto' (1.6). As Cardwell has suggested (1982, 238), Miss Twinkleton would also know the account given in the popular schoolbook often ridiculed by Dickens, Thomas Day's *Sandford and Merton* (1783–9; and numerous editions throughout the nineteenth century).

The handmaidens

the bill] Six months' tuition at such an establishment could cost from eleven to twenty pounds, and accounts would list stationery (a Bible, copy-books, pens, ink, a mending-box); Latin and Greek at about a guinea; a seat in church a shilling or two; the servants' charge at two or three shillings; a half-year's board, and tuition in English, writing, history and so on, at eight or nine guineas.

It would have made

It would have made a pretty picture] Miss Kitty Kimmeens, the pupil in 'Tom Tiddler's Ground', in which Miss Twinkleton's school is anticipated, 'remained behind, for her relations and friends were all in India', and when the holidays began 'five of the six pupils kissed little Kitty Kimmeens twenty times over (round total, one hundred times, for she was very popular), and so went home' (*CS*). The plate which illustrates this scene, 'Good-Bye, Rosebud, Darling', and all the plates that follow were not seen by Dickens, who died after the first three numbers of the novel had been published. The titles of these illustrations were composed by the artist (Kitton, 1899, 214).

sly faces carved on spout and gable] 'The silent High-street of Rochester is full of gables, with old beams and timbers carved into strange faces' ('The Seven Poor Travellers', *CS*).

If Rosebud in her bower

If Rosebud in her bower] An allusion to the romance of Henry II and

Rosamund Clifford, the 'fair Rosamund in her bower' of countless poems. Dickens tells the story in chapter 12 of *CHE*.

"Ah! But I fear

"I never thought of Jack!"] What is perhaps a preparatory sketch of this moment, although differing in tone and detail, appears in the *Book of Memoranda* (14; Kaplan could not trace Dickens's use of the sketch):

> Set of circumstances which suddenly bring an easy, airy fellow into ^near^ relations with people he knows nothing about, and has never even seen. This through his being thrown in the way of the innocent young personage of the story. "Then there is Uncle Sam to be considered," says she. "Aye, to be sure," says he, "so there is! By Jupiter, I forgot Uncle Sam. He's a rock ahead, is Uncle Sam. He must be considered, of course; he must be smoothed down; he must be cleared out of the way. To be sure. I never thought of Uncle Sam. – By the bye, who *is* Uncle Sam.

"Why, sister Rosa

"Why, sister Rosa, sister Rosa, what do you see from the turret?"] One of the frequent allusions in Dickens to the fairy tale of 'Blue Beard' (originally collected by Charles Perrault in 1697 and first translated into English in 1729). 'Blue Beard' tells of a bride who discovers the secret of her husband's murdered wives, and fears for her own life. Pleading time for prayer and solitude, she calls to her sister to look out for her two brothers whom she hopes will rescue her:

> 'Sister Anne' (for that was her name) 'go up I beg you, upon the top of the tower, and look if my brothers are not coming; they promised me that they would come to day' . . . Her sister Anne went up upon the top of the tower, and the poor afflicted wife cried out from time to time, 'Anne, sister Anne, do you see any one coming?' And sister Anne said, 'I see nothing but the sun, which makes a dust, and the grass, which looks green.'
>
> (cited in *Tales of Passed Times by Mother Goose*, Englished by [Robert Samber], 7th edn, 1795)

The brothers do arrive, and save their sister by killing Blue Beard.

Let them be

Among the mighty store of wonderful chains] Edwin's decision is important as the ring may have been intended as a clue for the solution to the mystery:

> all discovery of the murderer was to be baffled till towards the close, when, by means of a gold ring which had resisted the corrosive effects of the lime into which he had thrown the body, not only the person murdered was to be identified but the locality of the crime and the man who committed it. So much

> was told to me before any of the book was written; and it will be recollected that the ring, taken by Drood to be given to his betrothed only if their engagement went on, was brought away with him from their last interview. (Forster 3.18.426)

Forster's account is one of the strongest arguments for Edwin's being dead. Jasper would remove the watch and shirt-pin but, not knowing about the ring, would leave it on the body where it would resist corrosion. That the 'one chain', forged in Edwin's decision to retain the ring, should be 'gifted with invincible force to hold and drag' may well uphold Forster's conclusion.

They walked on

They walked on by the river.] The Esplanade, on the east of the Medway, lies under the castle walls and is pleasantly approached from the Cathedral Close.

She pulled hurriedly

And out of that look he vanished from her view.] Alterations in MS of this sentence include '<and never looked upon him> <and never thought [that he was to?] vanish from her view>'. This is not enough of a clue to be sure of whether Rosa will see Edwin again or not. Cardwell believes that even though 'the evidence is inconclusive' the scales are heavily weighted 'on the side of Edwin's death' (1969, 272).

Chapter 14

WHEN SHALL THESE THREE MEET AGAIN?

The title derives from the opening line of *Macbeth*: 'When shall we three meet again?'

Christmas Eve in

Christmas Eve in Cloisterham.] Christmas as depicted in *MED* is more like the modern festival, focusing on shops and public amusements, than that celebrated at Dingley Dell, where Boxing Day was not celebrated and the party broke up after breakfast on the morning of the 26th.

who come back from the outer world at long intervals to find the city wonderfully shrunken in size] Dickens has described Rochester in this way in 'Dullborough Town' (*UT*):

> Of course the town had shrunk fearfully, since I was a child there. I had entertained the impression that the High-street was at least as wide as Regent-street, London, or the Italian Boulevard at Paris. I found it little better than a lane. There was a public clock in it, which I had supposed to be the finest clock in the world: whereas it now turned out to be as inexpressive, moon-faced, and weak a clock as ever I saw.

Seasonable tokens

Twelfth Cake, culminating in the figure of a Harlequin . . . to be raffled for at the pastrycook's] The importance to the baker of this centrepiece of the festivities on Twelfth Night is explained in a *HW* essay:

> he is secretly at work in the production of a full set (we forgot how many he told us made a set) of the richest and most elaborately decorated and 'dramatised' Twelfth Cakes which the juvenile world of England has ever yet beheld. The man's half crazy. His wife says he gets no sleep with thinking of his cakes. The other night he started up in bed, and cried out "Sugar-frost and whitening!" till his night-cap stood on end. (4, Christmas Number, 6)

The Wax-Work which made so deep an impression on the reflective mind of the Emperor of China] This may well be a witty allusion to Lien Chi Altangi, the Chinese philosopher who visits London and records his impressions in Goldsmith's *Letters from a Citizen of the World to His Friends in the East* (1760). The philosopher is generally amazed at the odd customs of the English. One of his letters in particular describes a man who exhibits himself as a waxwork. Perhaps Dickens conflated his memory of Goldsmith with some contemporary events: during the 1860s the Emperor of China featured frequently in the British press because of his overthrow and subsequent reinstatement; and in 1868 a delegation of Chinese dignitaries paid an official visit to London. A correspondent in *The Times* complained of the lack of publicity accorded the dignitaries and commented: 'For all we hear of them they might be a group of private gentlemen who had come to London to see the Tower and Madame Tussaud's waxworks' (16 October 1868, 8; also see 9 July, 12).

Small waxwork exhibitions which toured the provinces were common in the eighteenth century and nineteenth century. Madame Tussaud herself travelled with her exhibition for many years until establishing it permanently in Baker Street in 1833. Like its predecessors (notably Mrs Salmon's Waxwork in Fleet Street), Madame Tussaud's exhibition featured models of British and foreign royalty, members of the nobility and historical figures. As well as displaying waxwork models of distinguished persons, Madame Tussaud's was famous as an attraction for distinguished and foreign visitors to London. This explains the first reading for 'Emperor of China': 'Crowned Heads of Europe' – an expression also descriptive of the wax models themselves. (See Thornbury and Walford, 1873–8, 1.45–6, 4.419; Timbs, 1855, 350.)

new grand comic Christmas pantomime] Dickens frequently recorded his delight in the pantomime, notably in his edition of Grimaldi's *Memoirs*, in a sketch on Astley's Amphitheatre in *SB*, and in a *HW* essay which describes how

> Harlequins, covered all over with scales of pure gold, twist and sparkle, like amazing fish; when Pantaloon (whom I deem it no irreverence to compare in my own mind to my grandfather) puts red-hot pokers in his pocket, and cries "Here's somebody coming!" or taxes the Clown with petty larceny, by saying "Now, I sawed you do it!" when Everything is capable, with the greatest ease, of being changed into Anything; and "Nothing is, but thinking makes it so." Now, too, I perceive my first experience of the dreary sensation – often to return in after-life – of being unable, next day, to get back to the dull, settled world; of wanting to live for ever in the bright atmosphere I have quitted; of doting on the little Fairy, with the wand like a celestial Barber's Pole, and pining for a Fairy immortality along with her. (2.292)

the High School] The King's or Cathedral Grammar School, founded by Henry VIII, was housed in handsome buildings in The Vines, but closer to the Nuns' House was Sir Joseph Williamson's Mathematical School in the High Street, founded in 1701 by Sir Joseph's bequest for a free school. The large red-brick building Dickens knew no longer exists.

"True," says Mr. Crisparkle

Do you come back before dinner?"] Macbeth reminds Banquo that 'Tonight we hold a solemn supper, sir/And I'll request your presence' (3.1.13).

His sister is at

and walk towards the upper inland country.] Away from the river and south.

"Entirely. I am not

his own sound mind in his own sound body] Juvenal, *Satires* 10.356: 'mens sana in corpore sano'.

Edwin Drood passes

Something of deeper moment than he had thought, has gone out of his life] Critics have argued that this insight into Edwin's consciousness is a premonition of both his dying and his survival. Dickens frequently reveals the minds of characters who are about to die (Jonas Chuzzlewit, Fagin, Ralph Nickleby, William Dorrit, Betty Higden), and, in Edwin's case, this convention may have been intended to soften our feelings towards him before his death (Cardwell, 1969, 133; Boege, 1950, 102). Conversely, the convention is applied to many characters who do not die, as with Charles Darnay (*TTC* 3.13) and Pip (*GE* 53).

As he only waits

he only waits for Mr. Grewgious now] Does Edwin in fact see Mr Grewgious before he departs?

Finding that his watch

his watch has stopped] The watch is of the kind that can be rewound when still going, but must be reset by a jeweller if allowed to run down. Fildes has noted beside this passage: '20 Thurs. Friday 7Pm Saturday Sunday' (Cardwell, 1972, 269). This is odd because the watch was thrown into the river in the early hours of Christmas day, a Sunday, and was found by Mr Crisparkle early on the Wednesday, the 29th. The number of days tallies, but not the dates.

He strolls about

the dinner hour] This would be roughly between 5.30 and 6.00 p.m.

He will soon be far away, and may never see them again, he thinks. Poor youth! Poor youth!] The MS correction is significant in regard to the dispute of whether Edwin is murdered or not: '<He> Poor youth! <He little, little knows how near a cause he has for thinking so.> Poor youth!' This issue is discussed in the Introduction (p. 6).

He straightens himself

for he seems to know her.] Commentators have suggested a relationship between Jasper and the opium-woman, based on this resemblance. But, if she has 'opium-smoked herself into a strange likeness of the Chinaman' in chapter 1, Edwin recognizes not a family resemblance, but the same fit he had seen overtake his uncle in chapter 2.

"Come from London

"Come from London] Only when the opium-woman swears in chapter 23 ' "I'll not miss ye twice" ' does the reader realize that Jasper had been to her den on Christmas Eve, when she had followed him home, missed him, and met up with Edwin instead.

"Do you eat

"Do you eat opium?"] Opium-eating, that is, drinking laudanum, was more usual than opium-smoking, a more complicated, and exotic, process (as described in the notes to chapter 1, pp. 29–30).

"The proverb says

"The proverb says that threatened men live long] 'Threatened folks live long' (Tilley F425). Is this a promise of Edwin's survival?

Still, it holds

Still, it holds to him] In *OMF* (4.6), Eugene Wrayburn's restless state of mind before he is attacked is described in similar terms:

> The rippling of the river seemed to cause a correspondent stir in his uneasy reflections. He would have laid them asleep if he could, but they were in movement, like the stream, and all tending one way with a strong current. As the ripple under the moon broke unexpectedly now and then, and palely flashed in a new shape and with a new sound, so parts of his thought started, unbidden, from the rest.

John Jasper passes

He says that his complexion is "Un-English."] A type of Podsnappery:

> Mr Podsnap's world was not a very large world, morally; no, nor even geographically: seeing that although his business was sustained upon commerce with other countries, he considered other countries, with that important reservation, a mistake, and of their manners and customs would conclusively observe, 'Not English!' when, PRESTO! with a flourish of the arm, and a flush of the face, they were swept away. (*OMF* 1.11)

the bottomless pit] Revelation 20.1: 'And I saw an angel come down from heaven, having the key of the bottomless pit and a great chain in his hand.'

Mr. Jasper is in beautiful

in beautiful voice this day.] Most nineteenth-century writers believed, perhaps erroneously, that opium stimulated artistic creation (Hayter, 1968, 43).

In the pathetic supplication] The response to the Commandments repeated during Holy Communion: 'Lord have mercy upon us, and incline our hearts to keep this law.'

as in this day's Anthem.] The anthem, sacred vocal music set to words from the Scriptures and sung at Morning and Evening Prayer, would be chosen by the choirmaster. On great festivals such as Christmas Eve, an elaborate piece would be selected.

These results are

a large black scarf of strong close-woven silk] In a letter to *The Times* (27 October 1905; printed in *The Times Literary Supplement*, 3 November 1905) Luke

Fildes recorded that he had questioned Dickens about this scarf because Jasper had previously been illustrated wearing a small black tie. Dickens asked him whether he could keep a secret, and then confided that Edwin was to be strangled with the scarf. Dickens did not expect that the reader would so quickly identify Jasper as the murderer, so it was decided deliberately to avoid a scene showing Jasper wearing the scarf (Cardwell, 1972, xxvi). Out of this correspondence arose the view (propounded by Howard Duffield in 1930 and supported by several critics, notably Edmund Wilson in 1940 and Margaret Cardwell, 1969, 1972) that John Jasper is a member of the Phansigars, popularly known as Thugs. During the nineteenth century the British police in India exposed and suppressed a religious sect whose worship of the goddess Kali obliged ritual murder. The comparison is interesting, and a fair amount of evidence has been offered to support the theory, but, as with so many of the proposed solutions to the novel, close examination shows it to be nothing more than an interesting and imaginative red herring. (For a full discussion, see Jacobson, 1977, 526–37.)

"One would think

you had been trying a new medicine] De Quincey found that a sudden increase in his intake of opium would cause 'preternatural paroxysms of intermitting power' when he would write brilliantly, but that he would suffer for it when the effects of the drug had worn off (Hayter, 1971, 16). Perhaps when Jasper is so distraught after Edwin's disappearance he is partly paying for indulgence in the den the day before. De Quincey also believed that opium intensifies susceptibility to sound because it is not by the ear that one communicates with music, he argues, but

> by the reaction of the mind upon the notices of the ear, (the *matter* coming by the *senses*, the *form*, from the mind,) that the pleasure is constructed: and therefore it is that people of equally good ear differ so much in this point from one another. ('The Pleasures of Opium', *Confessions*)

"Why, naturally

You are always training yourself to be, mind and body, as clear as crystal] Revelation 21.11: 'Having the glory of God: and her light was like unto a stone most precious, even like a jasper stone, clear as crystal.'

I am a muddy, solitary, moping weed.] Perhaps a memory of *Hamlet* 1.5.32–3: 'the fat weed/That roots itself in ease on Lethe wharf'.

No such power

Chimnies topple in the streets] Reminiscent of the unruly night in *Macbeth* when Duncan is murdered:

Our chimneys were blown down; and, as they say,
Lamentings heard i' th' air, strange screams of death,
And prophesying, with accents terrible,
Of dire combustion and confus'd events
New hatch'd to th' woeful time; the obscure bird
Clamour'd the livelong night. Some say the earth
Was feverous and did shake. (2.3.53–9)

Chapter 15

IMPEACHED.

Visitors in want

The Tilted Wagon] Several public houses have been offered as originals for the Tilted Wagon, so called because its sign would probably be a wagon with a canvas cover. At the top of Strood Hill stood the Coach and Horses inn (Matz, 1923, 227), but if Neville avoided the busy west–east road to London and Dover and went south towards Maidstone and the Weald of Kent he would come to the Upper Bell on Blue Bell Hill, about six miles from Rochester (Gadd, 1928, 188–90).

"If eight men

"If eight men, or four men, or two men, set upon one] Perhaps an echo of Falstaff's 'men-in-buckram' speech (*1 Henry IV* 2.4.167–81):

Gadshill: We four set upon some dozen—
Falstaff: Sixteen at least, my lord . . .
Gadshill: As we were sharing, some six or seven fresh men set upon us—
Falstaff: And unbound the rest, and then come in the other.
Prince: What, fought you with them all?
Falstaff: All! I know not what you call all, but if I fought not with fifty of them, I am a bunch of radish. If there were not two or three and fifty upon poor old Jack, then I am no two-legg'd creature.

to set his mark upon some of them.] Genesis 4.15: 'And the Lord set a mark upon Cain, lest any finding him should kill him.'

"Where is your nephew

"Where is your nephew?" . . . "Why do you ask me?"] Genesis 4.9: 'And the Lord said unto Cain, Where is Abel thy brother? And he said, I know not: Am I my brother's keeper?' Some critics, notably G. K. Chesterton, argue that Neville might have unknowingly done the deed after all, under the mesmeric control of

Jasper (just as Franklin Blake, under the influence of opium, unknowingly steals the Moonstone diamond). Chesterton suggests that when Dickens told Forster that the murderer would describe his experience 'as if "some other man" had undergone it' he may have meant that when the murderer confesses his crime it will in fact have been 'the act of another man' (1928, 225).

Mr. Sapsea being

Mr. Sapsea being informed] This scene is a pastiche of the examination by Dogberry and Verges of Borachio and Conrade in *Much Ado about Nothing* 4.2.

He washed his hands as clean as he could] The allusion is to Pilate who, when he 'saw that he could prevail nothing, but that rather a tumult was made, he took water, and washed his hands before the multitude, saying, I am innocent of the blood of this person: see ye to it' (Matthew 27.24).

With the earliest light

All the livelong day] The sequence of days is a little complicated here:

The discovery of Edwin's loss occurs on Sunday, Christmas Day, 25 December.
'All the livelong day' refers to the same day, 25 December.
'When the next day dawned' refers to Monday, 26 December.
'Setting his watches for that night again' is Monday night of 26 December, and it is on this day that Jasper returns home to find Grewgious waiting for him. The watch that Crisparkle sees that same night is recovered the next morning, on Tuesday, 27 December, and has been lying in the weir, presumably removed from Edwin on Christmas Eve, for two and a half days.

jack-boot] The boot, worn by cavalry soldiers, came above the knee, serving as protection, and was a version of the large boot worn by fishermen and rivermen.

cressets] A vessel of iron made to hold oil, or an iron basket holding pitched coal or wood, and burnt for light in the open air.

no trace of Edwin Drood revisited the light of the sun.] An echo of *Hamlet* 1.4.53: 'Revisits thus the glimpses of the moon'.

All that day

John Jasper worked and toiled.] De Quincey points to the 'subtle powers lodged in' opium to enable one to endure great effort. That opium has such an effect is debatable, but De Quincey claims that 'under any call for extraordinary exertion' one can 'sustain through twenty-four consecutive hours the else drooping animal energies', and that, 'most certainly, knowing or suspecting all this, I should have inaugurated my opium career in the character of one seeking *extra* power and enjoyment, rather than of one shrinking from *extra* torment' ('The Pains of Opium', *Confessions*).

"One of this young couple

"I speak to you and he IS gone."] Forster records that 'discovery by the murderer of the utter needlessness of the murder for its object, was to follow hard upon commission of the deed' (3.18.426). It has been suggested that the scene is influenced by the deathbed warning against passion discussed in Ann Radcliffe, *The Mysteries of Udolpho* (1794, 1): only when the drive of a single passion has been realized are pity and remorse aroused through horror of the deed committed (Cardwell, 1969, 104–5).

Mr. Grewgious heard

Mr. Grewgious heard a terrible shriek, and saw no ghastly figure, sitting or standing: saw nothing but a heap of torn and miry clothes upon the floor.] The image of a man whose form is reduced to a bundle of clothes persists throughout Dickens's work. For example, recollecting having witnessed the execution of Mr and Mrs Manning in November 1849, he remarked that the body of the dead man was like 'a limp, loose suit of clothes as if the man had gone out of them' ('Lying Awake', *RP*).

Chapter 16

DEVOTED.

The chapter takes its title from its last sentence, the declaration in Jasper's diary, ' "And that I devote myself to his destruction" '. The *Book of Memoranda* records a similar idea: 'Devoted to the destruction of a man. Revenge built up, on Love . . .', which was '[Done in Hunted Down]' (8). Another idea in the *Book of Memoranda* used in 'Hunted Down' and again in *MED* is the description of the villain, Julius Slinkton, who has 'his hair parted straight up the front of his head, like an aggravating gravel-walk. Always presenting it to you' (13). In Fildes's illustration to the second monthly number, 'On Dangerous Ground', Jasper, too, has his hair parted down the middle.

The extensive changes in this chapter, three out of four of which relate to Crisparkle's visit to the weir, are insertions to assure the required length of the number (Cardwell, 1969, 279).

"You must take

jelly] Mrs Tope has prepared a consommé.

"Do you know

"Do you know," said Jasper, when he had pushed away his plate] Dickens wrote to James T. Fields on 14 January 1870 telling him that Forster thought the second number of his new novel was a 'clincher', and added:

> There is a curious interest steadily working up to No. 5, which requires a great deal of art and self-denial. I think also, apart from character and picturesqueness, that the young people are placed in a very novel situation. So I hope – at Nos. 5 and 6 the story will turn upon an interest suspended until the end. (*Nonesuch* 3.760)

The 'curious interest' may lie in the manner of 'Jasper's artful use of the communication on his recovery' (noted in work plans), which begins here, and is 'suspended until the end' as he works out the plans that shelter him from suspicion.

"Such a thing

a seven days' wonder] A confusion of the Seven Wonders of the World and of 'a nine days' wonder'.

"How did I come

"How did I come here!"] From here to 'as if it were tangible' is not in MS. It has been suggested that the words from Milton coming so strangely 'unbidden' may suggest an external will imposing mesmeric control.

Then, he stood

airy tongues that syllable men's names] From Milton, *Comus* 205–9:

> What might this be? A thousand fantasies
> Begin to throng into my memory
> Of calling shapes, and beck'ning shadows dire,
> And airy tongues that syllable men's names
> On sands and shores and desert wildernesses.

He brought the watch

His notion was, that he would find the body] For those who believe Edwin is dead, the watch, chain and shirt-pin discovered in the weir are evidence that an attempt was made on his life. If he had escaped, his taking no steps to bring the wrongdoer to justice would incur grave responsibility, in law and to Neville (Saunders, 1962, 24–5). On the other hand, if Edwin has escaped, he may well have gone to Grewgious to seek asylum. The murder of a Harvard professor which Dickens learnt of in January 1868 has been unconvincingly proposed as the source for the novel (Garner, 1983). The only aspect of the murder which might have inspired Dickens is that the professor's gold watch was found in the river.

With these discoveries

Before coming to England he had caused to be whipped to death sundry "Natives" – nomadic persons . . . always of great virtue . . . and always reading tracts of the obscurest meaning] The whipping to death of 'Natives' alludes in part to the Governor Eyre controversy (see notes to chapters 6 and 17, pp. 85–6, 145–6). It is also informed by Dickens's attitude towards whipping as a mode of punishing criminals: he condemns it as a 'barbarous device' in an extended passage on the subject in his *HW* essay of 1852, 'Lying Awake' (6.145–8).

Of the 'Natives' themselves, Dickens had expressed his opinions on the romantic notion of the noble savage and the work of British missionaries in foreign countries in *HW* and *BH.* A vogue for the exhibition in England of savages imported mostly from Africa, North and South America, and the polar regions (Laplanders and Eskimos) began in the early nineteenth century and reached its peak in the 1840s and 1850s. The American painter George Catlin, in partnership with the showman Arthur Rankin, exhibited in 1843–4 a group of Ojibbeways, the first of many American Indians to tour London and the provinces. Catlin had lived among Indians for several years and had studied their culture. He attempted to impress upon the British public that the Indians possessed social graces and a morality, dignity and intelligence which qualified them as civilized. Unfortunately, his Ojibbeways caused disturbances as they toured the sights of London, and the public began to protest at their uncivilized habits and lack of cultivation. Catlin's faith in racial egalitarianism and the nobility of the savage was not representative of his day. Popular opinion by the mid-century favoured a belief in white superiority, a belief which Dickens espoused (Altick, 1978, 268–87). In 'The Noble Savage', a *HW* essay of 1853 occasioned by the visit to London of some Zulu tribesmen, Dickens praises Catlin's sincerity of belief but lampoons the coarse reality. In particular, he rejects the romantic patronization of 'natives':

> I beg to say that I have not the least belief in the Noble Savage. I consider him a prodigious nuisance, and an enormous superstition. His calling rum fire-water, and me a pale face, wholly fail to reconcile me to him. I don't care what he calls me. I call him a savage, and I call a savage a something highly desirable to be civilised off the face of the earth . . . My position is, that if we have anything to learn from the Noble Savage, it is what to avoid. His virtues are a fable; his happiness is a delusion; his nobility, nonsense. (7.337, 339)

The reference to 'reading tracts' alludes to another frequent object of Dickens's ridicule: the work in foreign countries of British missionaries and philanthropists to convert the heathen to Christianity (see *BH* 16). The Religious Tract Society was formed in 1799 by Anglicans and nonconformists to distribute pamphlets on moral and religious subjects; the activity was particularly characteristic of Evangelicals.

brought Mrs. Crisparkle's grey hairs with sorrow to the grave.] Genesis

42.38: 'if mischief befall him by the way in which ye go, then shall ye bring down my gray hairs with sorrow to the grave'.

the last man] The phrase derives from Thomas Browne, *Religio Medici* 1.58: 'My desires onely are (and I shall be happy therein,) to be but the last man, and bring up the Rere in Heaven.' Thomas Campbell and Thomas Hood wrote poems entitled 'The Last Man'. Hood explains the phrase:

So there he hung and there I stood,
The LAST MAN left alive,
To have my own will of all the earth:
Quoth I, "now I shall thrive!"
But when was ever honey made
With one bee in a hive! (29)

in the words of BENTHAM, **where he is the cause of the greatest danger to the smallest number."**] 'The greatest happiness of the greatest number is the foundation of morals and legislation' (Jeremy Bentham, *Introduction to the Principles of Morals and Legislation*, 1780; 1789). *HT* is an attack upon certain aspects of Utilitarianism, the philosophy formulated by Bentham, with which Dickens first became familiar during his reporting in Parliament, when many Members of the first Reformed House of Commons were influenced by Bentham.

These dropping shots

These dropping shots] 'To drop' means to knock down with a blow (Wright, 1898, 2.183), as when Boffin in *OMF* reports that ' "if Mrs Boffin hadn't thrown herself betwixt us, and received flush on the temple. Which dropped her, Mr Lightwood. Dropped her" ' (1.8).

blunderbusses of blunderheadedness] The contrast is between old-fashioned inaccurate weapons and modern developments in firearms. Blunderbusses were not much used after the eighteenth century; precision arms, dependent on new techniques in rifling barrels, breech-loaders, repeating systems and so on were developed during the first half of the nineteenth century.

On the suspicions

and Jasper laboured night and day.] 1 Thessalonians 2.9: 'For ye remember, brethren, our labour and travail; for labouring night and day, because we would not be chargeable unto any of you, we preached unto you the gospel of God'; and 2 Thessalonians 3.8: 'Neither did we eat any man's bread for nought; but wrought with labour and travail night and day, that we might not be chargeable to any of you'.

"Mr. Crisparkle," quoth

The days of taking sanctuary are past.] The Right of Sanctuary in the Middle Ages was ecclesiastical and secular: the criminal who took refuge in a church could not be removed from it but could take an oath of abjuration and go forward to a seaport. The Reformation drastically curtailed these rights, and in 1623 sanctuary for crime was abolished, although it lingered on in some instances for another hundred years.

"It is very lamentable

"It is very lamentable, sir] The passage from here to 'returned the Dean' is not in MS.

'Not at all

we clergy need do nothing emphatically."] The cautious attitude of the Dean has been identified as a topical issue by Cardwell (1982, 238), who cites an article in the *Spectator* (42, 9 October 1869): 'The Duty of Keeping the Church Insignificant'. The article criticizes *The Times* for encouraging Gladstone to appoint as bishops men with safe, inoffensive views:

> the *Times* seems to think it good policy to make the Church as insignificant as possible . . . it is the true policy of the Premier, hints the *Times*, to make choice of poor, weakish men, men who will be safe to do nothing great, and nothing particularly bad, who fill their charges and their sermons with the old lukewarm milk-and-water, a little more watery and less milky than ordinarily, and altogether be tame, harmless, feeble, insignificant, and neglected . . .

The principles of appointment designed to protect the Establishment, the *Spectator* continues, deny the opportunity for men of 'conviction', 'real power' and 'genius and energy' to redeem the church from insignificance, for:

> If the Church is to be saved only at the price of being insignificant, she is to be saved at the price of uselessness, for what good can an insignificant Church do? . . . A Church which does not assail, a Church which hides in a corner and smoothes decently over all the difficulties of life, is condemned already. There is nothing in it to save but a name. (1172)

Dickens's addition in MS of the word 'clergy' underlines the object of his satire.

So, Minor Canon Row

Minor Canon Row knew Neville Landless no more] A slip: Dickens forgetfully calls Minor Canon Corner by its real name in Rochester. Perhaps 'no more' foreshadows Neville's death. The phrase has a biblical tone: 'Yet a little while, and the world seeth me no more' (John 14.19).

and he went whithersoever he would, or could, with a blight upon his name and fame.] Neville is here identified with Cain (as he is in the next chapter when Crisparkle argues with Honeythunder):

> And Cain said unto the Lord, My punishment is greater than I can bear.

> Behold, thou hast driven me out this day from the face of the earth; and from thy face shall I be hid; and I shall be a fugitive and a vagabond in the earth; and it shall come to pass, that every one that findeth me shall slay me. And the Lord said unto him, therefore whosoever slayeth Cain, vengeance shall be taken on him sevenfold. And the Lord set a mark upon Cain, lest any finding him should kill him. (Genesis 4.13–15)

It was not until

he took his Diary from a pocket of his coat] In *The Moonstone* the Herncastle family lawyer, Mr Bruff, asks the question that could well be asked in *MED*:

> Why – even supposing he did take the Diamond – should Franklin Blake make himself the most prominent person in the house, in trying to recover it? You may tell me he cunningly did that to divert suspicion from himself. I answer that he had no need to divert suspicion – because nobody suspected him. He first steals the Moonstone (without the slightest reason) through natural depravity; and he then acts a part, in relation to the loss of the jewel, which there is not the slightest necessity to act, and which leads to his mortally offending the young lady who would otherwise have married him. (2.3)

And That I devote myself to his destruction."] Almost the same words are used in 'Hunted Down' (*RP*): Meltham is determined to overcome Slinkton if ' "absolutely certain that you could never elude him in this world . . . he devoted himself to your destruction with his utmost fidelity and earnestness" '. 'Sworn to avenge it', 'One Object in Life' and 'A Kinsman's Devotion' in the manuscript list of projected names and titles underline the significance of Jasper's obsession.

Chapter 17

Fifth monthly number
August 1870

PHILANTHROPY, PROFESSIONAL AND UNPROFESSIONAL.

The original title was 'Philanthropy in Several Phases'. The writing of number 5 was not easy in regard to the timing of Datchery's introduction into the scheme. Chapter 19, 'Shadow on the Sun-Dial', was written before chapter 18, 'A Settler in Cloisterham', and then transposed, thus avoiding an 'undramatic interpolation breaking the tension of the reader's feeling for Rosa' without altering chronology (Cardwell, 1969, 289).

In his college-days

the phrenological formation] The pseudoscience of phrenology was an empirical system of psychology formulated by the Viennese neuro-anatomist, Franz Joseph Gall (1757–1828). It attempted to correlate various functions of the brain with particular areas of the cerebral cortex, and was based on the theory that certain areas of the brain are especially connected with certain intellectual functions. The brain was thought to have thirty-seven separate 'organs' which controlled the moral, intellectual, emotional and sexual traits of an individual, and the size of each organ was thought to vary in relation to the development of the associated trait. On account of its claims to be able to ascertain disposition, capability and character, phrenology was seen to be a social philosophy promoting self-determination. For these reasons its theories were applied to education, penology and religion, and it had a wide following in the nineteenth century. By the 1830s many phrenological societies had been established, and there was a proliferation of literature on the subject (Davies, 1955, passim).

the Professing Philanthropists were uncommonly like the Pugilists.] Honeythunder, in this context, is reminiscent of Mr M'Choakumchild, the teacher in *HT* who is a 'professed pugilist', and who

> had a genius for coming up to the scratch, wherever and whatever it was, and proving himself an ugly customer. He would go in and damage any subject whatever with his right, follow up with his left, stop, exchange, counter, bore his opponent (he always fought All England) to the ropes, and fall upon him neatly. He was certain to knock the wind out of common sense, and render that unlucky adversary deaf to the call of time. (1.2)

to "pitch into"] Pugilistic slang meaning to assail and attack. In *GE* Pip feels guilty about having knocked down Herbert Pocket, knowing that 'village boys could not go stalking about the country, ravaging the houses of gentlefolks and pitching into the studious youth of England, without laying themselves open to severe punishment' (12).

Professors] *AYR* referred to 'professors' of pugilism as 'melancholy relics of a departed fashion' (3.133). The pugilistic world introduced here belongs to an earlier part of the century, and is distinct from the public-school manliness associated with Muscular Christianity. It is the pugilism of the Regency and of the Game Chicken in *DS*, derived from ideas promulgated in the early 1700s by Jim Figg, the first British bare-knuckle champion, and also by Jack Broughton, successor to the title, who in 1743 designed a set of rules which made boxing less brutal and more attractive to the upper classes in England. Thus did the Noble Art take on a glamour which appealed to such figures as Byron in the early part of the century. The Revised London Prize Ring Rules which developed from Broughton's original concept pertained from the middle of the eighteenth century for a hundred years until the improving Victorian spirit gave birth to the Marquess of Queensberry's famous rules in the 1860s; these humanized competition in the ring and formed the basis of the present-day conduct of the sport.

Edwin and Rosa for the last time? Done already

Kinfrederel

Edwin Disappears

The Mystery Done already

(Mystery of Edwin Drood. – No. V.)

Chapter XVII

Philanthropy <in several phases> professional and unprofessional

Chapter XVIII

<Shadow on the Sun Dial>

A Settler in Cloisterham

Chapter XIX

<A Settler in Cloisterham>

Shadow on the Sun Dial

Chapter XX

<Let's talk>

<Various Flights> Divers Flights

a turn-up] Pugilistic slang for a boxing contest.

Novice] A beginner in pugilism. In a speech to the Royal General Theatrical Fund (28 March 1866) Dickens 'found the Lord Mayor so thoroughly up in' the theatre that he 'recognized in him what would be called in fistic language, a very ugly customer – one, I assure you, by no means to be settled by any novice not in thorough good theatrical training' (*Speeches* 358–9).

circles of the Fancy.] The 'Fancy' usually refers to the followers of prize-fighting, but it includes as well the fighters, patrons, trainers, the crowds, and all enthusiastic sporting characters. According to a jingle in a sporting magazine of 1820,

> *Fancy's* a term for every blackguardism –
> A term for favourite men and favourite cocks –
> A term for gentlemen who make a schism
> Without the lobby or within the box –
> For the best rogues of polish'd vulgarism,
> And those who deal in scientific knocks –
> For bull-dog breeders, badger-baiters – all
> Who live in gin and jail, or not at all.
> (Ford, 1971, 147–8)

a moral little Mill] A 'mill' is a pugilistic encounter, and a 'Grand Mill' is a major prize-fight. A *HW* article describes a 'mill' in the Jewish quarter of London fought 'between Lurky Snaggs and Dan Pepper (the "Kiddy"), for one hundred pounds a side' (6.103).

the sporting publicans] Bets on fights were often taken in public houses.

Resolutions might have been Rounds.] Three rounds were fought, the first two of three minutes' duration, and the last of four minutes, with an interval, between each round, of one minute. The resolution is the conclusion of the fight.

an eminent public character, once known to fame as Frosty-faced Fogo] The phrase, deleted in proof, is characteristic of the several deletions in this chapter in that when Dickens was forced to 'lop and crop' he customarily cut the comic passages (Butt and Tillotson, 1968, 22).

'Frosty-faced Fogo' is an example of the 'noms-de-guerre' acquired by pugilists. The nicknames sometimes derived from the fighter's trade, as with 'the Bath Butcher' (Sam Martin) and 'George the Brewer' (Inglesden), and sometimes from his home, as in the case of 'West-country Dick' (Richard West) and 'the Brummagem Youth' (Phil Sampson from Birmingham). Other nicknames referred to physical characteristics: 'the Black' or 'Snowball' (Molyneux); 'No Neck' (Diggon) and 'White-headed Bob' (Ned Baldwin). Jack Fogo, whose nickname derived from his pockmarked face, was not himself a boxer but a sporting writer and organizer of fights. He worked for *Bell's Life*, a magazine rather 'short on politics . . . [but] long on crime reports and ring affairs'. During the Regency period he was a popular figure in the 'boozing dens of the Fancy', and his use of puns, sporting slang and pedantic literary allusions earned him the reputation of the poet of the prize-ring (Ford, 1971, 55, 177).

the magic circle with the rope and stakes.] Competitors boxed in a roped ring of about twelve to twenty-four feet square.

Suet Pudding] Suet pudding (made of flour and suet and boiled in a cloth) is pugilist slang for the fat around the loins.

the Philanthropists had not the good temper of the Pugilists, and used worse language.] One of the maxims of the pugilists was 'keep your temper' (Winn, 1897, 382).

to bore their man to the ropes] Honour is inherent in boxing rules: wrestling or roughing at the ropes is unacceptable; foul blows and unfairness can disqualify a competitor (Winn, 363).

to hit him when he was down, hit him anywhere and anyhow] No fighter may 'hit his adversary when he is down, or seize him by the ham, the breeches, or any part below the waist: a man on his knees, to be reckoned as down' (Winn, 369, 375).

"Now, Mr. Crisparkle

"Now, Mr. Crisparkle," said Mr. Honeythunder] The argument between Crisparkle and Honeythunder was influenced by the Governor Eyre controversy which remained a live issue at least until the end of 1869, by which time Dickens had begun to write *MED*. John Bright, the probable original of Honeythunder (see notes to chapter 6, pp. 84–5), joined the group of philanthropists and missionaries who formed the Jamaica Committee in order to bring Eyre to trial and punishment. Bright and the Peace Society were vociferous in demanding an inquiry into the case. When Bright was attacked in the House of Commons, he insisted that he had not in fact pre-judged Eyre. His reply, which was widely reported, sounds very like a speech of Honeythunder's:

> He reiterated his belief that Mr. Gordon had been cruelly murdered. In condemning the Governor he had taken the latter's own statement. He grieved to say that there were many persons in this country who did not feel the same sense of wrong and injustice when anything like this happened, if it were inflicted only upon those unfortunate 'niggers,' as they would if white men had suffered in a similar manner. He regarded every life among those men – before the law and before the sovereign authority of the Queen – as important as any life in this country or in the House, and it was idle to tell him that when he stood on a platform before thousands of his countrymen, he was to consider, because they were black, the lives of 2,000 subjects of the Queen as nothing in comparison with the feelings of Governor Eyre and his accomplices. (Smith, 1881, 2.5.166–7)

Professors Thomas Huxley, Goldwin Smith, Thorold Rogers and Henry Fawcett all sided with Bright against Eyre, and the phrase 'Professors of

Philanthropy' would seem to allude to these men. Honeythunder's angry references to Cain and Abel allude to the rhetoric employed by Baptists and non-conformists who addressed public meetings on behalf of the Jamaica Committee. The speakers denounced murder and attempted to arouse sympathy for the murdered Jamaicans and their executed Baptist leader, George William Gordon. Supporters of the Jamaica Committee assumed Eyre's guilt in much the same way as Honeythunder assumes Neville's.

"Here is a man

"swept off the face of the earth by a deed of violence.] Genesis 6.7: 'And the Lord said, I will destroy man whom I have created from the face of the earth'; also Exodus 10.5: 'And they shall cover the face of the earth, that one cannot be able to see the earth'. Honeythunder embraces Podsnappery:

> Mr Podsnap had even acquired a peculiar flourish of his right arm in often clearing the world of its most difficult problems, by sweeping them behind him (and consequently sheer away) with those words and a flushed face. For they affronted him. (*OMF* 1.11)

"Murder!" proceeded Mr. Honeythunder

Abel! Cain! I hold no terms with Cain.] The murder of Abel by Cain was evoked by those who spoke against Governor Eyre. But the similarities with Genesis are themselves relevant to the novel. When his offerings are rejected, Cain 'was very wroth, and his countenance fell. And the Lord said unto Cain, Why art thou wroth? and why is thy countenance fallen? If thou doest well, shalt thou not be accepted? and if thou doest not well, sin lieth at the door' (Genesis 4.5–7). The passage brings to mind the jealous anger Neville feels towards Edwin, the warning and guidance given by Crisparkle, and the accusation of murder levelled against Neville, who is punished by expulsion from Cloisterham:

> And Cain talked with Abel his brother: and it came to pass, when they were in the field, that Cain rose up against Abel his brother, and slew him. And the Lord said unto Cain, where is Abel thy brother? And he said, I know not: Am I my brother's keeper? . . . And now art thou cursed from the earth . . . a fugitive and a vagabond shalt thou be in the earth. (Genesis 4.8–12)

"The Commandments say

"The Commandments say no murder.] Exodus 20.13 and Deuteronomy 5.17: 'Thou shalt not kill.'

"And they also say

"And they also say, you shall bear no false witness] Exodus 20.16 and Deuteronomy 5.20: 'Thou shalt not bear false witness against thy neighbour.'

Mr. Crisparkle rose

Mr. Crisparkle rose . . . by a layman."] This passage was deleted in proof. Saunders believes that the deletion was prompted by a reluctance to disclose that Jasper had been in communication with Honeythunder, who does seem to know a good deal about the case (1962, 8–9). Baker wonders whether Honeythunder was 'eventually to join with Sapsea, and thus make a team of jackasses' (1951, 181).

"I may regard

its first duty is towards those who are in necessity and tribulation, who are desolate and oppressed] Reference is to the Litany: 'We beseech thee to hear us, good Lord, That it may please thee to succour, help, and comfort, all that are in danger, necessity, and tribulation.'

"Well, sir," returned

"I don't go about measuring people for caps.] The proverb is 'If the cap fits, wear it'.

"They are," repeated

"They are," repeated Mr. Crisparkle] This speech is much corrected in MS (not noted in Cardwell).

I will not bow down to a false God of your making] Exodus 20.3 and Deuteronomy 5.7–8: 'Thou shalt have no other gods before me . . . Thou shalt not bow down thyself to them, nor serve them: for I the Lord thy God am a jealous God.'

You make the platform discovery that

War is a vast calamity] An allusion to the bullying pacifism of Exeter Hall, especially in association with the Governor Eyre controversy.

you would punish the sober for the drunken.] While Dickens was aware of the serious problem of alcoholism among the poor, he disliked the missionary zeal of teetotal associations, believing that drunkenness was usually the result of misery. On the same principle he raised his voice against sabbatarians who sought to impose moral improvement through denial of the few amusements available to poor people (see Pope, 1978, 70–7).

to turn Heaven's creatures into swine and wild beasts!] In the *Odyssey* (10.210), the sorceress Circe lives on the island of Aeaea surrounded by wild beasts who fawn on new arrivals. With the aid of a magic cup, she changes the companions of Odysseus into swine.

run amuck like so many mad Malays] Perhaps Dickens had in mind here his *HW* article of 1855 in which he criticized the egoism and hypocrisy of sabbatarians and temperance advocates:

> We oppose those virtuous Malays who run a-muck out of the House of Peers or Exeter Hall, as much as those vicious Malays who run a-muck out of Sailors' lodging-houses in Rotherhithe. (12.4)

The use of the image in both cases would seem to derive from a passage in De Quincey's *Confessions.* Describing a Malay visitor to whom he had given some opium, De Quincey remarks that the Malay afterwards 'fastened . . . upon my dreams, and brought other Malays with him worse than himself, that ran "a-muck" at me, and led me into a world of troubles'. De Quincey adds a footnote on his use of the word 'a-muck':

> See the common accounts in any Eastern traveller or voyager of the frantic excesses committed by Malays who have taken opium, or are reduced to desperation by ill luck at gambling. ('The Pleasures of Opium')

An air of retreat

prisonous] The 'poisonous' in proof is a printing error. *OED* gives *LD* as the first usage: 'His son began . . . to be of the prison prisonous and of the streets streety' (1.6).

"I wish your eyes

"I wish your eyes were not quite so large, and not quite so bright] It has been suggested that Neville dies by violence in an attempt to capture the real murderer of Edwin Drood, thus vindicating his honour. But it seems more likely that he is being prepared for death in the way of the 'traditional Romantic sickness-unto-death' reflecting a crisis of identity or extraordinary effort of will (Kaplan, 1975, 157). Neville is in the tradition of Smike, Richard Carstone and Little Nell, among others, who have a type of mark of death upon them. When, a few lines down, Neville assures Mr Crisparkle that a word from him ' "would rally me" ' the omission of the reading in MS and proof, 'all my forces', following the insistent ' "But I *have* rallied" ', may suggest that he does not have the strength to do so. Whether Neville survives or not is one of the unsolved mysteries of the novel.

"If I could have

to be so tied to a stake] An echo of *Macbeth* (5.7.1–2):

> They have tied me to a stake; I cannot fly,
> But bear-like I must fight the course.

"Excellent circumstances

what need I have of study in all ways.] The law, generally a fatal career in Dickens, would be an obvious choice for a young man required to earn his living in a profession. In *BH* it is the choice of Richard Carstone, who studies law not for itself but because he is obsessed by the Court of Chancery. It may be that Neville's decision to study law has some bearing on the plot.

"And yet," returned Neville

"this seems an uncongenial place to bring my sister to!"] If Helena is to be her brother's companion in London, she cannot also be Mr Datchery in Cloisterham.

Mr. Crisparkle, with a significant

the yet unfinished and undeveloped railway station] The great station at London Bridge was opened in 1836 as the terminus for the Greenwich line, with many additions and alterations made thereafter.

"I beg your pardon

"the beans."] Recalling the tale of Jack and the Beanstalk referred to in chapters 3 and 21.

"I have noticed

" – my name is Tartar."] 'Tar' is the slang term for a sailor. 'Tartar' is both an old cant name for a strolling vagabond and the term applied to a military valet (Tartar was the school fag of Crisparkle). 'To catch a Tartar' means to tackle one who unexpectedly proves too formidable: perhaps this is what Tartar was intended to be for Jasper. Dickens might also have had in mind the Tartar frigate illustrated on the crockery belonging to Captain Cuttle in *DS* 4 (the passage is quoted in the notes to chapter 22, p. 167).

"I have noticed (excuse me)

you seem to like my garden aloft here.] An early·anticipation of Tartar's garden appears in a speech Dickens made to the Gardeners' Benevolent Institution on 9 June 1851:

> Probably there was no feeling in the human mind stronger than the love of gardening. The prisoner in his dismal cell would endeavour to raise a flower from the chinks in the floor of his dungeon; the invalid or lodger in the garret took delight in the pot of flowers on the parapet, or endeavoured to cultivate his scarlet runners in communication with the garret of his neighbour over the way. (*Speeches* 133)

In chapter 21, Dickens seems to be describing his own garden aloft, his Swiss chalet at Gad's Hill (see p. 166).

"Not at all

being an idle man."] Because Datchery describes himself as ' "an idle dog who lives upon his means" ' (chapter 18), it has been supposed that he is Tartar in disguise.

"No? I take it as a compliment

I was bred in the Royal Navy] Dickens imagined himself creating just such a character as Tartar in a letter of 1866 in which he offers advice on how the part of a sailor should be acted in Dion Boucicault's *A Long Strike* (1866):

> The very notion of a sailor, whose life is not among those little courts and streets, and whose business does not lie with the monotonous machinery, but with the four wild winds, is a relief to me in reading the play. I am quite confident of its being an immense relief to the audience when they see the sailor before them, with an entirely different bearing, action, dress, complexion even, from the rest of the men. I would make him the freshest and airiest sailor that ever was seen. (4 September 1866, *Nonesuch* 3.482)

In a speech of 14 June 1852, Dickens declared:

> I always hold in great respect our Army and Navy, and not least when it is by no means inappropriate to remember that no agriculture, no commerce, no art, could long be pursued if England were unable to defend herself, to repel invasion, and to make her name, as it ought to be, a name of fear to the tyrants of the world. (*Speeches* 144)

"Well, I had had twelve

a little Corvette.] A type of cruiser, a corvette is a flush-decked warship bearing one tier of guns, in contrast to the larger 'man of war' mentioned in chapter 22.

Mr. Grewgious, his bedroom

his gaze wandered from the windows to the stars, as if he would have read in them something that was hidden from him . . . but none of us so much as know our letters in the stars yet . . . and few languages can be read until their alphabets are mastered] An allusion to a current catchphrase, 'a message from the stars'. It apparently originated with a professor from Oxford named Philips. In his address to the British Association in 1865 he spoke of the recent discovery of spectral analysis:

> What message comes to us with the light which springs from the distant stars, and shoots through the depths of space to fall upon the earth, after tens, or hundreds, or thousands of years? It is a message from the very birth-place of light, and tells us what are the elementary substances which have influenced the reflection of the ray. Spectral analysis . . . has taught our countrymen to scrutinize not only planets and stars, but even to reveal the constitution of the nebulae. (cited in Timbs, 1871, 21)

Dickens deleted and then reinstated in proof the paragraph on Grewgious looking at the stars.

Chapter 18

A SETTLER IN CLOISTERHAM.

This is a much-discussed chapter partly because of the problem of Datchery's identity. Also, some critics have suspected that the chapter has been mistakenly transposed with chapter 19, a possibility which Cardwell's edition (1972) invalidates. Dickens overwrote the chapter and then deleted in proof several passages (restored by Cardwell) showing Datchery's curiosity about Jasper.

At about this time

At about this time, a stranger appeared in Cloisterham] Neville is now in London and has met Tartar, who does not disappear until after Rosa's flight. Helena has joined her brother, or is about to do so, for Rosa is alone at the Nuns' House in the next chapter. Bazzard, 'off duty . . . just at present' (chapter 20), is the only character available for disguise as the stranger in Cloisterham. But why should he, a stranger himself, bother with disguise at all, unless it is to hide his identity from someone about whom the reader does not know (Cardwell, 1969, 178)? Perhaps Datchery is simply himself: all the candidates proposed, apart from Bazzard as the only likely one, can be discounted (Gantz, 1977, 72–8). It is fair to assume that he is a criminal investigator of some sort. Dickens's interest in such characters was influenced by his acquaintance with Inspector Charles Field of Scotland Yard, the original of Inspector Bucket in *BH*. It is Field who, thinly disguised as 'Inspector Wild', appears as the hero of a series of articles in *HW*. Bucket assumes different personae during the course of his duties, and if Datchery's thick shock of hair is a wig hiding his real identity it may be that he has taken on a role to effect his purpose (see Collins, 1962, 210). Perhaps Datchery is a private investigator, as Field was towards the end of his career. This is not to suggest yet another identity for Datchery but, rather, to state that, since Datchery is clearly investigating the disappearance of Edwin Drood, he may have assumed a plain-clothes role. That there may be some other, more personal, connection between Datchery and the mystery cannot be denied.

blue surtout] A frock-coat on which the collar descends below the top of the waistcoat and the tails reach above the knee; it would be tightly buttoned beneath the collar to show off the figure.

the Crozier (the orthodox hotel] The connection between a 'crozier' and a 'mitre' suggests that this is the Mitre at Chatham, a historically interesting inn at which Lord Nelson put up when on duty in Chatham (the room he occupied being known as 'Nelson's Cabin'). The Mitre was well known to Dickens during his boyhood. He recalls it in 'The Holly Tree' (*CS*):

> There was an Inn in the cathedral town where I went to school . . . It was the Inn where friends used to put up, and where we used to go to see parents, and to have salmon and fowls, and be tipped. It had an ecclesiastical sign, – The Mitre, – and a bar that seemed to be the next best thing to a bishopric, it was so snug.

pint of sherry] An alarming measure, but the drink was diluted with water.

This gentleman's white head

This gentleman's white head was unusually large] Dickens disapproved of the devices used by Wilkie Collins in *No Name* (1862) of 'disguised women or the like' (*Nonesuch* 3.534). Where Dickens himself gives a wig to a character it becomes a comic prop, as in *NN* when Sir Matthew Pupker, wearing a flaxen wig, 'fell into such a paroxysm of bows, that the wig threatened to be jerked off every instant' (2). The crudity of Rigaud's disguise is immediately detected by Cavalletto, when told ' "of a soldier with white hair –hey? – not hair like this that he carries – white – who lives retired secretementally, in a certain place . . . He is a soldier with grey hair – But! . . . he is also this man that you see" ' (*LD* 2.28).

as a Newfoundland dog might shake his] The *Book of Memoranda* notes 'Characters. The Newfoundland-Dog man, and teazing capricious woman' (20). This is an amusing image of Datchery – was the 'teazing capricious woman' to appear later? Between 1865 and 1870, Dickens owned such a dog (Ford, 1952, 278–9; Johnson 1055).

a . . . buffer] A slang term for a dog or fellow; also, a chief boatswain's mate, one who acts as a 'buffer' between the Commander and the upper deck. The nautical association has aroused the suspicion that Datchery is Tartar in disguise.

"Now you know my name

"Dick Datchery] 'Datchery' may derive from Smollett's Lieutenant Hatchway (*The Adventures of Peregrine Pickle*, 1751). In Lady Lytton's *Cheveley* (1839) there is a man called Datchet who unexpectedly turns up to give evidence against the villain at his trial.

So when he had done his dinner

like the children in the game of hot boiled beans and very good butter] The cry of 'Hot boil'd beans and very good butter,/If you please to come to supper!' starts a seeking game which requires that an object be found, and, as the seeker moves closer to it, he gets progressively 'hotter' and, as he moves away, he is 'cold' (Opie, 1969, 153).

He was getting very cold

a hideous small boy was stoning it through the railings] Deputy's habit of throwing stones is reminiscent of Tom, the chimney sweep, in Charles Kingsley's *The Water Babies* (1863), who, when a 'smart little groom rode into the court', was 'just hiding behind a wall, to heave half a brick at his horse's legs, as is the custom of that country when they welcome strangers' (1).

"Indeed?" said Mr. Datchery

"Indeed?" said Mr. Datchery, with a second look of some interest.] Deletion in proof of this sentence excised an indication of Datchery's special interest in Jasper.

The boy instantly darted

taking off his hat to give that shock of white hair of his another shake] This habit recalls Mr Pancks in *LD*, who 'carried his hat under his arm for the liberation of his restive hair' (2.30), and is not necessarily an indication that Datchery wears a wig.

The poor dear gentleman

Perhaps Mr. Datchery had heard] The passage from here to 'unmixed in his mind' was deleted in proof, thus suppressing Datchery's interest in Jasper.

"There, I confess

a diplomatic bird] Why is Datchery so secretive about his background? In the 'Sapsea Fragment', Poker flatters Sapsea with the same results (see Appendix, p. 183).

"Might I ask His Honor

"Might I ask His Honor," said Mr. Datchery . . . white hair streaming.] This long passage of conversation, restored by Cardwell (1972), was deleted in proof. If Datchery's knowing that Jasper is 'concentrating his life on avenging the loss' does not come from Mrs Tope's account, how would he have learnt about this assertion made in the Diary?

"But proof, sir

the end crowns the work.] The phrase is a commonplace; compare: 'It is the end that crownes us, not the Fight' (Robert Herrick, 'The End', *Hesperides*, 1648). Also:

> The end crowns all;
> And that old common arbitrator, Time,
> Will one day end it.
> *Troilus and Cressida* 4.5.224–6

"And without betraying

what I call the secrets of the prison-house] From *Hamlet* 1.5.13–16:

> But that I am forbid
> To tell the secrets of my prison-house,
> I could a tale unfold whose lightest word
> Would harrow up thy soul.

"And by-the-bye

like Apollo shooting down from Olympus to pick up his forgotten lyre] As god of song and music, Apollo plays the lyre at the banquets of the gods.

"*that* is one of our small lions.] The expression derives from the practice of taking visitors to see the lions which used to be kept in the Tower of London, and refers to sights worth seeing, or to celebrities. The Tower menageries were abolished in 1834.

"I never was brought

"Mister Sapsea is his name . . .] A traditional rhyme, written on fly-leaves, by which schoolchildren identify their books, and quoted by Captain Cuttle in *DS* when introducing himself to Mr Toots: ' "Cap'en Cuttle is my name, and England is my nation, this here is my dwelling place, and blessed be creation" ' (32).

Here, Deputy (preceded by

a flying oyster-shell)] Oysters were not always the luxury they are now: at a penny a pound, a hundred years ago, they were accessible to the working man.

Chapter 19

SHADOW ON THE SUN-DIAL.

Again Miss Twinkleton has

her valedictory address] 'Valedictory', a Latin derivative, is typical of Miss Twinkleton's pedantic phraseology.

Cloisterham is so bright

Cloisterham is so bright and sunny in these summer days] For a consideration of Dickens's use of the pastoral, see Robison (1978, 414–15).

travel-stained pilgrims] These may be on their way to the shrine of William of Perth at Rochester Cathedral (see note to chapter 3, p. 52) or, more probably, to the shrine of Thomas Becket at Canterbury, as are Chaucer's pilgrims:

> 'My lord the Monk,' quod he, 'be myrie of cheere;
> For ye shul telle a tale trewely.
> Loo! Rouchestre stant heer faste by!
> Ryde forth, myn owen lord, brek nat oure game.'
> ('The Monk's Prologue', 3114–17)

the dust of the earth] Genesis 2.7: 'And the Lord God formed man of the dust of the ground, and breathed into his nostrils the breath of life; and man became a living soul.'

city kennels] The gutters which carry sewage down the margins of the road, or down the centre.

their yet unused sickles swathed in bands of straw.] The blade would be bound, when not in use, to prevent accidents on the sharp edge.

the Cloisterham police] Their reluctance to ask the itinerant farmworkers to 'move on' is reminiscent of the policeman in 'Our Watering Place' (*HW* 3.434) who 'never on any account [interferes] with anybody – especially the tramps and vagabonds'. England was badly policed before 1829, when Peel's Act established the Metropolitan Police. Later Acts established municipal and county police with increased government control through an inspectorate backed by financial sanctions, so that by mid-century a full-time paid force policed the whole country (Collins, 1962, 8).

On the afternoon

the Nuns' House stands . . . in grateful shade] Eastgate House in Rochester faces north, so the south-facing garden at the back gets the afternoon sun; but this is late afternoon, and part of the garden would lie in the shade of the trees.

Possessed by a kind of

many of its windows] In fact, not many windows overlook the garden of Eastgate House.

She has never seen

he is dressed in deep mourning. So is she.] That is, dressed entirely in black. Mourning-dress etiquette, influenced by the widowed Queen Victoria, who wore full mourning during the forty years of her widowhood, was rigid and detailed. Respectable middle-class women would include mourning dress as an essential part of their wardrobe, as family mourning followed the same pattern as that of the Court. Towards the end of the century a black armband was sufficient to indicate mourning for men; Jasper, as a member of the Cathedral community, would in any event wear black most of the time. Rosa would adopt the more elaborate full mourning prescribed for women (see Taylor, 1983, passim).

This time he does not

his face looks so wicked and menacing] For a discussion of Jasper as the traditional figure of death, see Hill, 1981, 141–4.

"Rosa, even when my dear boy

but worshipped in torment for yours] The MS reading 'yours' (for 'years') was restored by Cardwell (1972). 'Years' is meaningless in the light of Rosa's youth, and the fact that Jasper has loved her for a long time is anyway clear (Cardwell, 1969, 319).

girded by sordid realities, or wandering through Paradises and Hells of visions] An allusion to his opium dreams, and certainly to De Quincey's two sections, 'The Pleasures of Opium' and 'The Pains of Opium', with their imagery of paradisal and infernal states. This scene may be influenced by a similar scene from Hugo's *The Hunchback of Notre-Dame.* The Archdeacon of Notre-Dame, oppressed by a grinding monotony of work, is, like Jasper, associated with devilish pursuits. He, too, is demented by desire for the young orphan who believes him to have murdered her lover. And when he declares his passion to Esmerelda, alone and defenceless in her prison cell, she recoils from him in horror:

> 'Haunted by it incessantly, incessantly hearing thy song ringing in my ears, incessantly seeing thy feet dancing upon my breviary, my dreams by night, as well as my thoughts by day, being full of thee. I was desirous to behold thee again, to touch thee . . . When I had seen thee twice, I wished to see thee a thousand times, to have thee always in my sight. Then – who can stop himself on the steep descent to perdition? . . . The extremity of guilt has its delirium of

rapture . . . I carry a dungeon within me; within me is the chill of winter, the chill of despair; darkness enwraps my soul. Knowest thou all that I have suffered?' (25)

"How beautiful you are!

I don't ask you for your love; give me yourself and your hatred] An intriguing story by Miss Jolly was published in August 1869 in *AYR*. 'An Experience' tells of an inversion in love: a devoted mother takes her revenge upon the doctor who fails to save her child's life – by making him fall in love with her. She finds that she is in love herself, but leaves him, saying that she could have married him for hate, but not ' "for such love as has arisen in my soul for you – if indeed it is love . . . never!" ' (2.288). John Beer (1984, 155–60) argues that Dickens's fascination with this story lies in a conflict of love and revenge in the bereaved mother; but that Dickens himself, as he wrote to his daughter Mamie, 'should have made the woman love the man at last' (*Nonesuch* 3.733). The relevance to *MED*, as Beer sees it, is that Rosa would be revealed to be in love with Jasper, but would be so dismayed by the uncle's arranging to remove his nephew that she would be in a dilemma, having to choose to continue 'to love the now remorseful uncle, or [give] her affections elsewhere, or simply [withdraw] completely'.

The fascination with the inverted love–hate relationship may have been unhappily affirmed by the affair with Ellen Ternan which was marked by anguished frustration. Recalling Ellen Ternan's confession that she 'loathed the very thought of this intimacy' (reported by Wright, 1936, 67), the inclination to find autobiographical sources for Jasper's passion is irresistible. Even though it is Helena who is named after Ellen, it has been observed that Rosa is more like the young actress (as is Bella Wilfer in *OMF*), and it may be that 'Dickens' customary practice of doubling or of creating complementary pairs of characters' has conflated two characters to represent different aspects of Ellen (see Lonoff, 1980, 167).

With an action of his hands

With an action of his hands, as though he cast down something precious.] The sundial in Fildes's illustration of 'Jasper's Sacrifices' still stands, beside a new wooden bench recessed into the wall at the back of Eastgate House, and near a sunken rose-garden. This scene is very like that in which Bradley Headstone proposes to Lizzie Hexam in *OMF*, a scene in which he cries out that she is the ruin of him with a 'passionate action of his hands' as if he were 'flinging his heart's blood down before her in drops upon the pavement stones' (2.15). Both men utter threats: when Lizzie refuses Headstone, he changes his manner and, 'bringing his clenched hand down upon the stone with a force that laid the knuckles raw and bleeding', warns her that ' "I hope that I may never kill him!" ' Once again there is a sense that these portraits are informed by Dickens's own experience of a frustrating passion for Ellen Ternan.

'Not a word

as certainly as night follows day.] A proverbial phrase, but most reminiscent of *Hamlet* 1.3.79–80: 'And it must follow, as the night the day,/Thou canst not then be false to any man.'

The handmaid coming out

he quietly pulls off his hat] The distancing, through the past tense, used in MS for this paragraph was evidently reconsidered, and the paragraph was rewritten in the present tense (Cardwell, 1969, 321).

A thunderstorm is coming on] In fact, the day continues dry and Rosa's flight to London is not interrupted by a storm.

Chapter 20

A FLIGHT.

After Dickens's death, Forster chose this title rather than one of the three alternatives listed in the work plans.

But where could she take

malevolence] MS and proofs read 'blackest malevolence'.

Rosa's mind

the last six months] Since the disappearance of Drood.

if he were dead] Is the qualification a slight hint?

She ran over in her mind

(for what could she know of the criminal intellect, which its own professed students perpetually misread, because they persist in trying to reconcile it with the average intellect of average men, instead of identifying it as a horrible wonder apart)] Dickens made frequent claims to possess an understanding of the 'criminal intellect' superior to that of 'its own professed students' such as lawyers, prison officers and the police. It is well known that his acknowledged expertise was based partly on his life-long fascination with criminal trials, prisons, executions and related scenes of horror, and partly on his wide reading in the field. His library included such works as: *A Select and Impartial Account of the Lives, Behaviour, and Dying-Words of the Most Remarkable*

Convicts, from 1700 to the Present Time, 3 vols (1745); Hepworth Dixon, *John Howard, and the Prison-World of Europe* (1850) and *London Prisons* (1850); Dr W. Dodd, *Thoughts in Prison . . .* (1815); Alexandre Dumas, *Crimes célèbres*, 8 vols (1841); *Trials at the Old Bailey* (1779–80); and *State Trials. . .*, 21 vols (1809–14).

Similar to this passage are Dickens's analyses of the criminal mind in 'The Demeanour of Murderers' (*HW* 13.505–7), 'Hunted Down' (*RP*) and *OMF* 3.11. Slinkton, the actual murderer in 'Hunted Down', and Headstone, the would-be murderer in *OMF*, are both obsessed by thoughts of their crimes, as Jasper is obsessed. The murderer in *LD*, Rigaud, is described as one of those people

> who have no good in them – none. That there are people whom it is necessary to detest without compromise. That there are people who must be dealt with as enemies of the human race. That there are people who have no human heart, and who must be crushed like savage beasts and cleared out of the way. (1.11)

Now that she was whirling

the train came into London over the housetops] As did the Greenwich line, opened in 1838. It ran from London Bridge Terminus and, for about a mile and a half, crossed a viaduct of about a thousand arches.

"Hiram Grewgious, Esquire

"Hiram] The name of the King of Tyre; in Hebrew, Hiram means 'my brother is high'; it was a favourite name in England from the seventeenth century.

a cab] *AYR* describes the various modes of transport available in London, where 'Cabs, both of the Hansom and Clarence build', are the 'staple conveyance of middle-class Riding London' ('Riding London', 9.485–6). A *HW* article by Dickens and others complained of the discomforts of travelling in London:

> It has never been clearly made out – except by prescription and precedent – why it is indispensable that a London cab should be dirty; why the palsied window-sashes must be artfully made not to fit the window; why one door must never open, and the other never shut; why there must be, at least, one broken window, replaced (in the genteeler sort of cab) with a wooden shutter . . . why the nose-bags of the horses must be under the seat; why there must be a view of the pavement through the chinks in the bottom; why the fare must sit in a foot-bath of foul straw; why the cab must be damp; why the driver must be dirty . . . ('Common-Sense on Wheels', 3.61).

There was music

There was music playing here and there . . . No barrel-organ mended the matter] The nuisance caused by the growing number of street-musicians who plagued London was a popular subject of complaint during the mid-century. Most of the itinerant musicians were foreign émigrés, and the variety of instruments on which they performed (tambourines, Pan-pipes, bagpipes, drums, string and wind instruments) was increased by the development of new types of mechanical organs and pianos. Mayhew records that street-musicians could be divided into

> the tolerable and the intolerable performers, some of them trusting to their skill in music for the reward for their exertions, others only making a *noise*, so that whatever money they obtain is given them merely as an inducement for them to depart. (3.158–9)

Dickens supported 'Bass's Bill', legislation passed in 1864 to protect householders from annoyance. It had little effect: the streets continued noisy, and complaints in the popular press continued (see, for example, 'Music and Misery', *AYR* 20.230–3).

and no big drum beat dull care away.] Edwin sings this song, 'Begone, dull Care', in chapter 2.

Guided by the painted name

a shaded lamp] That the lamp is placed 'far from him' suggests that he does not want to be noticed in his vigil. In Fildes's illustration, 'Mr. Grewgious Experiences a New Sensation', the lamp is on the table. *OED* cites 1865 and *OMF* as the first instance of this use of a lamp or candle covered with a shade: 'he was standing with some papers in his hand by a table with shaded candles on it' (3.5). But Dickens had explained and used the lamp before, in *GE*:

> I stood with my lamp held out over the stair-rail, and he came slowly within its light. It was a shaded lamp, to shine upon a book, and its circle of light was very contracted; so that he was in it for a mere instant, and then out of it. (39)

"I will!" cried Mr. Grewgious

"Confound his politics] There are various versions of the National Anthem, and these words appear in one. Grewgious's own version of the National Anthem ('God Save our Gracious King') is by Henry Carey (1693?–1743). The second stanza reads:

> O Lord our God arise,
> Scatter his Enemies,
> And make them fall;
> Confound their Politicks,
> Frustrate their Knavish Tricks,
> On him our Hopes we fix,
> God save us all.

"Your rest too must be provided for

sooth to say] An archaism revived chiefly by Scott (*OED*).

"Lord bless my soul!"

"what a new sensation for a poor old Angular bachelor] This exclamation provided Fildes with the caption for the illustration, 'Mr. Grewgious Experiences a New Sensation'. The cosy background was drawn from a room in Staple Inn, and the original of the capacious armchair in which Rosa is ensconced was owned by the artist (Kitton, 1899, 212).

"No, he goes his ways

In fact, he is off duty here, altogether, just at present] This statement is the basis of the belief that, if Bazzard is not in London, he is in Cloisterham disguised as Datchery. The revision in MS of the first reading, 'he is off duty at present', suggests that Dickens was concerned to emphasize the absence of Bazzard.

"I didn't quite mean that

There are some other geniuses that Mr. Bazzard has become acquainted with, who have also written tragedies, which likewise nobody will on any account whatever hear of bringing out, and these choice spirits] Cardwell notes that this is possibly an allusion to the Syncretic Society, of which Dickens's friend R. H. Horne was a member (1972, xv; 1982, 239). In fact, there is no doubt that the allusion is informed by Dickens's dislike of a book Horne edited and by the breakdown of their friendship in 1869. The title of Horne's book is hinted at in Grewgious's expression, ' "these choice spirits" ', an echo of *Julius Caesar* 3.1.164: 'The choice and master spirits of this age'. *A New Spirit of the Age* (2 vols, 1844) contains an essay on Sheridan Knowles and William Macready in which Horne disparages the 'acted dramatists' of his day at the expense of the 'unacted dramatists'. Horne himself was the author of numerous unacted plays, many of them tragedies with titles suggestive of Bazzard's *The Thorn of Anxiety*. Horne belonged to the Syncretic Society, established in 1839: all the members wrote plays which theatrical managers refused to produce, and all wished to break the monopoly of the patent theatres (see *Letters* 4.78, n. 5). Bazzard's inflated notion of his genius and his sense of injustice (as related by Grewgious) are reminiscent of the aggrieved assertions of Horne in *A New Spirit of the Age*:

> . . . there have been men in whom all the passionate energies and imaginings of our nature would burst forth. These men belonging to literature, and not to the stage, have been rightly designated as "unacted dramatists," and the press gave to the world what the corrupted stages were too sunken in their own earthy ruins to be able to believe in, or even recognize as having any affinity with their own existence. The spirit of the drama no longer trod, but was trodden into "the boards," and therefore a set of unacted dramatists arose, and will some day be seen and heard.
>
> . . . "Who then are these unacted dramatists?" The answer must be – "Nearly all the best authors." . . . all are treated with nearly the same exclusion.

. . . The Drama is a root; a theatrical show is a mere blossom. One is borne of its age, the other grows through it. (2.99, 101)

After Dickens read *A New Spirit of the Age* (which contains a not entirely favourable essay on him), he wrote to a friend, alluding to two unacted dramas: 'Horne's book is Syncretic. Shadows of Martinuzzi, Gregory the Seventh, and Co. darken its pages, and make the leaves hideous. Don't you feel that, rather? (19 March 1844, *Letters* 3.78–9). Horne wrote frequently for *HW* and was a valued contributor, but Dickens considered him a careless writer and revised and corrected much of his work. Horne thought his genius unappreciated in England and went to Australia in 1852, leaving his wife behind. On his return in 1869, Dickens (who had separated from Catherine Dickens in 1858) broke off relations with him to express his indignation at his abandonment of his wife (see Lohrli, 1973, 309).

"Strictly between ourselves

"it has a dreadfully appropriate name. It is called The Thorn of Anxiety.] In view of the personal attack on R. H. Horne, the title is appropriate not for the reason Grewgious gives but on account of the implications of its biblical source, 2 Corinthians 12.7:

> And lest I should be exalted above measure through the abundance of the revelations, there was given to me a thorn in the flesh, the messenger of Satan to buffet me, lest I should be exalted above measure.

With that, Mr. Grewgious

the hotel] Identified as Wood's Hotel, on the north side of Furnival's Inn. It was a respectable family hotel housed in a stately four-storeyed building fronted by pillars (Matz, 1922, 218). Dickens very probably patronized it during his three-year residence in Furnival's Inn (see note to chapter 11, p. 111).

"Yes, you may be sure

the stairs are fire-proof] In the early days of fire-proofing, fire-watching was an essential part of the services offered by fire brigades. In the early nineteenth century methods for suppressing fire in the metropolis were crude and disjointed, and it was not until the 1860s that a select committee initiated changes in the Lighting and Watching Act, and in 1865 the Metropolitan Fire Brigade Act was passed. Preventive measures were often privately initiated, as seems to be the case at Wood's Hotel, but these came to be defined by local authorities and Building Acts. Fire-proofing at the time involved the use of certain types of flooring, effective partitions within the building, general good construction, and no exposed ironwork.

Chapter 21 Sixth monthly number
September 1870

A RECOGNITION.

Forster chose this title after reinstating deleted passages from the previous chapter to make up a short new chapter. The page lengths of chapters 19 and 20 had been reduced, and blank spaces were left at the end of chapters 18, 19 and 20; thus the sixth number could be made up to thirty pages (Cox, 1966, 37).

"Miss Twinkleton was so uneasy

by the very first train to be caught in the morning.] This would have been at about 7.00 a.m. (*Bradshaw's Railway Guide*, nos. 34, 309, 374).

"Perhaps," hinted Mr. Grewgious

I could relate an anecdote in point, but that it would be premature."] Perhaps this anecdote is something Grewgious knows about Jasper?

Mr. Crisparkle concentrated

a handsome face, much sunburnt] In *LD* Frederick Dorrit assumes that Arthur Clennam is a sailor because of his tanned face (1.8).

"My old fag!"

"My old fag!"] Fagging in English public schools is a system under which, with the approval of the authorities, junior boys perform certain duties for seniors, with the purpose of promoting discipline among the boys themselves. In *BH* Jarndyce had been the fag of Boythorn (9).

If Heaven, Rosa thought

If Heaven, Rosa thought, had but sent such courage and skill to her poor mother's aid!] It was Forster's view that Rosa would marry Tartar (3.18.426).

Mr. Tartar told her

Mr. Tartar told her he had been a sailor, roving everywhere for years and years.] An echo of the account by Othello of how Desdemona listened to 'the story of my life/From year to year' and 'lov'd me for the dangers I had pass'd;/ And I lov'd her that she did pity them' (1.3.129, 168–9).

[Dickens left this side blank]

(Mystery of Edwin Drood. – No. VI.)

Chapter XXI

A Gritty state of things comes on

Chapter XXII

The Dawn again

Chapter XXIII

She was thinking further

his far-seeing blue eyes looked as if they had been used to watch danger] It has been argued that this moment is comparable with that when Datchery directs his 'wistful gaze' at the Gate House (chapter 23), and therefore it is Tartar who goes to Cloisterham disguised as Datchery. This is, if anything, a red herring, although what the reader may suspect is that Grewgious may have commandeered the sailor, who does seem to be out of London – but not a hint of a reason is given.

happening to raise her own eyes, she found that he seemed to be thinking something about *them*.] Reminiscent of Ruth Pinch and John Westlock in *MC*, when he feels the light touch of her 'coy little hand' and looks down 'to assure himself he had it on his arm. But his glance, stopping for an instant at the bright eyes, forgot its first design, and went no farther' (45).

This a little confused Rosebud

his garden in the air] The magic garden in the air recalls the story of Jack and the Beanstalk. Here the image relates to the moment when Jack has climbed the beanstalk up into the clouds, finds himself in a strange country, and meets the fairy who directs him to the house of the Giant who killed his father. (For a study of the urban pastoral in the novels, see Robison, 1978; also, see Frank, 1976, 190–1, for a discussion of Tartar's chambers as an epitome of 'civilization without its discontents'.) There is perhaps another source for Tartar's garden. Dickens wrote part of *MED* in his Swiss Chalet at Gad's Hill, and in a letter to Mrs James T. Fields, he described what it was like to write there. Although the garden is in Kent, not in London, it is a kind of garden in the air:

> Divers birds sing here all day, and the nightingales all night. The place is lovely, and in perfect order. I have put five mirrors in the Swiss chalet (where I write) and they reflect and refract in all kinds of ways the leaves that are quivering at the windows, and the great fields of waving corn, and the sail-dotted river. My room is up among the branches of the trees; and the birds and the butterflies fly in and out, and the green branches shoot in, at the open windows, and the lights and shadows of the clouds come and go with the rest of the company. The scent of the flowers, and indeed of everything that is growing for miles and miles, is most delicious. (25 May 1868, *Nonesuch* 3.650)

Chapter 22

A GRITTY STATE OF THINGS COMES ON.

This was chapter 21 in the work plans, but when Forster gathered deleted material for the new chapter, 'A Recognition', it became chapter 22. Because Dickens was unlikely to have seen proofs for this and the next chapter, MS takes on a special interest (Cardwell, 1969, 213). The first few pages are heavily corrected in MS (not noted by Cardwell).

Mr. Tartar's chambers

Mr. Tartar's chambers] When Captain Cuttle prepares Walter's upper room in Solomon Gills's shop for Florence Dombey, he transforms it 'into a species of land-cabin' (50). The shop is like Tartar's chambers, for Solomon lives there in 'skipper-like state':

> Old prints of ships with alphabetical references to their various mysteries, hung in frames upon the walls; the Tartar Frigate under weigh, was on the plates; outlandish shells, seaweeds, and mosses, decorated the chimney-piece; the little wainscotted back parlour was lighted by a skylight, like a cabin. (4)

According to Mamie Dickens, her father 'had some of the sailor element in himself':

> One always hears of sailors being so neat, handy, and tidy, and he possessed all these qualities to a wonderful extent. When a sea captain retires, his garden is always the trimmest about, the gates are painted a bright green, and of course he puts up a flag-staff. The garden at Gad's Hill was the trimmest and the neatest, green paint was on every place where it could possibly be put, and the flag-staff had an endless supply of flags. (1885, 41)

ever seen under the sun, moon, and stars.] Deuteronomy 4.19: 'And lest thou lift up thine eyes unto heaven, and when thou seest the sun, and the moon, and the stars, even all the host of heaven'.

London blacks emancipated for ever] 'Blacks' were the particles of smut or soot prevalent in smog-ridden London, here with a suggestion of the emancipation of slaves, and, perhaps, a glance at the Governor Eyre controversy.

gone out of the land] Reminiscent of Exodus 20.2: 'I am the Lord thy God, which have brought thee out of the land of Egypt, out of the house of bondage'.

household gods] Lares and Penates, whose images were kept in the *atrium* or central room of the house, were divinities supposed to preside over the households of ancient Rome.

like a seedsman's shop] Reminiscent of the 'premises in the High-street' (in Rochester) where the corn-chandler, Mr Pumblechook, keeps his seeds in 'tied-up brown paper packets' neatly stored away in 'many little drawers in his shop' (*GE* 8).

his nicely balanced cot just stirred in the midst] 'Cot' here means 'hammock' (from Hindi *khat*, meaning bedstead, couch or hammock).

Everything belonging to Mr. Tartar] Naval custom and terminology accentuate the atmosphere of a sea-cabin.

Mr. Tartar doing the honors

Mr. Tartar doing the honors] This section, up to Rosa's call to Helena, is written in MS on a slip pasted over the original, a partial reading of which is offered by Cox (1974, 313):

> There ministered to Mr Tartar . . . his servant in these chambers, a . . . with a shaggy red beard and whiskers . . . his big head . . . the conventional hair as with rays . . . appeared to be shining . . . pantaloons of canvas, with shoes of buff . . . when first seen by the visitors.
> . . . Said Mr Tartar, 'He is a Triton.'
> 'Don't you mean a sailor?' said Mr Crisparkle . . .
> 'I don't indeed. He is a jack of all trades, but he was apprenticed . . .

'Jack' was the popular term for a sailor; that Lobley is a 'jack of all trades' may suggest for him a variety of purposes in the novel. Tartar calls him a 'Triton', a reference to the sea deity, son of Neptune and Amphitrite, who could calm the ocean and abate storms; Triton is generally represented blowing on a shell, and has the powerful body of a man from the waist up, with the tail of a dolphin.

When a man rides an amiable hobby] An allusion to Sterne, *Tristram Shandy* (1760–7): 'So long as a man rides his hobby-horse peaceably and quietly along the king's highway, and neither compels you or me to set up behind him, – pray, Sirs, what have either you or I to do with it?' (1.7).

"You see, Neville," Helena pursued

If Mr. Tartar would call to see him openly] This is a little puzzling: Tartar's absence from London is hinted at the end of the chapter, when Rosa seems to be losing her spirits waiting for him at the window.

"You know how I love you

I would sooner see you dead at his wicked feet."] *The Merchant of Venice* 3.1.73–9: 'The curse never fell upon our nation till now . . . I would my daughter were dead at my foot, and the jewels in her ear; would she were hears'd at my foot, and the ducats in her coffin!'

As Mr. Grewgious's idea

Southampton Street, Bloomsbury Square] As Southampton Street (now Southampton Row) borders on Holborn, Rosa would be close to Staple Inn. From 1851 to 1860, Dickens himself lived nearby, at Tavistock House, Tavistock Square.

BILLICKIN] Her remote relation to Bazzard may give her a significance in the novel's resolution; the Billickin's name means a 'dipper' or small utensil (Bleiler, 1984, 137).

"There is this sitting-room

with gas laid on.] For lighting – coal was burnt for warmth. Interiors of private houses, hitherto lit by candle or oil-lamp, were fitted with gas from the 1840s onwards. Electric light began to be used in the 1880s and 1890s.

The gas-fitter ... must go right under your jistes] The *Book of Memoranda* (2) records what Forster claims was a verbatim report from a 'confidential servant at Tavistock House' who, 'having conferred on some proposed changes in his bed-room with the party that was to do the work, delivered this ultimatum to her master' (3.12.245–6):

> 'The gas-fitter says, sir, that he can't alter the fitting of your gas in your bed-room without taking up almost the ole of your bed-room floor, and pulling your room to pieces. He says, of course you can have it done if you wish, and he'll do it for you and make a good job of it, but he would have to destroy your room first, and go entirely under the jistes.'

Forster himself did not note the connection with *MED*; Ford drew attention to the parallel in 1952 (277).

Mr. Grewgious looked

in this pickle.] In a sorry state of disorder: 'How cam'st thou in this pickle?' (*The Tempest* 5.1.281).

Mrs. Billickin then sent into

she could never go anywhere without being wrapped up)] As with Mrs Wilfer in *OMF*, who

> was much given to tying up her head in a pocket-handkerchief, knotted under the chin. This head-gear, in conjunction with a pair of gloves worn within doors, she seemed to consider as at once a kind of armour against misfortune (invariably assuming it when in low spirits or difficulties), and as a species of full dress. (1.4)

"Yes, sir," returned Mrs. Billickin

"it is open as the day] The simile is 'as honest as the day' or, as in the proverb, 'It is as clear as the day'.

"Five-and-forty shillings

It is not Bond Street nor yet St. James's Palace] Bond Street is an elegant street in Mayfair, and St James's Palace is one of the palaces of the Royal Household.

Mewses must exist.] The thousands of animals used for horse-drawn transport in London created a sanitary problem. In hot weather the smell was intolerable, as was the plague of flies from numerous mews and stables (an unfortunate necessity as Mrs Billickin explains, detracting from the desirability of her lodgings). The proximity to mews is, as in the case of Miss Tox in *DS*, an indication of genteel poverty:

> Miss Tox inhabited a dark little house that had been squeezed . . . into a fashionable neighbourhood at the west end of the town . . . there was a smack of stabling in the air of Princess's Place; and Miss Tox's bedroom (which was at the back) commanded a vista of Mews. (7)

The same odours and appurtenances of mews are betrayed when Arthur Clennam in *LD* calls on the pretentious but impecunious Mrs Gowan, a resident of Mews Street, Grosvenor Square:

> To the sense of smell, the house was like a sort of bottle filled with a strong distillation of mews; and when the footman opened the door, he seemed to take the stopper out. (1.10)

Words *has* arisen as to tradesmen] She does not want tradesmen to come to the house but will herself arrange for the purchase and delivery of goods; her reason is that tradesmen walk on her freshly cleaned doorstep (whitened with 'hearthstone'), not that she wants a commission for lodgers' purchases.

Coals is either *by* the fire, or *per* the scuttle.] She would charge either for keeping a fire going or for supplying scuttles of coal to be used by the lodger as required.

sharing suspicions] The owner of the dog might suspect that the landlady is in collusion with the thief (stolen dogs were resold or often sold back to their owners).

By this time

agreement-lines] A brief, informal contract, now called letters of agreement.

earnest-money] A sum paid to secure a bargain, now called a deposit.

"No, Mr. Grewgious, you must

down the airy] The 'area' is the enclosed sunken court, shut off from the pavement by railings and approached by a flight of steps giving access to the basement of houses.

But commit myself to a solitary female statement, no, Miss!] Mrs Lirriper shares this concern:

> Whoever would begin to be worried with letting Lodgings that wasn't a lone woman with a living to get is a thing inconceivable to me, my dear . . . nor is being of your own sex any safeguard, as I have reason, in the form of sugar-tongs to know, for that lady (and a fine woman she was) got me to run for a glass of water, on the plea of going to be confined, which certainly turned out true, but it was in the Station-house. ('Mrs Lirriper's Lodgings', *CS*)

Rosa reddening as if

baronial] A peer signs only with the name of his title.

"It occurred to me

Temple Stairs] King's Bench Walk leads down to the river and to Temple Stairs. The 'young men' among the lawyers and would-be lawyers in the Inns of Court kept boats here, as Pip does in *GE* (10).

"I was never up the river

"I was never up the river," added Rosa] Perhaps one of the most charming of Fildes's illustrations is 'Up the River' showing this excursion, with a glimpse of Putney Church and the old wooden bridge; coincidentally, this scene is similar to that depicted by Seymour for the monthly wrapper of *PP* (Kitton, 1899, 211). In a letter of 1851, Dickens describes a day on the river near Slough 'with Charley and three of his schoolfellows'. They went down 'all rowing hard' and 'dined in a field', with Dickens anxious lest he return them drunk to school (11 July, *Nonesuch* 2.326).

Within half an hour

Lobley] Possibly a derivation of 'loblolly', an oatmeal gruel, a rustic or nautical dish or kind of ship's medicine; it also means a rustic boor. A 'loblolly boy' is a ship's surgeon's assistant and dispenser (Cox, 1974, 313).

down by Greenhithe] A small town south of the Thames near Gravesend often used for the lying-off of private yachts. Situated about halfway between London and Rochester, Greenhithe is an interesting location for Tartar's yacht to berth if he is to become involved in events in the novel.

He was the dead image of the sun in old woodcuts] The sun, a recurrent motif in Renaissance woodcuts and emblem scenes, is usually depicted as wearing much the same round-faced, sweet jollity as Lobley in Fildes's illustration.

danced the tight rope the whole length of the boat like a man to whom shoes were a superstition and stockings slavery] Boots and shoes were worn as little as possible on board ship in the nineteenth century and early part of the twentieth century. Going barefoot hardened the soles of the sailors' feet so that wearing shoes became uncomfortable. If landed to march, it was not uncommon 'to see some of them at the end of the day getting along on bare feet, their boots around their necks' (Admiral Sir Gerald Dickens, 1957, 6).

Miss Twinkleton brought

Stateliness mounted her gloomy throne upon the Billickin's brow] Perhaps a reminiscence of *Paradise Lost* 1.600–4:

> . . . but his face
> Deep scars of thunder had intrenched, and care
> Sat on his faded cheek, but under brows
> Of dauntless courage, and considerate pride
> Waiting revenge.

"I will not hide

Though not Professed but Plain] Most private households would prefer a 'good plain cook' – a phrase used in newspaper advertisements – to a professional cook trained to prepare fancy foreign dishes.

"It is not, Miss

the Mill I have heard of, in which old single ladies could be ground up young] From the popular song, 'Manchester's Improving Daily':

> The spinning-jennies whirl along,
> Performing strange things, I've been told, sir,
> For twisting fresh and making young
> All maids who own they're grown too old, sir.
> (cited in Vicinus, 1974, 297)

Cardwell quotes this song and suggests it is a common fancy (1982, 239). It undoubtedly is, but the image derives from contemporary events. The press widely reported accounts of factory operatives being caught up, crushed and killed in the machinery of cotton mills. Reform of the Factory Act was urged in order to provide adequate safeguards for the equipment (see 'More Grist to the Mill', *HW* 11.605–6). There also seems to be an allusion here to John Stuart Mill. Apart from his association with Exeter Hall and the Governor Eyre controversy (referred to elsewhere in the novel), he had recently published *The Subjection of*

Women (1869). In the light of Dickens's lack of sympathy with Mill's support for the rights of women, the mention of 'old single ladies' is sarcastic.

The Billickin gracefully

shuttlecock between these two battledores.] The game now called badminton.

on the daily-arising question of dinner] Lamb's fry is 'the production of lamb's castration' (as the *OED* delicately phrases it). Butcher's meat is distinct from that of a poulterer; without refrigeration, the day on which meat is purchased would be important (thus Mrs Billickin's concern about 'killing days'). Sweetbreads, the pancreas or thymus gland of an animal, were esteemed a delicacy, as would be duckling in the early months of the year.

All this did not improve

She cut the love scenes] Just as Miss Pupford always excludes 'Cupid from recognition' when reading to her pupils in 'Tom Tiddler's Ground' (for this story as an early study for Miss Twinkleton's school, see Introduction, p. 2). Dickens himself once encountered just such a headmistress: in an anecdote recorded by Gladys Storey, he was reading aloud to an audience which included a group of schoolgirls and their headmistress the scene in *MC* in which Pecksniff is mistakenly received by Mrs Gamp in her capacity as midwife. Pecksniff realizes that 'he was supposed to have come to Mrs. Gamp upon an errand touching – not the close of life, but the other end'. Storey continues:

> At this juncture the headmistress was observed beckoning to the pupils sitting near her, the majority of whom were too intent upon listening and watching Dickens to look her way. ' "What, Mr Whilks!" cried Mrs Gamp. "Don't say it's you, Mr Whilks, and that poor creetur Mrs Whilks with not even a pin-cushion ready. Don't say it's you, Mr Whilks!" ' That finished it. The school-marm, with purple face and rigid, shocked expression, rose from her seat and, with head in the air, bundled her charges out of the hall as quickly as possible, that their innocent ears should hear no more. Dickens himself, having grasped the situation, appeared highly amused. (1939, 114)

Ironically, Dickens was himself guilty of cutting both love scenes and potentially indelicate phrases, as Margaret Cardwell has demonstrated in her edition of *Martin Chuzzlewit* (1982, xli, 606, 621, 671).

Chapter 23

THE DAWN AGAIN.

Jasper's return here to the setting of the opening chapter compares with Macbeth's return to the witches' coven.

Although Mr. Crisparkle

more than half a year gone by] Late summer will soon become autumn, the season with which the novel begins.

False pretence not being

he lived apart from human life.] Macbeth knows that 'troops of friends,/I must not look to have' (5.3.25–6); Macready's interpretation (which Dickens knew well) concentrated on Macbeth's withdrawal from companionship. In *The Dream of Eugene Aram, the Murderer*, the poem by Hood which has similarities to *MED* (see Introduction, p. 3), Aram 'sat remote from all,/A melancholy man!' (17–18).

the nicest mechanical relations and unison] The choirmaster shares the ability to function mechanically with Bradley Headstone, the schoolmaster who attempts murder in *OMF*: Headstone 'could do mental arithmetic mechanically, sing at sight mechanically, blow various wind instruments mechanically, even play the great chu. ch organ mechanically' (2.1).

Drowsy Cloisterham

dismissed by the bench of magistrates] The history of Neville's contact with the law can be summarized: when Neville was brought back from his walking tour to go before the Mayor, Crisparkle undertook to keep him at his own home (chapter 15). The next day the watch and shirt-pin were discovered and Crisparkle took Neville to the Mayor again (chapter 16). Investigations ensued, and 'Neville was detained and redetained', then 'set at large' (chapter 16), but he soon after left Cloisterham. It is not clear whether Neville has been actually imprisoned, and that to ensure his release his case has been examined by a bench of magistrates.

The Cathedral doors

two or three services] He is free for two or three Matins and Evensongs, and would only have to be back on the morning after next.

His travelling baggage

a hybrid hotel in a little square behind Aldersgate Street, near the General Post Office . . . It announces itself, in the new Railway Advertisers] Although usually thought to be the Falcon Hotel in Falcon Square (Dexter, 1900; 1930, 52), the hotel would be almost impossible to identify among the many little squares with 'hybrid hotels' sprinkled behind Aldersgate. Such hotels multiplied in cities connected by rail with other centres; Bradshaw's *Railway Guide* ran advertisements describing, for example, 'The Cathedral Hotel and Tavern' as being 'central and cheerfully situated' with 'superior accommodation at moderate charges' for hot and cold baths and well-aired beds (no. 34, 1 September 1844). Dickens describes such an advertisement in a *HW* essay:

> I go to Mrs Skim's Private Hotel and Commercial Lodging House, near Aldersgate Street, City, (it is advertised in "Bradshaw's Railway Guide," where I first found it), and there I pay, "for bed and breakfast, with meat, two and ninepence per day, including servants." (2.97)

Some lodging-house keepers refused to appear in Bradshaw – Mrs Lirriper, for example:

> My dear, you never have found Number Eighty-one Norfolk Street Strand advertised in Bradshaw's *Railway Guide*, and with the blessing of Heaven you never will or shall so find it. Some there are who do not think it lowering themselves to make their names that cheap. ('Mrs Lirriper's Lodgings', *CS*)

a pint of sweet blacking for his drinking] 'Blacking' (shoe polish) was a jocular phrase for poor-quality wine or porter.

high roads, of which there will shortly be not one in England.] The advent of the railway led to the decline of coach travel by road.

"Well, there's land customers

there's land customers, and there's water customers.] Reminiscent of *The Merchant of Venice* (1.3.23): 'ships are but boards, sailors but men; there be land-rats and water-rats, water-thieves and land-thieves – I mean pirates'.

But she finds the candle

cabbage-nets] Small nets in which to boil cabbage.

"I thought I never should have

dead, and gone to Heaven."] A cliché, used by Edwin in chapter 2.

"I didn't suppose

"I didn't suppose you could have kept away, alive, so long] She would know to what extent her customer was addicted. The pattern of dosage varies, from weekly or longer intervals in the early stages, to three or four times a day later on, although even then the state is not uniform (Hayter, 1968, 57). The novel is not exact as to the degree of Jasper's addiction.

"We are short to-night!"

the all-overs] A cant expression for an indefinite feeling of unease.

But this is the place to cure 'em in] De Quincey ends the section on 'The Pleasures of Opium' with an apostrophe which, when compared to this passage, gives Jasper's plight an ironic pathos:

> O just, subtile, and mighty opium! . . . eloquent opium! that with thy potent rhetoric stealest away the purposes of wrath, and, to the guilty man, for one night givest back the hopes of his youth, and hands washed pure from blood; and, to the proud man, a brief oblivion for
>
> Wrongs unredress'd, and insults unavenged;
>
> that summonest to the chancery of dreams, for the triumphs of suffering innocence, false witnesses, and confoundest perjury, and dost reverse the sentences of unrighteous judges; thou buildest upon the bosom of darkness, out of the fantastic imagery of the brain, cities and temples.

Entering on her process

beginning to bubble and blow] The witches in *Macbeth* are echoed: 'Double, double toil and trouble;/Fire burn, and cauldron bubble' (4.1.10–11).

"I've got a pretty many

first and last] A cliché meaning all the time and what with one thing and another.

"But you got on

"But you got on in the world, and was able by-and-bye to take your pipe with the best of 'em, warn't ye?"] The nervous system will adjust itself to a slow accumulating tolerance-level so that escalating dosage is required (Berridge and Edwards, 1981, 278–9). Doubtless the Princess Puffer administers a less potent mixture in order to get him to talk during the semi-conscious period before sleep, which she wants to lengthen.

"That may be the cause

and speaks in his ear.] *Footfalls on the Boundary of Another World* (1860), by Robert Dale Owen, was studied by Dickens while writing *MED* (Stonehouse 86).

The work describes psychic experiences, ghosts, visitations and similar phenomena. The scene here seems to be influenced by the following passage from Owen:

> Occasionally it has been found that dreams may be actually framed by the suggestions of those who surround the bed of the sleeping man. A remarkable example in the case of a British officer is given by Dr Abercrombie, in which they could produce in him any kind of dream by whispering in his ear, especially if this was done by a friend with whom he was familiar. (141–2)

"Just like me!

I did it over and over again.] A passage in the MS of *OMF* (Pierpont Morgan Library) is strikingly similar in tone to Jasper's anxious mood:

> But he must be up and doing. He must be ever doing the deed again and again, better and better, with more and more of precaution, though never in a swifter way. His head had got to ache with the sound of the blows; in their monotonous repetition, they had begun to go to a horrid tune; he could vary the preliminaries and the attendant circumstances in doing the act again; but the act, if his mind had ever been able to change the manner of it, would be changed no more. The same blows without diminution of number or force. The same effects from the blows, the same slipping of his foot upon the grass, the same strained face fallen back and turned up to the moon, the same face drifting down the stream.

The similarity between Headstone and Jasper is further strengthened by the manner in which they both strive compulsively towards the crime:

> But, as he heard his classes, he was always doing the deed and doing it better. As he paused with his piece of chalk at the black board before writing on it, he was thinking of the spot ... He was doing it again and improving on the manner, at prayers, in his mental arithmetic, all through his questioning, all through the day. (4.7)

"It was a journey

"It was a journey, a difficult and dangerous journey.] There have been several attempts to describe this 'journey' in terms of the architecture of Rochester Cathedral; the allusion here may be to the space in stone-vaulted cathedrals between the leaded roof and the vaulting where dark galleries can be crossed across narrow ledges (Clark, 1930, 151; also see Pythian-Adams, 1934, 181–2).

Look down, look down! You see what lies at the bottom there?"] Compare *The Dream of Eugene Aram, the Murderer.*

Aram looks down at his victim:
Two sudden blows with a ragged stick,
   And one with a heavy stone,
One hurried gash with a hasty knife, –
   And then the deed was done:
There was nothing lying at my foot
   But lifeless flesh and bone! (86–90)

Also compare the stanzas from Southey's ballad, 'Jaspar' quoted in notes to chapter 2 (pp. 34–5).

"Well; I have told you

when it was really done, it seemed not worth the doing, it was done so soon."] *Macbeth* 1.7.1–2: 'If it were done when 'tis done, then 'twere well/It were done quickly'.

He answers first

I came to get the relief] Not only from his life, but also from the yearning for the drug. The effects of opium blend with the psychology of the smoker: the relief from his life and from the craving are one.

"Time and place

"Time and place are both at hand."] *Macbeth* 1.7.51–4:

Nor time nor place
Did then adhere, and yet you would make both;
They have made themselves, and that their fitness now
Does unmake you.

"That's what I said to you

It has been too short and easy. I must have a better vision than this] Is there no catharsis after the event? If Jasper has murdered Edwin, why is he still driven to opium dreams? When he says ' "and yet I never saw *that* before" ', does he see the dead body of his victim? Has reality impinged on fantasy? The journey that Jasper has made repeatedly in his dreams seems to have happened, but ' "when it was really done, it seemed not worth the doing, it was done so soon" '. He repeats this complaint: ' "when it comes to be real at last, it is so short that it seems unreal for the first time" '. The opium-woman's insistence that there is a fellow-traveller is confirmed in Jasper's impatient ' "how could the time be at hand unless the fellow-traveller was?" ' The vision he now has is disappointing, the ' "poorest of all" ', because there has been ' "no struggle, no consciousness of peril, no entreaty" '. The something that ' "must be real" ', the ' "poor, mean, miserable thing" ' imposes itself. Is this what he looks down upon, is this what he has 'darted forward . . . to point at' on the ground 'as though at some imaginary object far beneath'? Why has he never seen the 'poor, mean, miserable thing' before? Has his dream never taken him to the end?

The woman, however

past all rousing] A similar incident occurs in *The Moonstone* when an experiment only half-succeeds because Jennings administers too much opium and Franklin falls asleep before he can re-enact his actions of a year ago: 'It was all over now . . . the sedative influence had got him' (2.4).

But she goes no further

But she goes no further away . . . daylight looks into the room.] These three paragraphs are written on a slip pasted over the original reading in MS. Part of what can be read underneath shows that Dickens deleted a complaint of the Princess Puffer: '. . . "you are too deep to talk too plain and you hold your secrets tight, you do!" ' (Cardwell, 1972, 209).

It has not looked

when he sits up, chilled and shaking, slowly recovers consciousness of where he is, and makes himself ready to depart.] In addition to the several parallels in this chapter with the witches in *Macbeth*, there are allusions to other witches in literature. In the romantic tradition, opium is associated with a hag or harlot. In 'The World of Dreams' by George Crabbe (1754–1832) the poppy appears as an allegorical harlot who subdues men with witchcraft:

How came I hither? Oh, that Hag!
   'Tis she the enchanting spell prepares;
By cruel witchcraft she can drag
   My struggling being in her snares:
Oh, how triumphantly she glares!
   But yet would leave me, could I make
Strong effort to subdue my cares. –
   '*Tis made!* – and I to Freedom wake! (36)

He repairs to the back

she can . . . buy bread within a hundred yards, and milk as it is carried past her.] She buys bread from a baker and milk from street-sellers who plied their trade during the summer months.

He comes forth

He is not going back into the country] There is no account of Jasper's movements between noon and six in the evening – just as there is no account of them in chapter 1 between the time he leaves the opium den in the morning and returns to Cloisterham several hours later.

The woman looks up

the chartered bore of the city] As Durdles is called in chapter 4 'the chartered libertine of the place' (from *Henry V* 1.1.48).

Mr. Datchery, with a sudden change

Mr. Datchery, with a sudden change of countenance, gives her a sudden look.] Who but Edwin could have informed Datchery of Jasper's opium habit so that he looks so suddenly at the Princess Puffer?

John Jasper's lamp

Mr. Datchery's wistful gaze] The word 'wistful' has aroused interest among commentators who have argued for Helena as Datchery because of the heart-felt concern expressed here (Nicoll, 1912, 158; Cross, 1928, 242–3; Saunders, 1919, 182–8).

His object in now

It is half-past ten by the Cathedral clock] About an hour and a half after Datchery saw the Princess Puffer at the Gate House.

"I said so

Jacks. And Chaynermen. And hother Knifers."] The East End of London, the haunt of sailors, was a violent place; Dickens describes a typical scene in 'Poor Mercantile Jack' (*UT*):

> . . . and what are we all about, when poor Mercantile Jack is having his brains slowly knocked out by pennyweights, aboard the brig Beelzebub, or the barque Bowie-knife – when he looks his last at that infernal craft, with the first officer's iron boot-heel in his remaining eye, or with his dying body towed overboard in the ship's wake, while the cruel wounds in it do "the multitudinous seas incarnadine"?

Mr. Datchery receives

a few uncouth chalked strokes on its inner side.] The old country way of keeping a record of accounts by marking a slate with chalk.

"I think a moderate

suits the action to the word] *Hamlet* 3.2.16: 'Be not too tame neither, but let your own discretion be your tutor. Suit the action to the word, the word to the action.'

A brilliant morning

A brilliant morning shines on the old city.] This paragraph, commencing the luminous last pages written by Dickens, has haunted many readers. Forster was moved to comment:

> On the 8th of June he passed all the day writing in the Châlet. He came over for luncheon; and, much against his usual custom, returned to his desk. Of the sentences he was then writing, the last of his long life of literature . . . the reader will observe with a painful interest, not alone its evidence of minute labour at this fast-closing hour of time with him, but the direction his thoughts had taken. He imagines such a brilliant morning as had risen with that eighth of June shining on the old city of Rochester. He sees in surpassing beauty, with the lusty ivy gleaming in the sun, and the rich trees waving in the balmy air, its antiquities and its ruins; its Cathedral and Castle. But his fancy, then, is not with the stern dead forms of either; but with that which makes warm the cold stone tombs of centuries, and lights them up with flecks of brightness, 'fluttering there like wings.' To him, on that sunny summer morning, the changes of glorious light from moving boughs, the songs of birds, the scents from garden, woods, and fields, have penetrated into the Cathedral, have subdued its earthy odour, and are preaching the Resurrection and the Life. (3.20.500)

the one great garden of the whole cultivated island] Kent, traditionally called the 'garden of England', is described in *PP* as the place 'where wild flowers mingle with the grass, and the soft landscape around forms the airiest spot in the garden of England' (21). There is perhaps an echo in this passage of the dying speech of John of Gaunt in *Richard II*:

> This royal throne of kings, this scept'red isle,
> This earth of majesty, this seat of Mars,
> This other Eden, demi-paradise,
> This fortress built by Nature for herself
> Against infection and the hand of war,
> This happy breed of men, this little world,
> This precious stone set in the silver sea,
> Which serves it in the office of a wall,
> Or as a moat defensive to a house,
> Against the envy of less happier lands;
> This blessed plot, this earth, this realm, this England.
> (2.1.40–50)

and preach the Resurrection and the Life] The opening words of the Burial Service: 'I am the resurrection and the life, saith the Lord: he that believeth in me, though he were dead, yet shall he live: and whosoever liveth and believeth in me shall never die.'

Comes Mr. Tope

attendant sweeping sprites] An echo of Puck's speech in *A Midsummer Night's Dream* 5.1.376–9:

Not a mouse
Shall disturb this hallowed house.
I am sent with broom before,
To sweep the dust behind the door.

and comes John Jasper leading their line] This order of procession is incorrect, as the smaller boys customarily take the lead (Cox, 1974, 314).

"Know him!

Better far, than all the Reverend Parsons put together know him."] In Bulwer-Lytton, *Eugene Aram* (1832), an old woman who betrays Aram's secret indulges in the sense of mystery her special knowledge brings: ' "I knows what I knows" ' she mutters and claims that ' "I could hang him" ' (5.1).

APPENDIX
THE SAPSEA FRAGMENT

The fragment was found by Forster among Dickens's papers after his death, and was given the title 'How Mr. Sapsea ceased to be a Member of the Eight Club. Told by Himself'. The rejected piece may have been a preliminary attempt for chapter 18, 'A Settler in Cloisterham' (Cardwell, 1971, xxviii), or it may have been written to make up the length of the first two numbers (Cox, 1966, 41).

A somewhat popular member

Kimber] Listed under 'Available Names' in the *Book of Memoranda.*

Another member of

Peartree] Also in the *Book of Memoranda.*

Between Peartree and Kimber

I will raise the veil so far as to say I KNOW she might] Sapsea has proposed marriage to the pretty younger daughter of Kimber. Her lack of veneration contrasts with Miss Brobity's.

the common herd] A common phrase, as in *Julius Caesar* 1.2.262: 'Marry, before he fell down, when he perceiv'd the common herd was glad he refus'd the crown, he pluckt me ope his doublet, and offer'd them his throat to cut.'

When I sold off

he was a brown hulking sort of revolutionary subject who had been in India with the soldiers and ought (for the sake of society) to have his neck broken.] Peartree was a member of the Royal College of Surgeons, and it was probably as a regimental surgeon that he learnt an independence of spirit that Sapsea does not appreciate. The heroism of the army in India at the time of the Indian Mutiny (1857) perhaps informs the passage.

As it was the first time

I kept myself in what I call Abeyance.] A legal term that had become a cliché.

"Gentlemen," I said

the sacred rites of hospitality] The phrase 'sacred rites' was a cliché in the eighteenth century; *OED* cites 1793 and Horsley's Sermons: 'Maintaining what in the new vocabulary of modern democracy is named the sacred rite of insurrection'.

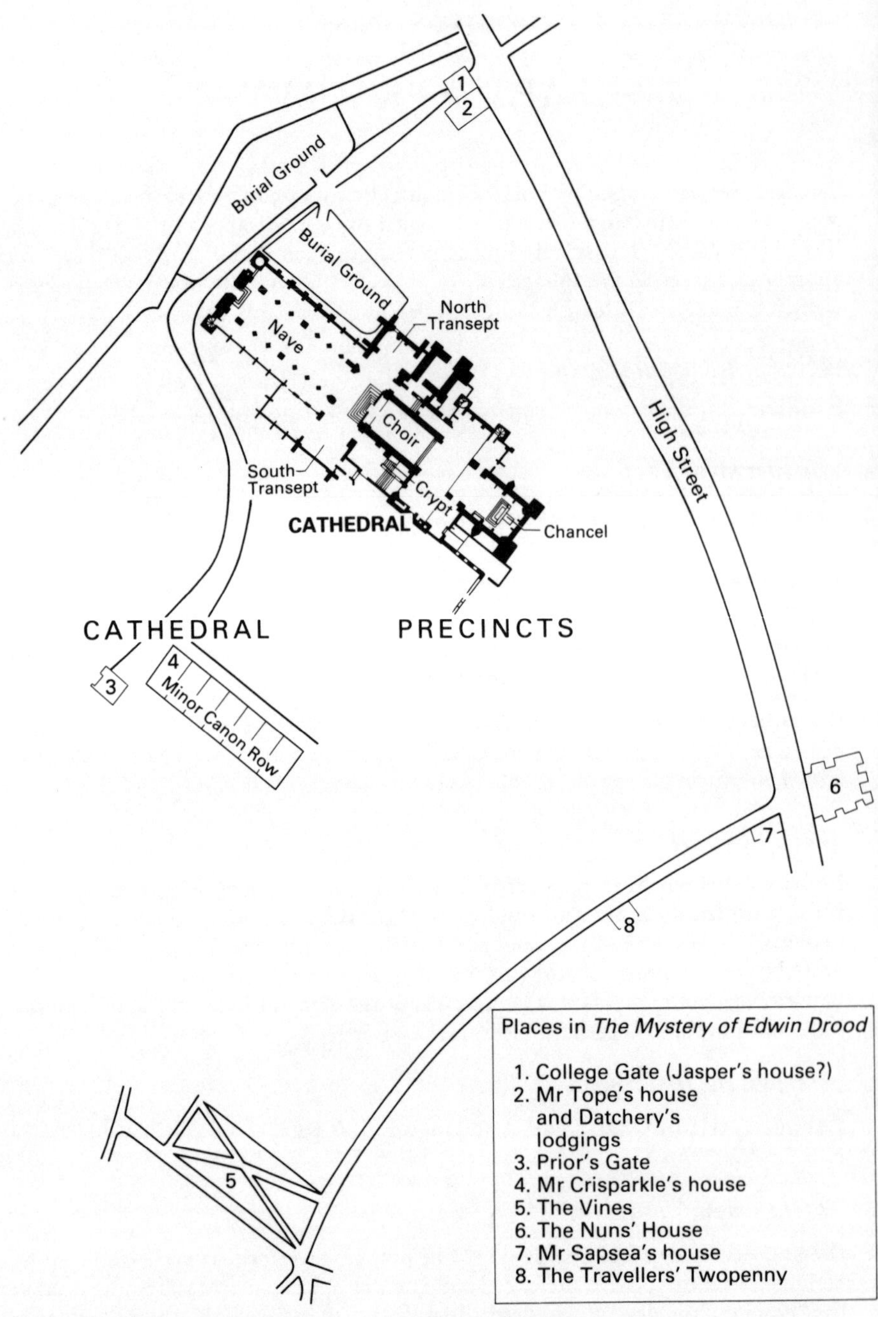

9 **Rochester** (after the Ordnance Survey of 1860), showing the Cathedral precincts and the High Street

SELECT BIBLIOGRAPHY

The manuscript and work plans of *The Mystery of Edwin Drood* are in the Forster Collection of the Victoria and Albert Museum, London.

(i) *Works by Dickens*

The Clarendon Dickens (Oxford: Clarendon Press, 1966–) is the edition cited in quotations from:

David Copperfield, ed. Nina Burgis (1981)
Dombey and Son, ed. Alan Horsman (1974)
Little Dorrit, ed. Harvey Peter Sucksmith (1979)
Martin Chuzzlewit, ed. Margaret Cardwell (1982)
Oliver Twist, ed. Kathleen Tillotson (1966)

The Norton Critical Edition (New York/London: W. W. Norton) is cited in quotations from:

Bleak House, ed. George Ford and Sylvère Monod (1977)
Hard Times, ed. George Ford and Sylvère Monod (1966)

The Penguin English Library (Harmondsworth: Penguin Books) is the source of quotations from:

A Tale of Two Cities, ed. George Woodcock (1970)
Barnaby Rudge, ed. Gordon Spence (1973)
The Christmas Books, ed. Michael Slater, 2 vols (1971)
Great Expectations, ed. Angus Calder (1965)
Nicholas Nickleby, ed. Michael Slater (1978)
The Old Curiosity Shop, ed. Angus Easson (1972)
Our Mutual Friend, ed. Stephen Gill (1971)
The Pickwick Papers, ed. Robert L. Patten (1972)

The Oxford Illustrated Dickens, 21 vols (London: Oxford University Press, 1947–58) is the source of quotations from:

American Notes and *Pictures from Italy*
A Child's History of England (this volume includes *Master Humphrey's Clock*)
The Christmas Stories (this volume includes 'A Lazy Tour of Two Idle Apprentices')
Sketches by Boz (this volume includes *Sketches of Young Gentlemen* and *Sketches of Young Couples*)
The Uncommercial Traveller and Reprinted Pieces (this volume includes *To be Read at Dusk, Hunted Down, Holiday Romance* and *George Silverman's Explanation*)

Memoirs of Joseph Grimaldi, edited by Dickens, ed. Richard Findlater (London: MacGibbon & Kee, 1968).

Miscellaneous Papers, ed. B. W. Matz, 2 vols (Vols 35 and 36 in the Gadshill Edition) (London/New York: Chapman & Hall, Charles Scribner's Sons, 1897–1908).

Collected Papers, Nonesuch Edition, 2 vols (London: Nonesuch Press, 1938).

The Letters of Charles Dickens, Pilgrim Edition, 5 vols to date (Oxford: Clarendon Press, 1965–). Vols 1 and 2, ed. Madeline House and Graham Storey; Vol. 3, ed. Madeline House, Graham Storey and Kathleen Tillotson; Vol. 4, ed. Kathleen Tillotson; Vol. 5, ed. Graham Storey and K. J. Fielding.

The Letters of Charles Dickens, ed. Walter Dexter, Nonesuch Edition, 3 vols (London: Nonesuch Press, 1938).
Letters from Charles Dickens to Angela Burdett-Coutts, 1841–1865, ed. Edgar Johnson (London: Jonathan Cape, 1953).
The Speeches of Charles Dickens, ed. K. J. Fielding (Oxford: Clarendon Press, 1960).
Charles Dickens' Book of Memoranda, ed. Fred Kaplan (New York: New York Public Library, 1981).

(ii) *Articles in* Household Words

Browne [or Brown], 'Barbarous Torture', 12 (13 October 1855), 247–9.
Cole, Alfred Whaley, ' "Cape" Sketches', 1 (14 September 1850), 588–91.
Collins, William Wilkie, *The Dead Secret*, 15 (3 January 1857), 12–18, and (except for 4 April) the following twenty-two numbers, ending 15 (13 June 1857), 565–70.
Collins, William Wilkie, 'Gabriel's Marriage', 7 (23 April 1853), 181–90.
Collins, William Wilkie, 'Sister Rose', 11 (28 April 1855), 292–303.
'Curious Epitaph', 1 (11 May 1850), 168.
Dickens, Charles, 'Cheap Patriotism', 11 (9 June 1855), 433–5.
Dickens, Charles, 'Chips', 1 (6 July 1850), 350–1.
Dickens, Charles, 'A Christmas Tree', 2 (21 December 1850), 289–95.
Dickens, Charles, 'The Demeanour of Murderers', 13 (14 June 1856), 505–7.
Dickens, Charles, 'Lively Turtle', 2 (26 October 1850), 97–9.
Dickens, Charles, 'Lying Awake', 6 (30 October 1852), 145–8.
Dickens, Charles, 'The Noble Savage', 7 (11 June 1853), 337–9.
Dickens, Charles, 'On Duty with Inspector Field', 3 (14 June 1851), 265–70.
Dickens, Charles, and Morley, Henry, 'Boys to Mend', 5 (11 September 1852), 597–602.
Dickens, Charles, and Morley, Henry, 'Mr. Bendigo Buster on Education', 2 (28 December 1850), 313–19.
Dickens, Charles, with Murray, Grenville, and Wills, W. H., 'Common-Sense on Wheels', 3 (12 April 1851), 61–6.
Dickens, Charles, with Murray, Grenville, and Wills, W. H., 'Foreigners' Portraits of Englishmen', 1 (21 September 1850), 601–4.
Dickens, Charles, and Wills, W. H., 'Chips: Small Beginnings', 3 (5 April 1851), 41–2.
Dickens, Charles, and Wills, W. H., 'The Doom of English Wills', 2 (28 September 1850), 1–4.
Dickens, Charles, and Wills, W. H., 'The Metropolitan Protectives', 3 (26 April 1851), 97–105.
Dixon, Edmund Saul, 'Over the Water', 7 (23 July 1853), 483–8.
Dixon, Edmund Saul, 'Poultry Abroad', 11 (26 May 1855), 399–402.
Dodd, George, 'Music Measure', 7 (28 May 1853), 297–301.
Dodd, George, 'Opium', 16 (1 August 1857), 104–8.
Dodd, George, 'Wood, and How to Cut It', 6 (19 February 1853), 541–5.
Gaskell, Elizabeth, *Morton Hall*, 8 (19 November 1853), 265–72.
Hannay, James, 'Graves and Epitaphs', 6 (16 October 1852), 105–9.
Hannay, James, 'Lambs to be Fed', 3 (30 August 1851), 544–9.
Hogarth, George, and Wills, W. H., 'Heathen and Christian Burial', 1 (6 April 1850), 43–8.
Horne, Richard H., 'A Time for All Things', 2 (22 March 1851), 615–17.
Horne, Richard H., 'What Christmas Is to a Bunch of People', 4 (Extra Christmas Number, 1851), 3–7.
Michelsen, Edward H., 'Chips: Chinese Players', 8 (19 November 1853), 281–3.

Morley, Henry, 'The Irish Use of the Globe', 2 (12 October 1850), 51–6.
Morley, Henry, 'More Grist to the Mill', 11 (28 July 1855), 605–6.
Morley, Henry, 'Our Phantom Ship: China', 3 (28 June 1851), 325–31.
Morley, Henry, and Gooder, J. C., 'What Is to Become of Chatham?' 14 (20 December 1856), 550–2.
Ollier, Edmund, 'Eternal Lamps', 8 (22 October 1853), 185–8.
Ollier, Edmund, 'Left Behind', 9 (22 July 1854), 543–6.
St John, Bayle, 'The Betrothed Children', 10 (23 September 1854), 124–9.
Sala, George Augustus, 'Cries from the Past', 11 (28 July 1855), 606–9.
Sala, George Augustus, 'Houses to Let', 5 (20 March 1852), 5–11.
Sala, George Augustus, 'Jack Alive in London', 4 (6 December 1851), 254–60.
Sala, George Augustus, 'The Key of the Street', 3 (6 September 1851), 565–72.
Sala, George Augustus, 'Old Clothes!', 5 (17 April 1852), 93–8.
Sala, George Augustus, 'Phases of "Public" Life', 6 (16 October 1852), 101–5.
Stone, Thomas, 'Dreams', 2 (8 March 1851), 566–72.
Stone, Thomas, 'Sleep', 2 (8 February 1851), 470–5.
Wills, W. H., 'The Monster Promenade Concerts', 2 (19 October 1850), 95–6.
Wills, W. H., 'The Schoolmaster at Home and Abroad', 1 (20 April 1850), 82–4.
Wills, W. H., with Costello, Dudley, and Wilson, T. H., 'The Magic Crystal', 2 (14 December 1850), 284–8.
Wills, W. H., and Hoare, Mrs, 'The Story of Giovanni Belzoni', 2 (1 March 1851), 548–52.

(iii) *Articles in* All the Year Round

Bulwer-Lytton, Sir Edward, *A Strange Story*, 6 (4 January 1862), 337–42.
'Gloves', 9 (27 June 1863), 425–30.
'A Grumble', 11 (19 March 1864), 136–8.
'A Handful of Humbugs', 10 (12 September 1863), 55–8.
Hollingshead, John, 'The Great Pugilistic Revival', 3 (19 May 1860), 133–8.
Jolly, Emily, 'An Experience', 2, NS (21 August 1869), 280–8.
'Milk', 13 (4 March 1865), 126–31.
'Thuggee in Ireland', 7 (28 June 1862), 374–8.
Yates, Edmund, 'Riding London', 9 (18 July 1863), 485–9.

(iv) *Other Material*

Adams, Henry, *The Education of Henry Adams: An Autobiography* (1907) (Boston/New York: Houghton, Mifflin, 1918).
Altick, Richard D., *The Shows of London* (Cambridge, Mass./London: Belknap Press of Harvard University Press, 1978).
Arnold, Ralph, *The Whiston Matter: The Reverend Robert Whiston versus the Dean and Chapter of Rochester* (London: Rupert Hart-Davis, 1961).
Aylmer, Felix, *The Drood Case* (London: Rupert Hart-Davis, 1964).
Aylmer, Felix, 'First aid for the *Drood* audience', *Dickensian*, 47 (1951), 133–9.
Baker, Richard M., *The Drood Murder Case: Five Studies in Dickens's 'Edwin Drood'* (Berkeley/Los Angeles, Calif.: University of California at Los Angeles Press, 1951).
Bearman, Robert, *Education in Nineteenth Century Stratford-upon-Avon* (Stratford-upon-Avon: The Shakespeare Birthplace Trust, 1974).
Beer, John, '*Edwin Drood* and the mystery of apartness', *Dickens Studies Annual*, 13 (1984), 143–91.

Belzoni, Giovanni Battista, *Narrative of the Operations and Recent Discoveries within the Pyramids...* (London: John Murray, 1820).

Berridge, Virginia, 'East End opium dens and narcotic use in Britain', *London Journal*, 4 (1978), 3–28.

Berridge, Virginia, 'Opium eating and the working class in the nineteenth century: the public and official reaction', *British Journal of Addiction*, 73 (1978), 7–112.

Berridge, Virginia, 'Victorian opium eating: responses to opiate use in nineteenth-century England', *Victorian Studies*, 21 (1978), 437–81.

Berridge, Virginia, and Edwards, Griffith, *Opium and the People* (London: Allen Lane, 1981).

Bewell, Alan J., 'Wordsworth's primal scene', *English Literary History*, 50 (Summer 1983), 321–46.

Bleiler, Everett F., 'The names in *Drood*', *Dickens Quarterly*, 1 (September 1984), 88–93, and (December 1984), 137–42.

Bond, Francis, *The Cathedrals of England and Wales* (London: Batsford, 1912).

Brumleigh, T. Kent, 'Notes on *Dombey and Son, Dickensian*, 38 (1942), 211–17.

Butt, John, and Tillotson, Kathleen, *Dickens at Work* (1957; revised edn London: Methuen, 1968).

C., D., 'A mystery of *Edwin Drood*', *Notes and Queries*, 186 (March 1944), 131–3, 184.

Carden, Percy T., *The Murder of Edwin Drood* (London: Cecil Palmer, 1920).

Cardwell, Margaret, '*Edwin Drood*: a critical and textual study'. Unpublished dissertation, Bedford College, University of London, 1969.

Cardwell, Margaret (ed.), *The Mystery of Edwin Drood*, Clarendon Dickens (Oxford: Clarendon Press, 1972).

Cardwell, Margaret (ed.), *The Mystery of Edwin Drood*, World's Classics (Oxford: Clarendon Press, 1982).

Chesterton, G. K., 'Introduction' to *The Mystery of Edwin Drood* (London: J. M. Dent, 1909).

Chesterton, G. K., 'On *Edwin Drood*', in *Generally Speaking* (London: Methuen, 1928).

Clark, W. A., Letter, *Dickensian*, 26 (1930), 151.

Coleman, John, 'Facts and fancies about *Macbeth*', *Gentleman's Magazine*, 266 (1889), 213–32.

Collins, Philip, *Dickens and Crime* (London: Macmillan, 1962).

Collins, Philip, *Dickens and Education* (London: Macmillan, 1965).

Collins, Philip, 'Inspector Bucket visits the Princess Puffer', *Dickensian*, 60 (1964), 88–90.

Cox, Arthur J., 'The *Drood* remains', *Dickens Studies*, 2 (1966), 33–44.

Cox, Arthur J., 'The haggard woman', *Mystery and Detection Annual* (Beverley Hills, Calif.: Donald K. Adams, 1972), 65–77.

Cox, Arthur J., ' "If I hide my watch –" ', *Dickens Studies*, 3 (1967), 22–37.

Cox, Arthur J., 'The morals of *Edwin Drood*', *Dickensian*, 58 (1962), 32–42.

Cox, Arthur J. (ed.), *The Mystery of Edwin Drood* (Harmondsworth: Penguin, 1974).

Cross, J. F., Letter, *Dickensian*, 24 (1928), 242–3.

Crosse, Gordon, 'A reminiscence of Macready in *Edwin Drood*', *Notes and Queries*, 12, series 2 (8 July 1916), 25.

Cruse, Amy, *The Victorians and Their Books* (London: Allen & Unwin, 1935).

Cunnington, Philis, and Lucas, Catherine, *Occupational Costume in England* (London: A. & C. Black, 1967).

Cunnington, C. Willett, and Cunnington, Philis, *Handbook of English Costume in the Nineteenth Century* (1966; 3rd edn London: Faber, 1970).

Davies, John, *Phrenology, Fact and Science* (New Haven, Conn.: Yale University Press, 1955).

[De Quincey, Thomas], *Confessions of an English Opium-Eater* (London: Taylor & Hessey, 1822).

Dexter, Walter, *The Kent of Dickens* (London: Cecil Palmer, 1924).

Dexter, Walter, *The London of Dickens*, 3rd edn illustrated (London: Cecil Palmer, 1930).

Dibdin, Charles, *Songs, Naval and National* (London: John Murray, 1841).

Dickens, Admiral Sir Gerald, *The Dress of the British Sailor* (London: National Maritime Museum, 1957).

[Dickens, Mary], 'Charles Dickens at home', *Cornhill Magazine*, NS, 4 (1885), 32–51.

Dilke, Charles Wentworth, *Greater Britain: A Record for Travel in English-Speaking Countries during 1866 and 1867* (London: Macmillan, 1869).

Dolby, George Charles, *Dickens as I Knew Him* (London: T. Fisher Unwin, 1885).

Downer, A. S., *The Eminent Tragedian, William Charles Macready* (Cambridge, Mass./London: Harvard University Press/Oxford University Press, 1966).

Duffield, Howard, 'John Jasper, strangler', *Bookman* (1930), 581–8.

Dyson, A. E., '*Edwin Drood*: "a horrible wonder apart" ', *Critical Quarterly*, 11 (1969), 138–57.

'East London opium smokers', *London Society*, 14 (1868), 68–72.

Elliotson, John, *Human Physiology* (London: Longman, 1840).

Fielding, K. J., '*Edwin Drood* and Governor Eyre', *Listener* (25 December 1952), 1083–4.

Fields, James T., *Yesterdays with Authors* (Boston, Mass.: 1900; reprinted New York: AMS Press, 1970).

Ford, George H., 'Dickens's notebook and *Edwin Drood*', *Nineteenth-Century Fiction*, 6 (1952), 277–8.

Ford, George H., 'The Governor Eyre case in England', *University of Toronto Quarterly*, 17 (October 1947), 219–23.

Ford, George H., 'Light in darkness: gas, oil, and tallow in Dickens's *Bleak House*', in *From Smollett to James: Studies in the Novel and Other Essays Presented to Edgar Johnson*, ed. Samuel I. Mintz, and others (Charlottesville, Va: University Press of Virginia, 1981), pp. 183–210.

Ford, John, *Prizefighting: The Age of Regency Boximania* (Newton Abbot: David & Charles, [1971]).

Forster, John, *The Life of Charles Dickens*, 3 vols (London: Chapman & Hall, 1872–4).

Forsyte, Charles, *The Decoding of 'Edwin Drood'* (London: Gollancz, 1980).

Francatelli, Charles E., *The Cook's Guide*, revised edn (London: Richard Bentley, 1888).

Frank, Lawrence, 'The intelligibility of madness in *Our Mutual Friend* and *The Mystery of Edwin Drood*', *Dickens Studies Annual*, 5 (1976), 150–95.

Gadd, Laurence, 'The "Tilted Waggon" ', *Dickensian*, 25 (1928), 188–90.

Gantz, Jeffrey Michael, 'Notes on the identity of Dick Datchery', *Dickens Studies Newsletter*, 8 (September 1977), 72–8.

Garner, Jim, 'The mystery of Edwin Drood', *Harvard Magazine*, 85 (1983), 44–8.

Hark, Ina Rae, 'Marriage in the symbolic framework of *The Mystery of Edwin Drood*', *Studies in the Novel: North Texas State University*, 9 (Summer 1977), 154–68.

Harris, Edwin, *John Jasper's Gatehouse* (Rochester: MacKays, 1931).

Hawthorne, Nathaniel, *Our Old Home*, 2 vols (London: Smith, Elder, 1863).

Hayter, Alethea (ed.), *Confessions of an English Opium-Eater* (Harmondsworth: Penguin, 1971).

Hayter, Alethea, *Opium and the Romantic Imagination* (London: Faber & Faber, 1968).

Hennelly, Mark M., Jr., 'Detecting Collins' diamond: from Serpentine to Moonstone', *Nineteenth-Century Fiction*, 39 (June 1984), 25–47.

Herbert, Christopher, 'De Quincey and Dickens', *Victorian Studies*, 17 (March 1974), 247–63.

Hill, Nancy K., *A Reformer's Art: Dickens's Picturesque and Grotesque Imagery* (Athens, Ohio: Ohio University Press, 1981).

Hill, T. W., 'Notes on *The Mystery of Edwin Drood*', *Dickensian*, 40 (1944), 198–204; 41 (1945), 30–7.

Holdsworth, William S., *Charles Dickens as a Legal Historian* (New Haven, Conn.: Yale University Press, 1928).

Hollington, Michael, *Dickens and the Grotesque* (Beckenham: Croom Helm, 1983).

Hope, W. H. St John, *The Architectural History of the Cathedral Church and Monastery of St Andrew at Rochester* (London: Mitchell & Hughes, 1900).

Horne, R. H. (ed.), *A New Spirit of the Age*, 2 vols (London: Smith, Elder, 1844).

Hoskins, Halford Lancaster, *British Routes to India* (London: Cass, 1966).

Hughes, William R., *A Week's Tramp in Dickens-Land* (London: Chapman & Hall, 1891).

Hugo, Victor, *Notre-Dame; A Tale of the Ancien Régime*, 3 vols (London: Effingham Wilson, 1833).

Hyam, Ronald, *Britain's Imperial Century, 1815–1914* (London: Batsford, 1976).

'In an opium den', *Ragged School Union Magazine*, 20 (1868), 198–200.

Isichei, Elizabeth, *Victorian Quakers* (London: Oxford University Press, 1970).

Jackson, Henry, *About 'Edwin Drood'* (Cambridge: Cambridge University Press, 1911).

Jacobson, Wendy S., 'A commentary on Dickens's *The Mystery of Edwin Drood*' Unpublished dissertation, University of Birmingham, 1975.

Jacobson, Wendy S., 'John Jasper and Thuggee', *Modern Language Review*, 72 (July 1977), 526–37.

Johnson, Edgar, *Charles Dickens: His Tragedy and Triumph*, 2 vols (New York/London: Little, Brown/Hamish Hamilton, 1952).

Kaplan, Fred, *Dickens and Mesmerism: the Hidden Springs of Fiction* (Princeton, NJ: Princeton University Press, 1975).

Kaplan, Fred, ' "The Mesmeric mania": the early Victorians and animal magnetism', *Journal of the History of Ideas*, 35 (1974), 691–702.

Kiernan, V. G., *The Lords of Human Kind* (London: Weidenfeld & Nicolson, 1969).

King, C. W., *The Natural History, Ancient and Modern, of Precious Stones and Gems, and of the Precious Metals* (London: Bell & Daldy, 1865).

Kitton, Frederick G., *Dickens and His Illustrators* (London: George Redway, 1899).

Lang, Andrew, *The Puzzle of Dickens's Last Plot* (London: Chapman & Hall, 1905).

Langton, Robert, *Charles Dickens and Rochester* (Rochester: Chapman & Hall, 1880).

Levin, Harry, 'The uncles of Dickens', in *The Worlds of Victorian Fiction*, ed. Jerome Buckley, Harvard English Studies 6 (Cambridge, Mass./London: Harvard University Press, 1975), pp. 1–35.

Lohrli, Anne, *'Household Words', a Weekly Journal 1850–1859, Conducted by Charles Dickens: Table of Contents, List of Contributors and Their Contributions* (Toronto: University of Toronto Press, 1973).

Lomax, Elizabeth, 'The uses and abuses of opiates in nineteenth-century England', *Bulletin of the History of Medicine*, 47 (1973), 167–76.

Longley, Katharine M., [book review], *Dickensian*, 77 (Summer 1981), 102–5.

Lonoff, Sue, 'Charles Dickens and Wilkie Collins', *Nineteenth-Century Fiction*, 35 (June 1980), 150–70.

Loudon, J. C., *On the Laying-out, Planting, and Managing of Cemeteries and on the Improvement of Churchyards* (London, 1843).

Martin, Robert Bernard, *The Dust of Combat* (London: Faber & Faber, 1959).

Martineau, Harriet, *Eastern Life Past and Present*, 3 vols (London, 1848).

Martineau, Harriet, *Letters on Mesmerism* (London: Edward Moxon, 1845).

Matchett, Willoughby, 'Mr Datchery', *Dickensian*, 4 (1908), 17–21.

Matchett, Willoughby, Letter, *Dickensian*, 10 (1914), 133–4.

Matz, B. W., *Dickensian Inns and Taverns* (London: Cecil Palmer, 1922).

Mayhew, Henry, *London Labour and the London Poor*, 4 vols, (London: Griffin, Bohn, 1861–2).

Meynell, Alice, 'How *Edwin Drood* was illustrated', *Century Magazine*, 5 (1884), 522–8.

Morbid Cravings: the Emergence of Addiction [exhibition catalogue] (London: Wellcome Institute for the History of Medicine, 1984).

Morley, John, *Death, Heaven, and the Victorians* (London: Studio Vista, 1971).

[Murray's] *A Handbook for Travellers in Kent and Sussex* (London: John Murray, 1858).

Nicoll, W. Robertson, *The Problem of 'Edwin Drood': A Study in the Methods of Dickens* (London: Hodder & Stoughton, 1912).

Oliver, John, *Dickens and Rochester* (Rochester: John Hallewell, 1978).

Opie, Iona and Peter, *Children's Games in Street and Playground* (Oxford: Clarendon Press, 1969).

Owen, Robert Dale, *Footfalls on the Boundary of Another World* (London: Trubner & Co., 1860).

Paden, W. D., *Tennyson in Egypt: a Study of the Imagery in His Earlier Work* (Lawrence, Kan.: Kansas University Press, 1942).

[Perrault], *Tales of Passed Times by Mother Goose*, trans. Robert Samber, 7th edn (London: T. Boosey, 1795).

Pope, Norris, *Dickens and Charity* (London: Macmillan, 1978).

Proctor, R[ichard] A[nthony], *Watched by the Dead* (London: W. H. Allen, 1887).

Pythian-Adams, 'A suggested solution of *The Mystery of Edwin Drood*', *Dickensian*, 30 (1934), 181–2.

Quarterly Review, [review of Edwin Chadwick's *A Supplementary Report on . . . Interment in Towns* and books on related subjects], 73 (1844), 438–77.

Robinson, Kenneth, *Wilkie Collins: A Biography* (London: Bodley Head, 1951).

Robison, Roselee, 'Dickens' everlastingly green gardens', *English Studies*, 59 (October 1978), 409–24.

Robson, W. W., ' "The Mystery of Edwin Drood": the solution?' *The Times Literary Supplement*, 11 November 1983, pp. 1246, 1259.

Rogers, Col. H. G. B., *Turnpike to Iron Road* (London: Seeley, Service, 1961).

Roughead, William, *The Rebel Earl and Other Studies* (Edinburgh: W. Green, 1926).

Sanders, Andrew, *Charles Dickens: Resurrectionist* (London: Macmillan, 1982).

Saunders, Montagu, 'Dickens, *Drood*, and Datchery', *Dickensian*, 15 (1919), 182–8.

Saunders, Montagu, *The Mystery in the Drood Family* (Cambridge: Cambridge University Press, 1914).

Shatto, Susan, ' "A complete course, according to question and answer" ', *Dickensian*, 70 (1974), 113–20.

Smith, George Barnett, *The Life and Speeches of John Bright*, 2 vols (London: Hodder & Stoughton, 1881).

Stone, Harry, *Dickens and the Invisible World: Fairy Tales, Fantasy, and Novel-Making* (New York/London: Macmillan, 1979; 1980).

Stonehouse, J. H. (ed.), *Catalogue of the Libraries of Charles Dickens and William Thackeray* (London: Piccadilly Fountain Press, 1935).

Storey, Gladys, *Dickens and Daughter* (London: Frederick Muller, 1939).

Strutt, Joseph, *The Sports and Past-times of the People of England* (London: William Reeves, 1830).

Taylor, Lou, *Mourning Dress: A Costume and Social History* (London: Allen & Unwin, 1983).

Tennyson, Hallam (ed.), *The Works of Alfred, Lord Tennyson*, 9 vols (London/New York: Macmillan, 1907–8).

Tennent, Sir James Emerson, *Ceylon: An Account of the Island, Physical, Historical, and Topographical*, 2 vols (London: Longman, Green, 1859).

Thornbury, Walter, and Walford, Edward, *Old and New London*, 6 vols (London: Cassell, 1873–8).

Tilley, Morris Palmer, *A Dictionary of the Proverbs in England in the Sixteenth and Seventeenth Centuries* (Ann Arbor, Mich.: Michigan University Press, 1950).

Timbs, John, *Curiosities of London* (London: John Camden Hotten, 1885).

Timbs, John, *Popular Science* (London: Charles Griffin, 1871).

Trollope, Anthony, *Clergymen of the Church of England* (London: Chapman & Hall, 1866).

Underhill, Francis, *The Story of Rochester Cathedral* (Gloucester: British Publishing Company, 1947).

Vicinus, Martha, *The Industrial Muse* (London: Croom Helm, 1974).

Walters, J. Cuming, *Clues to Dickens's 'Mystery of Edwin Drood'* (London/ Manchester: John Heywood, 1905).

Walters, J. Cuming, *The Complete 'Mystery of Edwin Drood'* (London: Chapman & Hall, 1912).

Wellesley, Frederick Arthur, *Recollections of a Soldier-Diplomat*, ed. Victor Wellesley (London: Hutchinson, 1947).

Westminster Review, 'London Churchyards' [by J. H. Elliott], 40 (1843), 149–82.

Williams, E[lijah], *Staple Inn* (London: Archibald Constable, 1906).

Wilson, Angus, 'Introduction', *The Mystery of Edwin Drood* (Harmondsworth: Penguin, 1974).

Wilson, Edmund, *The Wound and the Bow* (Cambridge, Mass.: Houghton Mifflin, 1941).

Winkles, H., *Winkles's Architectural and Picturesque Illustrations of the Cathedral Churches of England and Wales*, 3 vols (London: Effingham Wilson & Charles Tilt, 1838–42).

Winn, R. G. Allanson, *Boxing* (London: G. Bell, 1897).

Workman, G. B., 'The reactions of nineteenth century English literary men to the Governor Eyre controversy'. Unpublished dissertation, University of Leeds, 1973.

Wright, Joseph, *The English Dialect Dictionary*, 6 vols (London: Henry Frowde, 1898).

Wright, Thomas, *The Life of Charles Dickens* (London: Herbert Jenkins, 1935).

Wright, Thomas, *Thomas Wright of Olney: An Autobiography* (London: Herbert Jenkins, 1936).

INDEX

INDEX

This is an index to The Companion to *'The Mystery of Edwin Drood'*: it is not an index to Dickens's novel. Variant readings in the manuscript and proofs are not indexed, nor are the work plans. References to Dickens's other writings and quotations from them are indexed only when they are considered to be of major significance in the annotation.

Literary allusions and references are indexed only when a note gives a probable allusion by Dickens: references which are merely illustrative, or which are examples of typical phrases, are not indexed. Allusions and references are given title entries in the following cases only: (i) anonymous works other than books of the Bible, nursery rhymes, nursery tales, and songs; (ii) works by Dickens.

Because of the density of information contained in the text, it has not been possible to index all *mentions* of names, places and so on. Notes on the names of characters are entered under the character's surname.

Filing order is word by word rather than letter by letter: thus 'Queen Victoria' precedes 'Queensberry Rules'.

The abbreviation *MED* is used for *The Mystery of Edwin Drood.*